Using UNIX System V

Release 3

Using UNIX System V

Release 3

The LeBlond Group—
Geoffrey T. LeBlond
Sheila R. Blust
Wes Modes

Osborne **McGraw-Hill**

Berkeley New York St. Louis San Francisco
Auckland Bogotá Hamburg London Madrid
Mexico City Milan Montreal New Delhi Panama City
Paris São Paulo Singapore Sydney
Tokyo Toronto

Osborne **McGraw-Hill**
2600 Tenth Street
Berkeley, California 94710
U.S.A.

For information on translations and book distributors outside of the
U.S.A., please write to Osborne **McGraw-Hill** at the above address.

A complete list of trademarks appears on page 479.

Using UNIX System V Release 3

2 3 4 5 6 7 8 9 0 DOC/DOC 9 9 8 7 6 5 4 3 2 1 0

ISBN 0-07-881556-8

Contents at a Glance

Contents

Acknowledgments

The authors would like to thank the following people and organizations: Ilene Shapera, for her insight and her extraordinary efforts to get the book published just the way we wanted it; Liz Fisher, for always being there when we needed her and for giving us that all-important push; Dusty Bernard and Kathy Krause, for pulling it all together; Ross Oliver, for his invaluable technical editing and sharp eye; Stephen Coffin, whose thorough technical editing helped us out of a tight spot; Bill LeBlond, who went the extra mile to help keep things running smoothly; The Santa Cruz Operation, for graciously providing SCO Xenix System V and UNIX System V which were used to produce this book; and DigiBoard, for providing the hassle-free DigiCHANNEL multiport board that strung the office together.

Introduction

Twenty years ago, in a remote corner of AT&T Bell Labs' New Jersey headquarters, a group of researchers devised an operating system for their own use, which they christened "UNIX." Although this first version of the UNIX operating system appears minuscule compared to more recent versions, it contained many of the essential features that have made UNIX the de facto standard for multi-terminal systems.

An operating system is a collection of programs that manages a computer's resources. For example, when you type a command from the keyboard, it is the operating system that reads and interprets the command. The operating system also lets you create and manage files, run programs, and access the devices attached to your computer (such as printers and disk drives).

UNIX was designed as a "multiuser" operating system. This simply means that many users can use one computer at the same time, with each person capable of accessing the computer's full power and resources. In addition, UNIX is "multitasking"—meaning that it is capable of running more than one program at a time. You can, for example, write a letter, print a report, and receive electronic mail all at the same time.

UNIX also provides hundreds of built-in commands, called *utilities* or *tools*. Each UNIX tool is a discrete program designed to do one specific task and do it well. In addition, UNIX is designed so that the output from one tool can become the input for another, so you can easily link tools together to customize your environment.

Finally, UNIX is open. UNIX offers an extensive development environment that you can use to create your own specially designed programs. And because of UNIX's maturity, there are thousands of programs available to perform almost any task.

Although UNIX got its start in academic and engineering environments, it has gradually made its way into general business use. Today UNIX is experiencing unprecedented popularity. UNIX is second only to MS-DOS in number of users with estimates of five to six million UNIX users, versus 14 to 15 million for DOS. The future bodes well for UNIX as its growth rate continues to outpace DOS and the rest of the computer industry.

About This Book

This book was written to help you get started with this unique and powerful operating system. Whether you are new to computers or an experienced computer user, this book will provide a good introduction to UNIX and its many programs.

The early chapters will help you get a feel for how UNIX works and will get you up and running quickly. The later chapters cover more advanced topics, which you can read about as you need them. The command reference at the back of the book provides extensive coverage of the most common UNIX commands.

This book provides a much-needed preliminary step to the UNIX manuals that accompany your system. While the manuals are brief and are often impenetrable to all but the most knowledgeable users, this book provides more extensive explanations and examples.

How This Book Is Organized

This book is divided into thirteen chapters as follows:

Chapter 1 gives a brief introduction to UNIX. It includes, for example, an explanation of what an operating system is, the history of UNIX, and UNIX features and benefits. It also discusses the future of the UNIX system.

Chapter 2 begins with a discussion of the hardware components of a typical UNIX system. It then describes how the software components work together within a system.

Chapter 3 takes you through the basic steps of using a UNIX system. In this chapter you will learn to log in to the system, change your password and execute some other simple commands, and log out.

Chapter 4 explains a number of commands that allow you to create and manipulate files and directories.

Chapter 5 introduces special UNIX functions such as the pipe, which allows you to send the output of one command to another, and the ampersand, which lets you run programs in the background. You will also learn about a class of UNIX utilities called filters, which, when combined, allow you to manipulate data in an unlimited number of ways.

Chapter 6 explains in detail how to use the visual text editor, **vi**. You can begin by learning the basics of **vi** and then go on to more advanced topics. Once you are comfortable using **vi**, you can use the "**vi** Quick Reference" at the end of the chapter to quickly and easily find a particular **vi** command.

Chapter 7 discusses the UNIX **nroff** and **troff** text formatters. It introduces the **mm** macro package, the **tbl** table formatter, and the **eqn** equation formatter.

Chapter 8 covers the UNIX **mail** utility in detail. This chapter tells you how to send mail to other users and other systems and how to read and manage mail you receive.

Chapter 9 introduces you to shell programming in the UNIX Bourne shell. It covers variables, programming, and modifying your Bourne shell environment.

Chapter 10 introduces the many features of the UNIX C shell. It covers the history feature, aliases, and C shell programming, including variables and modifying your C shell environment.

Chapter 11 covers the UNIX C compiler and the **make** utility. This chapter tells you how to compile C programs with **cc** and how to manage large programs with **make**.

Chapter 12 addresses topics pertinent to a multiuser system, such as system administration, getting information about other users, and system and user processes.

Chapter 13 is a command reference that provides descriptions and examples of the utilities discussed in other chapters and many additional utilities.

Conventions Used in This Book

Throughout this book, certain conventions are used to make the text easier to read and understand:

■ Most filenames, directory names, and commands in UNIX are in lower case. UNIX is *case sensitive*. For example, the command **MORE** is not the same as the command **more**. In this book, filenames, directory names, and commands are in bold and are all lower case, as in "the directory **/usr/spool/mail**," or "the command **rm file∗**." If all or part of a name or command is in upper case, there is a specific reason for it, and it is to be typed in upper case.

■ User input is generally set off from the text and printed in bold listing font, as in the following:

```
% cat tuna
```

■ Computer output is generally set off from the text and printed in listing font, as follows:

```
cat: cannot open tuna
```

■ In many examples a prompt symbol (usually %, $, or &) appears before a line of user input. UNIX displays the prompt to tell you that it is waiting for you to type a command. When typing input from examples, do not type the prompt character.

■ Keys appear in small capital letters, for example, BACKSPACE or TAB. When two keys must be pressed simultaneously, those keys are separated by hyphens, for example, CTRL-C.

■ A control character (a key pressed in combination with the CTRL key) is often represented on the screen preceded by a caret, for example, CTRL-D may be represented as

```
^D
```

■ Throughout this book, we use the RETURN key. This key may be labeled either ENTER or ⏎ on your keyboard.

■ Some terminals may not have a BACKSPACE key. It is often simulated by pressing CTRL-H, although it may be assigned to any key on your keyboard.

■ The TAB key, if it does not exist on your terminal, may often be simulated by pressing CTRL-I, although it also may be assigned to any key on your keyboard.

■ In Chapter 7, **troff** output that looks similar to regular text is set off with horizontal lines, as in the following:

Report writing is a fine art. Be short and concise and get your point across in as few words as possible. Make it brief and to the point. Avoid repetition.

■ There are many notes in this book. Notes are items of special importance and are set off to make them easily seen, as in the following:

▶**NOTE**   Messages that are "deleted" are not really removed from your mailbox until you use the **quit** command to leave **mail**.

■ This book also includes tips to provide you with a little more information to help you understand UNIX better. They are set off, as in the following:

▶**TIP**   In UNIX, although a filename may be up to 14 characters, a long filename may be tedious if it is typed often.

■ Differences between System V UNIX and Berkeley UNIX are noted. Features exclusive to Berkeley UNIX are set off as follows:

▶**BERKELEY VERSION**   The mail program on Berkeley UNIX is called **mail** as well, but this version has more features and more flexibility than AT&T **mail**.

In Conclusion

Corporations are discovering what the academic and engineering communities have known for quite some time — UNIX offers a unique combination of features in a powerful open system environment. In addition, UNIX offers a level of maturity that is unmatched by any other operating system.

This book was designed to make it as easy as possible for you to become productive with UNIX. In addition to the solid instruction on UNIX that is the foundation of this book, we have also tried to give you some background on where UNIX is and where it is going in its evolution.

Mastering the UNIX environment is not a snap. But you can rest assured that it is worth the effort.

Additional Help From Osborne/McGraw-Hill

Osborne/McGraw-Hill provides top-quality books for computer users at every level of computing experience. To help you build your skills, we suggest that you look for the books in the following Osborne series that best address your needs.

The "Teach Yourself" Series is perfect for people who have never used a computer before or who want to gain confidence in using program basics. These books provide a simple, slow-paced introduction to the fundamental uses of popular software packages and programming languages. The "Mastery Skills Check" format ensures your understanding concepts thoroughly before you progress to new material. Plenty of examples and exercises (with answers at the back of the book) are used throughout the text.

The "Made Easy" Series is also for beginners or users who may need a refresher on the new features of an upgraded product. These in-depth introductions guide users step-by-step from the program basics to intermediate-level usage. Plenty of "hands-on" exercises and examples are used in every chapter.

The "Using" Series presents fast-paced guides that cover beginning concepts quickly and moves on to intermediate-level techniques and some advanced topics. These books are written for users already familiar with computers and software who want to get up to speed fast with a certain product.

The "Advanced" Series assumes that the reader is a user who has reached at least an intermediate skill level and is ready to learn more sophisticated techniques and refinements.

"The Complete Reference" Series provides handy desktop references for popular software and programming languages that list every command, feature, and function of the product along with brief but detailed descriptions of how they are used. Books are fully indexed and often include tear-out command cards. "The Complete Reference" series is ideal for both beginners and pros.

"The Pocket Reference" Series is a pocket-sized, shorter version of "The Complete Reference" series. It provides the essential commands, features, and functions of software and programming languages for users of every level who need a quick reminder.

The "Secrets, Solutions, Shortcuts" Series is written for beginning users who are already somewhat familiar with the software and for experienced users at intermediate and advanced levels. This series provides clever tips, points out shortcuts for using the software to greater advantage, and indicates traps to avoid.

Osborne/McGraw-Hill also publishes many fine books that are not included in the series described here. If you have questions about which Osborne books are right for you, ask the salesperson at your local book or computer store, or call us toll-free at 1-800-262-4729.

Other Osborne/McGraw-Hill Books Of Interest To You

We hope that *Using UNIX System V Release 3* will assist you in mastering this popular operating system and will also pique your interest in learning about other ways to better use your computer.

If you're interested in expanding your skills so you can be even more "computer efficient," be sure to take advantage of Osborne/McGraw-Hill's large selection of top-quality computer books that cover all varieties of popular hardware, software, programming languages, and operating systems. While we cannot list every title here that may relate to UNIX and to your special computing needs, here are just a few books that complement *Using UNIX System V Release 3*.

ANSI C Made Easy by Herbert Schildt is a step-by-step in-depth introduction to ANSI C that's filled with numerous hands-on exercises and examples. This book thoroughly covers fundamentals and moves on to intermediate level programming techniques.

C: The Complete Reference, Second Edition by Herbert Schildt is a handy desktop resource for novice and experienced programmers, and covers ANSI C libraries, C library functions by category, algorithms, applications, and C's newest direction: C++. In short, it's an encyclopedia to the C programming language.

Using C++ by Bruce Eckel is a fast-paced, practical guide to this leading-edge language that includes object-oriented programming. Beginning concepts are quickly discussed before concentrating on intermediate level techniques and some advanced topics.

For the best way to get started in telecommunications or to get more out of the on-line services available today, see *Dvorak's Guide to PC Telecommunications* by John C. Dvorak and Nick Anis. This book/disk package, written by the internationally recognized computer columnist John Dvorak with programming whiz Nick Anis, shows you how to instantly plug into the world of electronic databases, bulletin boards, and on-line services. The package includes an easy-to-read comprehensive guide plus two disks loaded with outstanding free software. It is an asset to computer users at every skill level.

Why This Book Is for You

Using UNIX System V Release 3 is a user's guide to UNIX for the beginning to intermediate computer user. The book is task-oriented and contains numerous examples. By working through the examples, you will build a working knowledge of UNIX.

Using UNIX is both a tutorial and reference work. If you are a new user, you will find that the early chapters get you up and running in UNIX quickly with an easy-to-read style. You can then read the chapters that follow, as you need them, to build your knowledge of UNIX. For intermediate users, this book includes a variety of tips and techniques that you can use to hone your UNIX skills. It also provides several reference sections that even an advanced user will find helpful.

Although the title of this book refers to UNIX System V Release 3, which implies "AT&T UNIX," this book is also useful for Berkeley UNIX. When a feature is unique to Berkeley UNIX, it is so marked.

Although this book is written primarily for users of the UNIX system, not system administrators, it does address key aspects of system administration in general terms to give you a feel for the issues involved and to help you make more effective use of the UNIX system.

Learn More About UNIX

There is an excellent selection of other Osborne/McGraw-Hill books available on UNIX that will help you build your skills and maximize the power of this widely-used operating system.

If you are just starting out with UNIX, look for *UNIX Made Easy* by Lurnix, a step-by-step, in-depth introduction to all versions of UNIX that includes plenty of hands-on exercises and examples.

For all UNIX users with System V Release 3.1, from beginners who are somewhat familiar with the operating system to veteran users, see *UNIX: The Complete Reference* by Stephen Coffin. This handy desktop encyclopedia covers all UNIX commands, text processing, editing, programming, communications, the Shell, the UNIX file system, and more.

For an informative guide to the newest version of AT&T's operating system, look for *UNIX System V Release 4: An Introduction* by Kenneth H. Rosen. This book provides a solid background in UNIX basics before covering the many new features and functions in Release 4.

A User Guide to the UNIX System, Second Edition by Dr. Rebecca Thomas and Jean Yates quickly leads beginners in intermediate techniques and even covers some advanced topics. There are 12 hands-on tutorials that cover UNIX System V Release 2.0 and Berkeley UNIX.

If you're an experienced C programmer who knows the fundamentals of UNIX System V Release 2.0, *Advanced Programmer's Guide to UNIX System V* by Dr. Rebecca Thomas, Lawrence R. Rogers, and Jean L. Yates may be just what you're looking for. You'll learn how to use the software tools in UNIX to write more effective programs.

1 An Overview of the UNIX Operating System

UNIX is the name of a computer operating system. In the last few years, UNIX has enjoyed a surge in popularity as affordable hardware capable of running it has become available and users have recognized its power and cost effectiveness. This chapter defines what an operating system is and then provides a brief overview of the UNIX system. If you already know what an operating system is, you may want to skip to the next section, "The History of UNIX."

What Is an Operating System?

An *operating system* is an integrated collection of programs that acts as a link between the computer and its users. There are three primary functions of an operating system:

■ To help create and manage a file system. A *file* is a collection of information stored in a computer. Files can contain programs, letters, lists, budgets, or anything else that you want to collect and store as a group. Operating systems have built-in tools for creating new files and adding to existing files. They also let you copy, move, erase, and rename files. Files are stored in a system of hierarchical directories called a *file system*. For the most part, the operating system hides all the details of how the file system interacts with the hardware, letting you concentrate on the more important aspects of managing your files.

■ To run programs. Computers consist of a CPU (central processing unit) and RAM (random access memory, temporary memory that loses its contents when you turn off the power to the CPU). A computer program consists of a sequence of instructions that are placed, for the most part, one after the other in RAM. The CPU reads and executes each instruction in sequence. An operating system controls the process of loading programs into RAM and executing them. You can have the operating system execute one of its many utility programs or a program supplied by another user or software developer.

■ To use the system devices attached to your computer. Some system devices that the operating system lets you access are terminals, printers, and disk drives.

The History of UNIX

UNIX was conceived in 1969 at AT&T's Bell Labs by a group of re-searchers who designed the system for their own use. Prior to this project, the group was involved in a massive operating system project known as MULTICS that was a joint development effort of AT&T, M.I.T., and General Electric. MULTICS was one of the first operating systems designed to handle several users simultaneously. Unfortunately, MULTICS grew to be so unnecessarily complicated and unwieldy that AT&T withdrew from the project.

Ken Thompson, Dennis Ritchie, and Rudd Canaday, all members of Bell Labs' original MULTICS design team devised a file system struc-ture that they implemented as the original version of UNIX. They began using this version of UNIX on a Digital Equipment PDP-7, a computer with only 18K of RAM (minuscule by today's standards), and then moved on to more powerful versions of the PDP-11 computer. UNIX gained more widespread use throughout AT&T and additional features were added to adapt it to company-wide use. In the process, UNIX grew in size and complexity.

Like most operating systems, UNIX was originally written in *assembly language*, a primitive but powerful set of instructions that interact directly with a computer's hardware. Because hardware differs significantly from one type of computer to the next, programs written in assembly language must be completely rewritten before they can be ported from one type of machine to another.

To make UNIX less machine dependent, one of the developers of UNIX decided in the mid-1970s to rewrite the system in the C programming language. C was developed as a general-purpose programming language that combines much of the power of assembly language (such as the ability to deal directly with characters, numbers, and addresses) with the convenience of higher-level programming languages (including the ability to perform logical tests, looping, and subprograms). Another advantage of C is its portability. Since C was and is available on a wide variety of computers, it's easy to port UNIX to other styles of machines.

UNIX Features and Benefits

UNIX offers a dynamic blend of portability, file and record locking, sophisticated user security, multitasking, advanced electronic mail and communications, networking, and remote file sharing. While other systems, such as OS/2, offer similar capabilities, UNIX is especially good at making these features work together smoothly and efficiently.

Portability

As mentioned, most operating systems are written in assembly language and are therefore not easily adapted to a different machine. Because UNIX is written in C, it can easily be ported to other computer systems. Today, UNIX runs on all types of computers, from Cray and Fujitsu supercomputers to IBM PCs, Apple Macintoshes, and even laptops.

The market for UNIX has grown in recent years partly because of its availability on microprocessor-based systems. Because of its portability, UNIX was one of the first operating systems available for such systems. In particular, Intel 80286- and 80386-based systems have been especially popular platforms for UNIX. In fact, many believe that the Intel 80386 chip has done more to advance the UNIX operating system than any other single advancement in hardware. By exploiting the protected mode of the 80386 chip, UNIX takes full advantage of the chip's 32-bit processing power—its raw speed and huge address space.

UNIX on 80386-based PCs brings to the desktop power that rivals minicomputers at a fraction of the cost. Whereas 15-terminal minicomputer systems used to cost in the neighborhood of $200,000 in the 1970s, a similar 80386-based PC system costs as little as $15,000 today. Single-user systems are available for less than $5000, making UNIX by far the least expensive cost per user.

Multiuser and Multitasking

One of UNIX's major advantages is that it was designed as a *multiuser* operating system. In a traditional UNIX system, a single computer does all the work for a number of dumb terminals—one computer with multiple users in a time-shared system. (Terminals are said to be *dumb* when they provide little or none of their own processing power, instead relying on the computer to which they are linked.) As a multiuser system, UNIX supports built-in protection schemes such as passwords and file permissions. This allows a group of users to have individual accounts, each with his or her own home directory for easy access.

As a *multitasking* operating system, UNIX can support many programs running at the same time on the same computer. It lets you run several programs simultaneously. This means, for example, that while running an application program such as a spreadsheet, you can launch another application such as a text editor to draft a letter, and still receive electronic mail that doesn't interfere with your work.

Hierarchical File Structure

In a multiuser environment, the number of files can multiply quickly. UNIX's hierarchical file structure lets you group files in a coherent and accessible fashion. The file structure resembles an inverted tree whose trunk is the root directory. Other directories, sometimes called *subdirectories,* branch from the root directory, with each directory containing one or more files. By grouping files in this way, you can easily locate them and perform operations on them. UNIX's file structure has become the foundation for other operating systems, including MS-DOS for IBM PCs. Chapter 4, "Files and Directories," covers UNIX's hierarchical file structure in more detail.

Utilities/Tools

In addition to the operating system itself, UNIX provides a host of built-in commands that are often called *utilities* or *tools.* These tools are executable programs that were written with the idea that each tool should do one job well. In addition, the output from one utility is expected to be the input for another.

The advantage of the tools approach is its flexibility. It allows you to customize your environment by taking separate programs and combining them to do specific jobs. See Chapter 5, "UNIX Command-Line Fundamentals," and Chapter 13, "Command Reference" for more on the UNIX utilities.

I/O Redirection and Pipes

By default, UNIX displays the output of most commands on the screen. For example, if you use the **ls** command, which lists the contents of a directory, UNIX displays the directory contents on the screen. You can have UNIX direct the output to a file, however, by using *I/O (input/ output) redirection.* I/O redirection simply means that you can reassign where a command or program gets its input and where it sends its output.

Piping is a special form of I/O redirection that lets you make the output from one command or program become the input to another. Like UNIX's hierarchical file structure, I/O redirection and piping have also become part of other operating systems. See Chapter 5, "UNIX Command-Line Fundamentals," for more on redirection and piping.

Shells

A *shell* is a command interpreter that controls the interaction between the user and the kernel. (The *kernel* is the core UNIX program that serves as an interface between the hardware and the operating system.) The two most popular shells for UNIX are the Bourne shell and the C shell. See Chapter 2 for more on shells and the structure of UNIX.

In addition to interpreting commands typed from the keyboard, shells can interpret commands stored in a file. When you store commands in a file, that file is known as a *shell script.* The commands you place in a shell script can be from among the many utility programs that UNIX provides. They can also be any of the special *flow control commands* that the shell offers for controlling the order of execution of commands in the shell script. For example, the Bourne shell offers the **for** command, which lets you execute a group of commands a specified number of times. You can use flow control commands in a shell script to create a variety of sophisticated applications programs. Chapter 9 covers the Bourne shell and Chapter 10 covers the C shell.

Text Processing

UNIX offers a comprehensive set of tools for creating, editing, and formatting documents. You can create documents that include simple text, tables of data, and even mathematical equations. The following sections describe UNIX's popular text processing utilities.

Editors

The original UNIX editor was **ed**, a simple line-oriented editor that accepts editing commands you enter and performs the requested operation on the contents of a particular line or group of lines of a text file.

Although the **ed** utility is offered on all UNIX systems, it is rarely used today because of the **vi** editor.

The **vi** (visual) editor is an interactive, full-screen editor that is the most popular editor among UNIX users today. As a full-screen editor, **vi** provides a window onto your text file that shows approximately 20 lines of text at a time. To edit text in **vi**, you simply move the cursor around the window by using single-character commands. After locating the cursor at a chosen spot within the text file, you then use **vi**'s editing commands to insert, delete, and change text as you like. You can also use other editing commands that affect groups of lines within the document or the document as a whole. See Chapter 6, "The vi Editor," for a more complete description of **vi**.

Text Formatting Tools

After creating a document with an editor, you need to format it for printing by using a text formatter. UNIX offers two principal text formatters: **nroff** for formatting text for line printers and **troff** for formatting text for laser printers and phototypesetters. Both **nroff** and **troff** offer the same basic set of formatting functions: text justification, line spacing, length control, line indention, page headers and footers, and so on. However, **troff** offers additional features that take advantage of higher-resolution printing devices. For example, with **troff** you can control type size and use a proportionally spaced font.

You format a document by using an editor to place formatting commands within the text. The **nroff** or **troff** utility interprets any text that begins with a period in the first column of an input line as a command. For example, the command **.ls 2** within your input file instructs **nroff** and **troff** to double space your document.

The **nroff** and **troff** utilities provide sets of macros for controlling your output. These macros are a set of ready-made functions that let you perform with a few simple commands what would otherwise take several **nroff** and **troff** commands. See Chapter 7, "Text Formatting with nroff and troff," for more on the **nroff** and **troff** text formatting utilities and their related macros.

Because documents often include tables, UNIX offers **tbl**, a special utility for formatting tabular information. You can use **tbl** to produce multiple-column lists, simple charts, and other tabular material. In addition, UNIX offers **eqn**, a utility for formatting mathematical equations. As with **nroff** and **troff**, you use an editor to place **tbl** and **eqn** commands in your document. The commands are then interpreted by **tbl** and **eqn** and translated into appropriate **nroff** and **troff** commands.

Mail

UNIX includes powerful electronic mail capabilities. Each user on a system has a *mailbox* to receive incoming mail, and the **mail** utility enables you to send and receive electronic mail from different mailboxes.

To send mail to another user on the same UNIX system, you just need to know the other user's account name. To send mail to a user on another UNIX system, you need to know that user's system or network address. Either way, once you have an appropriate address, you can easily send a message to other users, even if they are across the country or around the world. Chapter 8 covers electronic mail in detail.

Software Development Tools

UNIX has a longstanding reputation as a powerful software development environment. In fact, UNIX and the C language offer among the richest set of development tools, including the Source Code Control System (SCCS), optimizing C compilers, and source-code debuggers. Many software development companies use a UNIX/C combination for developing software even though their programs will ultimately run on non-UNIX systems (commonly referred to as a *cross-development system*). Chapter 11, "Program Development with C," discusses how to create and run a C program as well as how to use several of UNIX's standard development tools.

Linking to Other Systems

UNIX provides powerful communications and networking software that can connect hundreds of UNIX terminals whether they are under the same roof or thousands of miles apart. UNIX offers the Transmission Control Protocol/Internet Protocol (TCP/IP), a Department of Defense standard protocol for networked systems. In addition, Network File System (NFS), developed by Sun Microsystems and adopted by many other vendors, allows UNIX systems to share disk drives, distribute files across a network, and run electronic mail across a variety of machines. NFS networks can mix different computers—such as DEC Vaxes, Sun workstations, IBM-compatibles, Apple Macintoshes—all running their own version of UNIX with NFS. With these standardized, public protocols, UNIX is bringing order to a complex communications marketplace.

Applications Programs

UNIX applications span a broad range of "horizontal" applications, such as spreadsheets, database management, communications, and word processing. These applications are horizontal in that they are intended to appeal to the entire UNIX marketplace. In addition, UNIX offers many "vertical" applications, such as financial modeling, robotics, Computer-Aided Design (CAD), Computer-Aided Manufacturing (CAM), Computer-Aided Software Engineering (CASE), and medical billing. These vertical applications are targeted to a particular segment of the UNIX market, such as financial managers, engineers, and doctors. The next sections describe some of the major categories of horizontal applications. See the section "Who Buys UNIX Systems?" for a discussion of vertical market applications.

Word Processing Although UNIX provides many powerful text-formatting and document-processing tools, they are not as interactive as most popular word processors for PCs. As UNIX has become more popular on PCs, many of the most popular word processors for DOS have made their way to UNIX, including Microsoft Word, WordPerfect, and Samna. In addition, SCO Lyrix, part of the SCO Office Portfolio series from the Santa Cruz Operation (SCO), is a popular word processor among SCO XENIX and UNIX users.

Database Management   UNIX plays host to many powerful database management programs. These include Oracle Corporation's ORACLE, Relational Database Systems' Informix, Relational Technology's INGRES, Fox Software's FoxBASE+ (a dBASE III PLUS work-alike), Unify Corporation's ACCELL/SQL, and others.

Spreadsheets   In the spreadsheet arena, UNIX offers several entries including Multiplan (developed by Microsoft and marketed by SCO), SCO Professional (a Lotus 1-2-3 work-alike from SCO), and 20/20 from Access Technology (a powerful spreadsheet with graphics, database management, and consolidation features). In addition, Lotus Development Corporation, the premier supplier of spreadsheets for PCs, has announced plans to provide its best-selling 1-2-3 spreadsheet for UNIX systems.

Versions of UNIX

UNIX exists in several versions today, including AT&T UNIX, Berkeley UNIX, and SCO XENIX. The following sections describe these different versions.

AT&T Versions

Over the years, AT&T has licensed numerous versions of the UNIX system. Initially, UNIX was offered mostly to academic institutions, as a distribution of Bell Labs' research effort rather than as a product. Recently, however, UNIX has become more popular and the release of each new version is treated with great anticipation by the UNIX community.

The earliest versions of UNIX were named for editions that came out of the Bell Labs' research department. For example, the Sixth Edition was the first licensed version of UNIX, distributed mostly to universities. The Seventh Edition was the first commercially licensed version of

UNIX by AT&T.In the late 1970s, AT&T changed its naming convention for new editions of UNIX to System III and System V. (System IV was developed but never licensed outside AT&T.) System V, the latest version of UNIX, was first introduced in January 1983. Since then, AT&T has added release numbers following the system number, as in System V Release 2 and System V Release 3.

Berkeley UNIX (BSD)

The University of California at Berkeley has been very active as a UNIX think tank since the late 1970s. It has produced many unique UNIX utilities and its own version of UNIX known as the Berkeley Software Distribution (BSD), or simply as Berkeley UNIX. The most recent version of Berkeley UNIX is BSD Release 4.3, which is the dominant version in the university and engineering communities. Compatibility between BSD and AT&T versions of UNIX is an ongoing problem. More recent editions of UNIX promise some relief as AT&T has moved to incorporate many BSD features into the UNIX standard (see the section "The Future of the UNIX System" in this chapter).

SCO XENIX

Because AT&T licensed UNIX software but not the UNIX trademark, licensees could not use the UNIX name on their versions of UNIX. XENIX is the name of a version of UNIX that was originally written by Microsoft in 1983 and then licensed to the Santa Cruz Operation (SCO). XENIX is a fully licensed version of AT&T UNIX optimized for microprocessor-based systems. SCO handles all the marketing of XENIX in a joint licensing agreement with Microsoft, which owns a 20% stake in SCO.

XENIX is available for 80286- and 80386-based systems and Micro Channel machines (IBM PS/2s and compatibles) and is installed on more than 90% of all microcomputers that run UNIX. XENIX consists of three parts, each sold separately:

■ The operating system, with the full set of utilities to perform system administration, edit files, run applications, and electronic mail

■ A development system, with the tools necessary to write C and assembly language programs

■ A text processing system, which includes the **nroff** and **troff** text formatters

In addition to the XENIX operating system, SCO offers several optional packages. These include SCO VP/ix (for running MS-DOS applications under XENIX), SCO MultiView (a multitasking windowing environment), SCO uniPATH SNA-3270 (a multiuser micro-to-mainframe SNA link product). SCO also offers the SCO Office Portfolio, a full package of integrated business applications that run on XENIX and other UNIX systems.

Due to AT&T's recent loosening of the UNIX trademark, SCO decided in August 1989 to use the name SCO UNIX in favor of XENIX on all of its future products.

Hardware Vendor Ports

UNIX is also available from a number of system manufacturers who have purchased the UNIX source code from AT&T and ported it to their systems. For example, Sun Microsystems, the leading maker of UNIX workstations, calls its version of UNIX SunOS. Similarly, Apple Computer offers AU/X for its Macintosh family of computers, and IBM offers AIX, a version of UNIX for its RISC-based computers, such as the IBM RT system.

The UNIX System Documentation

Most every UNIX system provides a copy of the *UNIX User's Reference Manual*. This is the official documentation for your system and describes the shells, utility commands, and programming interfaces for the system. (The term "man page" is often used to refer to an entry in the *User's Manual*, though the entry might actually occupy more than one page.)

In addition, AT&T offers a "standard" set of documents that describe UNIX System V. These books, which are written by AT&T and published by Prentice-Hall, are AT&T's official reference works on AT&T and are available at most major bookstores. Here are some of the more important books currently available in the UNIX System V library:

■ *UNIX System V Release 3.2 User's Guide* gives an overview of the UNIX system with tutorial sections on using text editors, mail, and simple shell programming.

■ *UNIX System V Release 3.2 Programmer's Guide Volumes I and II* provide an overview of UNIX's programming environment and include tutorials on its programming tools.

■ *UNIX System V Release 3.2 Programmer's Reference Manual* provides information for UNIX programmers, including a description of UNIX system calls, file formats, libraries, and subroutines.

■ *UNIX System V Release 3.2 System Administrator's Guide* describes how to perform administrative tasks on a UNIX system.

■ *UNIX System V Release 3.2 System Administrator's Reference Manual* provides more technical information for system administrators, including commands, file formats, and more.

All of these books are also available for UNIX on 80386-based systems, in which case the title begins with "UNIX System V/386."

Many UNIX systems allow you to access an online help facility that you can use to find out about UNIX commands and their available options. On some systems, the online help facility includes all the pages in the *UNIX User's Reference Manual*. To access the online manual, use the **man** command.

Other Standard Operating Systems

Besides UNIX, two other important standard operating systems are MS-DOS and OS/2. MS-DOS from Microsoft Corporation is the leading single-user, single-tasking operating system for 16-bit personal computers and is important to UNIX users because of the wealth of applications programs available for it. In addition, some versions of UNIX can run existing DOS applications in a UNIX environment, using products such as VP/ix from Interactive Systems Corporation or DOS-Merge from Locus Computing. This feature is particularly attractive to MS-DOS users who want to bring their applications to UNIX.

OS/2, also from Microsoft, is a single-user, multitasking operating system for 16-bit computers, although it will soon be offered for 32-bit computers. Besides multitasking, OS/2 and UNIX share other features, including, for example, a hierarchical file structure and interprocess communication. Here are some of the major differences between OS/2 and UNIX:

■ **Single User**   Although OS/2 was designed as a multitasking operating system, it was also designed for a single user, with more priority given to performance of the system for that user.

■ **Portability**   Microsoft did not develop OS/2 with portability in mind. The OS/2 core contains a larger volume of assembly language than UNIX's, which is written almost entirely in C. In addition, Microsoft wrote OS/2 to exploit the features of the Intel 80286 processor.

■ **Presentation Manager**   This is a subsystem of OS/2 that manages the windows-based graphics user interface. Presentation Manager is a standard component of the OS/2 operating system. UNIX systems as a whole do not offer a graphics user interface, although this is about to change.

Who Buys UNIX Systems?

For years, UNIX was viewed as the ugly duckling of operating systems. People thought it belonged to the province of engineering and research and development labs with technically proficient users. It is true that as UNIX evolved many of its commands and options became too complex for the average user. Yet phone companies and the federal government standardized on UNIX, while hundreds of value-added resellers (VARs) and dealers prospered by selling low-cost UNIX multiuser systems.

Today the UNIX marketplace is diverse and growing rapidly. A market research firm predicts that by 1993 nearly 1.7 million PCs and workstations will be running UNIX, an increase of over 900% from 1987. In fact, some surveys estimate that in the 1990s as much as 20% to 25% of the market will be UNIX-based systems.

UNIX is widely used in the workstation environment, where Sun Microsystems and Apollo Computer are the major players. Workstations come in several configurations, but all sport fast RISC (reduced instruction set computing) chips, high-resolution monitors, high-capacity hard disks, and special versions of UNIX. Workstations are used for a wide variety of applications, including CAD (computer-aided design), CAE (computer-aided engineering), software engineering, software development, animation, and communications. Figure 1-1 shows a picture of the Sun family of workstations.

Early on, AT&T licensed the UNIX system to universities at minimal cost. Consequently, UNIX has become the favored choice of computer

Figure 1-1. *The Sun family of workstations (courtesy of Sun Microsystems, Inc.)*

science departments in most major universities across the country. Each year, tens of thousands of computer science students graduate with experience using UNIX.

In addition, the U.S. government has standardized on UNIX because of its availability on a wide range of systems. The government has been particularly active in establishing standard protocols for networking UNIX systems.

UNIX has also been very popular with value-added resellers (VARs) who fill the demand for customized multiuser applications for which MS-DOS is not a major consideration. These include telephone companies, universities, accounting departments, and workstation environments.

VARs typically specialize in vertical markets like health care, accounting, and legal offices. For a low cost per user, they can put together multiuser computer systems custom-fit to the vertical market's needs. Because UNIX is available on so many different hardware models, VARs have a larger audience than they would with another operating system.

A typical system for a UNIX VAR is a fast Intel 80386-based PC with a large hard disk running SCO XENIX/386. In order to allow several users to use the system at once, VARs often use a multiport board like the one in Figure 1-2, to which users can attach several terminals.

The Future of the UNIX System

In many ways, the key to UNIX's future lies in standardization. Several efforts are under way to merge the best features of UNIX variants into one UNIX system. For example, the Institute of Electrical and Electronic Engineers (IEEE) has developed the portable operating system standard (POSIX) that establishes a standard set of system calls and library routines for UNIX. In addition, AT&T and Sun Microsystems have joined to create a system that meets many of the requirements of POSIX and also incorporates many features of the BSD and XENIX systems. An important part of this system is OPEN LOOK, a graphics user interface. AT&T and Sun expect that the final system, UNIX System V Release 4, will be available in 1990.

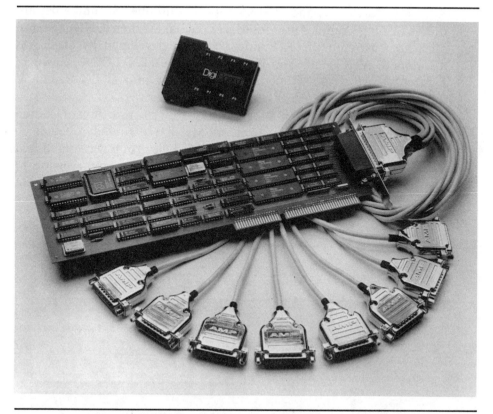

Figure 1-2.   *An eight-port intelligent Input/Output board for 80286- and 80386-based UNIX systems (courtesy of DigiBoard, Incorporated)*

Graphics User Interfaces

The UNIX system was not designed for graphics-display devices. Instead, UNIX is geared towards supporting many users through inexpensive character-based terminals. Nevertheless, the UNIX community pioneered the use of graphics in workstations. UNIX is the favored system for the high-end scientific and engineering workstation market.

UNIX's character-based approach has its advantages. For the experienced user, a character-based system is quick and convenient. It also lends itself to the software tools approach for which UNIX was designed. However, to make proficient use of a character-based system, the user must know quite a bit.

In an effort to expand UNIX's appeal, a number of companies are now providing graphics user interfaces (GUIs) for their UNIX systems. Most are based on the X Window System, developed by M.I.T. As mentioned, AT&T and Sun are producing OPEN LOOK shown in Figure 1-3, which AT&T plans to incorporate into UNIX System V Release 4.

In response to the efforts of AT&T and Sun, a consortium of leading original equipment manufactures (OEMs) have banded together to form the Open Systems Foundation (OSF). This group was established in May, 1988 to produce a standardized but more open version of UNIX. Members of OSF include IBM, Digital Equipment Corporation

Figure 1-3. *A view of the OPEN LOOK graphics user interface from Sun and AT&T (courtesy of Sun Microsystems, Inc.)*

(DEC), Apollo, Hewlett-Packard, and Toshiba, among others. As part of their alternative UNIX standard, OSF has proposed a graphics user interface standard known as Motif. Currently, the only Motif-compatible GUI shipping is Open Desktop from SCO. Other members of OSF have not yet announced their plans for shipping Motif-compatible GUIs.

Yet another forthcoming graphics user interface for UNIX is PM/X from Microsoft. This is a version of Presentation Manager that originated with the OS/2 operating system. The advantage of PM/X is that software vendors will be able to port their OS/2 applications to UNIX easily, thereby making available the various applications programs that are expected for OS/2 within the next few years.

_____

In its 20-year history, UNIX has developed a level of maturity unmatched by other multiuser, multitasking operating systems. It provides a wealth of commands, text-formatting tools, and communications facilities as well as a rich software development environment. In recent years and with its recent advances in graphics user interfaces, UNIX has overcome the stigma of being primarily an academic- and research-oriented operating system and has passed into general business use.

2 The Structure of UNIX

UNIX is a large and complex operating system that runs on a wide variety of hardware platforms from PCs to mainframes. It includes literally hundreds of commands with thousands of associated options. Nevertheless, UNIX has a consistent structure that applies regardless of the hardware platform on which it is running. Whether you approach UNIX as a system administrator or as an end user, it helps to understand that basic structure, the various components of which are described in this chapter.

A Typical UNIX Hardware System

Because of the extraordinary variety of hardware platforms on which UNIX runs, there is no typical UNIX hardware system. However, there are certain hardware components that you'll find in every UNIX system. Some components, such as the system unit, you may never have to deal with directly. Others, such as terminals, you will undoubtedly become well acquainted with. The major hardware components of a UNIX system are explained below.

■ The *system unit* holds the system's central processing unit, or CPU (the processing center of the computer, on which the system software runs) and the disk drives where the system software is kept on a permanent basis.

■ You use a *backup storage device*, such as a floppy disk or magnetic tape drive, to copy software and file systems to and from the computer, usually to make backup copies of files or file systems in case they are accidentally removed or destroyed.

■ The *console* is a terminal with a display and keyboard that is connected directly to the system unit. System error messages are displayed on this terminal. System administration and operation are usually controlled from the console, though the console can often function as an ordinary user terminal. The console may actually be part of the system unit in the case of a workstation or microcomputer.

■ *Modems* are devices that use phone lines to connect remote terminals to a UNIX system or to connect one UNIX system to another.

■ *Communications lines* connect the system to mainframe computers or to other UNIX-based systems. Your UNIX system may or may not be connected to other computers.

■ *User terminals* have a keyboard and a screen display and are either directly connected to the system unit or connected via modems and telephone lines. You use the terminals to communicate with the system unit by typing from the keyboard. You can use many different brands and models of terminals with UNIX systems, from simple ASCII terminals to high-powered graphical workstations. While keyboards are set up in roughly the same way, they may vary slightly from terminal to terminal. Also, each type of terminal acts slightly differently. You will have to learn the keyboard setup and idiosyncrasies of your terminal.

■ *Printers* produce hard-copy output. You can use many different kinds of printers with a UNIX system, from simple impact printers (such as dot-matrix printers and letter-quality printers) to laser printers and phototypesetters.

Software Components

There are many tasks involved in running an operating system, each of which must be controlled by some aspect of the UNIX software. For example, a UNIX system can support many users at the same time, each one running different programs — an ability called *multitasking*. The software that manages this scheduling is not invoked by users, but runs automatically whenever UNIX is active. Other software must be employed by users to do specific tasks, such as word processing, text formatting, mathematical calculations, and interuser communications.

The Kernel

The core of the UNIX system is called the *kernel*. The kernel communicates directly with the system hardware, and therefore must be adapted to the unique architecture of each hardware platform. It is the kernel that insulates users from the differences in diverse hardware.

Besides communicating with the hardware, the kernel coordinates the many internal functions of the operating system. One of these functions is allocating memory and other system resources to the processes going on at any given time. Because UNIX is a multiuser, multitasking operating system, the kernel must manage all of the scheduling and memory management involved in such a complex environment. The kernel ensures that many programs or applications can run at the same time without interfering with one another.

The kernel also keeps track of who is logged in where and keeps track of the contents and locations of all of the files on the file systems. Once the shell has translated users' commands into instructions that the computer can carry out, it is the kernel that carries out these instructions. The kernel also maintains records of the system activity and each user's employment of the system for accounting purposes.

The Shell

The *shell* is a part of the operating system software that acts as a link between the commands you type and the activities that the kernel can carry out. When you type a command, the shell translates that command name into a set of machine language *system calls,* which are requests for the kernel to perform some task. Each UNIX command is really just an easy-to-remember name for some specific set of system calls. The purpose of a shell is to make the operating system friendlier. It is much easier for users to remember command names than the set of system calls that underlie them.

There are a few different shells available on most UNIX systems—for example, the Bourne shell, C shell, and Korn shell. Each one has slightly different characteristics and special features. If you have a choice of shells on your computer, you can choose the one with the features you like best.

The UNIX Utilities

UNIX utilities (often called *commands*) are programs that carry out specific tasks for system users. As mentioned, there are hundreds of different utilities, though not all of them are available on all UNIX systems. What follows is an overview of the things that you can do with UNIX utilities:

- Text editing
- Text formatting
- Spell checking
- Mathematical calculations
- File and directory management
- System administration
- Maintaining file and system security
- Sending output to printers
- Program development
- Filtering data

Because the utilities perform such a wide variety of functions, many users just rely on the utilities. However, you can create your own programs if you wish to accomplish more complex or specialized tasks. Figure 2-1 illustrates the interactions between the various components of the UNIX system, including the kernel, shell, and UNIX utilities.

File Systems

Data is grouped together in collections called *files*. There are several kinds of files:

■ *Ordinary text files*, in which users store data

■ *Programs*, which are files of machine code

■ *Special files*, which are files set up for the various devices on the system, such as terminals and printers

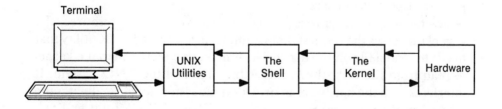

Figure 2-1.   *The components of the UNIX system*

Each file on a UNIX system is stored in a directory, which is a collection of files and other directories. A system of directories and files is called a *file system*. Each UNIX system contains at least one file system. Having files organized in file systems permits much more efficient searches for particular files. The main directory that contains all other directories and files in a UNIX system is called the *root directory*. In the root directory are directories that contain the user work areas and files of machine code necessary to run the UNIX utilities.

Processes

Every time you execute a utility or a program in UNIX, you initiate a *process*. As a multiuser, multitasking operating system, UNIX is capable of running multiple processes simultaneously. The UNIX kernel controls the timing and priority of execution of processes. It allows processes to be created (for example, by loading a utility for execution) and terminated.

There are two types, or levels, of processes in UNIX: user processes and system (or kernel) processes. Whenever you execute a UNIX utility (for example, to display the amount of available disk space), you initiate a user process. System processes, on the other hand, are initiated by the kernel to maintain the smooth control of the operating system. For example, the kernel initiates a system process (or system call) whenever a program needs memory to execute. System processes are, for the most part, transparent to users.

Every time a user process needs to access a system resource, the kernel processes the request. For example, if you run a UNIX utility that needs to read a file on the disk drive, it makes a system call to the kernel to read from the disk; the kernel is the driver of the UNIX system. It interfaces with the hardware to provide a file system and coordinates the execution of processes. See Chapter 12, "The UNIX Multiuser Environment," for more on processes.

CPU Scheduling

UNIX is a timesharing operating system. As such, each user must have the illusion of having the complete computer to him- or herself. Since there is only a single processor in most standard UNIX systems, however, only one process can run at a time. This means that processes must be activated and deactivated at high speed so that they appear to run uninterrupted. Every few ticks of the system clock (a few milliseconds), the UNIX system interrupts the current process and switches execution from that process to another process, a mechanism known as *preemptive scheduling*. Because of the CPU's speed, the period when the CPU is switching between processes is very small. Everything about a process's context is saved so that when UNIX returns to the process, it can continue running the process just as before.

In order for processes to appear to run in an uninterrupted fashion, the kernel must schedule processor time in a "fair" manner. To do so, it uses a round-robin approach. That is, it skips from one process to the next by using a priority system. In general, system processes have a higher priority than do user processes, to ensure smooth running of the system. No single process will complete as quickly using a round-robin approach, but the processing power of the system is more evenly distributed among the users of the system.

The many parts of a UNIX system work together to form a very powerful computational tool. Since you must use the UNIX hardware in order to use the software, you will gradually come to use most of the hardware on your system without really trying. The software, however, will take some time to learn and is what this book is all about.

3 *Getting Started*

The first step in using UNIX is always to log in to the computer. *Logging in* means identifying yourself to the computer, which then gives you access to your home directory, where you can execute UNIX commands and create, store, and edit files. To do this, you need a user or login name and a password, which you should obtain from the system administrator. Once you have these things, you are ready to begin.

Since UNIX is a command-oriented operating system, you need to know the names and functions of commands before you can use UNIX to do anything. This chapter explains and demonstrates some simple commands that will help you start using UNIX.

Login

Your terminal or PC should be turned on and you should see a login prompt, which will look something like the following.

```
login:
```

What appears before the word "login" may differ, but all that matters is the "login" portion. If this prompt does not appear on your terminal, press the RETURN key, several times if necessary, and the prompt should appear. Once you see the prompt, type your user or login name exactly as it has been assigned to you by the system administrator, matching upper- and lowercase letters. Since UNIX is sensitive to case, the login name **User1** is different from the login name **user1** or **USER1**.

Password

To keep unauthorized people from accessing UNIX accounts, you are required to enter a password before you can log in to your account. After entering your login name and pressing RETURN, you will see the password prompt:

```
Password:
```

Now type your password, again exactly as it has been assigned to you. So that your password cannot be read by other users, it will not appear on the screen as you type it. Some accounts, usually public accounts to be used by a number of users, do not require a password. If your account is public, you will not see the password prompt and can ignore the instructions regarding passwords.

   If you have typed both your login name and password correctly, you will be logged in to your account. If you made a mistake typing either your login name or your password, you will see this error message:

```
login incorrect
login:
```

You should type both your login name and your password again, at their respective prompts.

Once you have successfully logged in, what happens varies depending on the system you are using. Most systems notify you at the beginning of a login session if there is electronic mail for you. If your system does this and if you have mail, you will see one of the two following messages:

```
You have mail.
You have new mail.
```

Later in this chapter, you will learn how to read your electronic mail.

Setting Your Terminal Type

Most likely, the next thing you will see is another prompt, this time asking you what type of terminal you have. UNIX needs to know what kind of terminal you have so that it can properly set up the screen for utilities such as vi, the visual screen editor. Each brand and model of terminal supported by UNIX has a unique code associated with it. The code is what you enter when UNIX prompts you for your terminal type. don't know the code for your terminal or PC, ask your system administrator. Usually, there will be a default terminal type, and the prompt will say **TERM =** followed by code for the default terminal type in parentheses. For example, if the default type is a WYSE 50, the prompt will say:

```
TERM = (wy50)
```

If your terminal type is the same as the default, you just need to press RETURN. If your terminal type is not the default, type the code for your terminal type at this prompt and press RETURN. If there is only one kind of terminal on your UNIX system or if you are working at the console, you may not be prompted for a terminal type.

After entering your terminal type, you might see a message confirming what type of terminal you have. You may also see some messages from your system administrator. Generally, these messages are just for your information and don't require a response.

The Prompt

After any messages have printed on your screen, you will see a *shell prompt*. This prompt is the signal that UNIX is ready to carry out your next command. A shell prompt could be a percent sign (%) or a dollar sign ($), depending on which login shell you have. A *shell* is an interface between you and the computer. This interface interprets the commands you type as instructions to run a certain program or programs. Your *login shell* is the shell in which you are placed when you first log in. In later chapters, you will learn some commands unique to the two most common shells, the Bourne shell and the C shell. However, the commands listed in this chapter will work no matter what shell you are in. Once you have successfully logged into your account and see a shell prompt, you are ready to try some sample commands.

Correcting Mistakes

There are several ways to correct mistakes you make as you type UNIX commands. Some of these ways will work for you, and some will not, depending on what type of terminal you have and what your UNIX system recognizes.

With the BACKSPACE key, you can back up one space at a time until you reach your mistake. As you back up, the letter the cursor is on will be erased. CTRL-H usually works exactly like the BACKSPACE key.

On some terminals, you can also use the # (pound sign) key to back up one space at a time. This key functions differently from BACKSPACE or CTRL-H. It doesn't back up the cursor; rather, it follows the erroneous character on the screen with the # character. The character preceding the # is then ignored when UNIX interprets the command. As you type the sample commands, try out these keys and see which ones work on your particular terminal.

You may type a whole line and decide that you don't want to execute the command or discover that you've made a mistake at the beginning of the line. In this case, you might want to erase the entire line in one fell swoop rather than one character at a time. Keys or key combinations that erase a whole line or nullify a command are called *line-kill* keys. One way to erase a whole line is by pressing CTRL-U. Depending on your system, CTRL-U may or may not actually erase the line from the screen. In any case, it will always stop the command from being executed. Another key that works on some systems is the DELETE (DEL) key. You may also use this key to stop a program from executing once it has already started. On some terminals, the @ key also functions as a line-kill key. Again, you will have to experiment with these keys to see which ones work for you.

▶**NOTE**   You can also determine which erase and line-kill keys work on your terminal by using the **stty** command. To learn how to use this command, see Chapter 13, "Command Reference."

Some Sample Commands

When you log in to a UNIX system, nothing happens until you give the computer a command. You do this by typing the name of the UNIX utility you want to use. All UNIX command names are one word long and almost all of them consist of only lowercase letters. Each time you type a command, you must press RETURN before it will be executed. Some commands, such as **date**, are actual English words. Others, like **ls**, are not. Most commands that are not English words, however, are fairly mnemonic. For example, **ls** stands for "list," **rm** stands for "remove," and **mkdir** stands for "make directory." It should be easy to memorize the names of the commands you use often. A convenient command reference is provided at the end of the book, so you can look up the names of commands that you use less often.

Different UNIX commands require different types of input and produce different types of output. Some commands require you to specify the name of a file or directory on which to operate, while others do not. Most commands can be followed by options, which are extra letters typed after hyphens that allow you to achieve different results with the same command. Whenever you type something else (either a file name or an option) after a command name, it must be separated from the command name by a space. In this chapter, you can try some commands that do not operate on files or directories, since at this point you probably don't have any files or subdirectories in your account.

Noninteractive Commands

Some commands cause something to print on the screen with no input from you besides the name of the command itself. These are called *noninteractive* commands and are the simplest commands. They are also a good place to start because they produce immediate and visible results. What follows are some sample noninteractive commands.

date   Type **date** and UNIX will print today's date and time (using a 24-hour clock), as in the following example:

```
% date
Thu May 24 15:12:59 PDT 1990
```

ls   Shorthand for "list," the **ls** command lists the contents of a directory. Type **ls** to see an alphabetized list of the files and other directories in your home directory. When you first log in, there may be no files in your home directory, in which case **ls** will return just a prompt. The following example shows a sample list of files and directories as displayed by the **ls** command. (Note that because filenames and directory names assume the same form, there is no overt distinction between them.)

```
% ls
accounts
letter.to.ed
mbox
personal
timetable
```

cal   The term "cal" is shorthand for "calendar." Type **cal** to see the present date and a calendar for the present months and the two adjacent months. To see a calendar for a whole year, type **cal** *year*. For instance, to see the calendar for the year 2000, type **cal 2000**. The following example illustrates the **cal** command with no year specified:

```
% cal
mon May   6 12:52:14 1990
```

```
          Apr                      May                      Jun
 S  M Tu  W Th  F  S      S  M Tu  W Th  F  S      S  M Tu  W Th  F  S
 1  2  3  4  5  6  7               1  2  3  4  5                  1  2
 8  9 10 11 12 13 14      6  7  8  9 10 11 12      3  4  5  6  7  8  9
15 16 17 18 19 20 21     13 14 15 16 17 18 19     10 11 12 13 14 15 16
22 23 24 25 26 27 28     20 21 22 23 24 25 26     17 18 19 20 21 22 23
29 30                    27 28 29 30 31           24 25 26 27 28 29 30
```

who   Type **who** for a list of users currently logged in to the computer. You will see an alphabetized list of users followed by the name assigned to the terminal they are using and the time they logged in, as in the following example:

```
% who
root          tty02          May 24 10:25
sheila3       tty1a          May 24 11:23
```

clear   Notice that, as you type commands, previous commands and their output remain on the screen and scroll off the top as the screen fills up. You can type **clear** to clear off all of the old commands and output and get a new prompt at the top of the screen. This can be advantageous if, for instance, you have just typed a mail message that you don't want anyone else to see. Unless you type **clear**, the message will remain on the screen until it scrolls off the top. Clearing the screen also makes it easier to focus on the output of the next command.

Interactive Commands

The commands you've just seen do not require you to do anything after typing the command name. Some *interactive* commands, on the other hand, ask you to respond to a question or make a choice at some point during program execution and will not continue until you respond. Here are some sample interactive commands.

passwd   You can use the **passwd** command to change your password from the one given to you by the system administrator to a new one of your choice. To do this, type **passwd**. If your login name were **brown,** you would then see the following:

```
Changing password for brown
Old password:
```

You now type your old password. Remember, the password will not print on the screen as you type it. If you type it incorrectly, the **passwd** program will not work and you will get this error message:

```
Sorry.
```

If you type the old password correctly, you will be asked to enter a new password as follows:

```
New password:
```

Before you get the prompt for a new password, you may see some instructions about what length or type of characters the new password should consist of. For example, you may be told that it should consist of a combination of upper and lowercase letters and numbers. Following these instructions will make your password harder to guess. You should not use your name or nickname or any word in the dictionary. (Someone who really wanted to find out your password could systematically check every word in the UNIX system dictionary to see if it matched your password.) On the other hand, you should select a password that will be easy for you to remember, since you should never write your password down. A word or name with numbers inserted between or in place of some of the letters is a good idea for a password.

Once you have selected a new password, type it at the prompt. Then you will be asked to reenter the new password. This ensures that you haven't typed the new password incorrectly. If the two match, **passwd** returns a shell prompt. If they don't match, it asks you to retype the new password. You can change your password as often as you like and should change it regularly to maintain the security of your account.

mail or mailx   The **mail** or **mailx** program, depending on what type of UNIX system you have, allows users to communicate with other users on the system or other connected UNIX systems. Mail will be discussed in more detail in Chapter 8, but this chapter briefly introduces reading and responding to your mail messages and sending mail of your own.

Follow these steps to send a mail message to yourself so that you have some mail to read while you try out the mail program. You can send mail to any other user whose login name you know by following the same steps but inserting their login name in place of yours.

Type **mail** *your login name*. The **mail** program now prompts you for the subject of your message as follows:

```
Subject:
```

You don't need to have a subject, but for now type something and press RETURN. What you type next will be the body of your message. Type as you ordinarily would, using the BACKSPACE and line-kill keys when necessary. If you type continuously, the text appears to wrap around to the next line automatically. However, your message will really be one long line which could be garbled when you try to read your mail. Therefore, you must press RETURN at the end of each line. When you finish typing your message, type CTRL-D as the first character on a line. Depending on how **mail** is set up for you, you will either be returned to a shell prompt after typing CTRL-D or you will get the **mail** prompt:

```
Cc:
```

To send copies of the message to additional users, you would enter the login names of those users at this prompt. For now, just press RETURN if you see this prompt, telling mail that you don't want to send any copies. Now you will be returned to the shell.

The following example shows how a user with the login name **marie** would send herself a message:

```
% mail marie
Subject: Practice mail
Hi!  I'm sending myself practice mail to see how the mail program
works. Bye!
^D
Cc:
%
```

Now that you've sent yourself some mail, you are ready to read your message and any others that you might have. To read your mail, simply type **mail** or **mailx**. Though you are sure to have at least one message now, sometimes you will have none, in which case UNIX will tell you so, and the mail program will not be executed. When there is mail for you, you will see a list of messages. The list contains the number of each message, according to the order in which it was received, the login name of the sender, the date and time the message was received, some information about its length, and its subject, if any. At the end of the list is the mail prompt, which is usually an ampersand (&) or a question mark (?) but may also be an underscore.

Once you see the list of messages, you can choose one to read. If you want to read message number 1, you can enter one of three things at the mail prompt:

■ You can press RETURN by itself. This displays the current message, which when you first enter the mail program is always number 1. By pressing RETURN again, you can see the subsequent message, and so on, until all of the messages have been displayed.

■ You can type **t** (shorthand for "type") followed by the number.

■ You can type just the message number.

The following example shows how the user Marie enters the **mail** program and reads the practice message she just sent herself:

```
% mail
Mail version 5.2 6/21/85.  Type ? for help.
"/usr/spool/mail/marie": 2 messages 2 new
 U  1 yourboss            Wed May 31 14:09 165/6809 "The new account"
>N  2 marie               Thu Jun  1 09:44  12/361  "Practice mail"
& t 2
Message 2:
From marie Fri Jun  1 09:44:13 1990
Date: Fri, 1 Jun 89 09:44:11 -0700
From: marie
To: marie
Subject: Practice mail

Hi!  I'm sending myself practice mail to see how the mail program
```

```
works. Bye!

& q
Saved 1 message in mbox
Held 1 message in /usr/spool/mail/marie
%
```

Once you select a message to read, **mail** displays that message, together with some information about the sender, the date sent and received, and the addressee. When the entire message has been displayed, you are returned to a **mail** prompt. Now you can either choose another message to read or respond to the one you just read. To respond to a message, type a lowercase "r" at the mail prompt. This initiates a new message that will be mailed only to the person who sent the original message. An uppercase "R" will mail the subsequent message to everyone who got a copy of the original message.

▶**NOTE**   The lower- and uppercase r's may work in the opposite way on your system. That is, a lowercase "r" may cause copies to be sent to everyone who got a copy of the original message, while an uppercase "R" sends the reply only to the sender of the original message.

To leave the mail program, you can use the **quit** (**q**) or **exit** (**x**) commands. If you type **q**, any messages you looked at will be saved in a file called **mbox** in your home directory. Those you did not read will remain in the *mail spool,* where new messages are held. If you leave the mail program by typing **x**, all messages, even those you already read or deleted, will be held in the spool.

Logging Out

When you want to leave the UNIX system, you need to log your terminal out. In this way, no one else can have access to your account and other users can use the terminal to log into their accounts. When you log out, whatever was on your screen will stay there for the next user to read. If you don't want this to happen, clear the screen with **clear** before logging out.

If your prompt is $, your login shell is the Bourne shell and you can log out with CTRL-D. If your prompt is %, your login shell is the C shell and you can log out by typing **logout**. CTRL-D sometimes logs you out in the C shell as well, but your account may be set up so as not to allow this. If your account is set up this way and you type CTRL-D, you will get this error message:

```
Use "logout" to logout.
```

To make sure you are logged out, wait until you see the login prompt on the screen again, indicating that the terminal is ready for another user to log in.

_____

In this chapter, you learned how to log in to your account, execute some simple commands, and log out. Basically, this is what every login session will consist of, the only difference being that the commands you use will be more complex. You have now had some hands-on experience with two types of UNIX commands: interactive and noninteractive. In the next few chapters, you will learn about some of the other types of commands, including those that create, edit, and remove files and directories.

4 *Files and Directories*

A UNIX file system consists of a hierarchical structure of both files and directories. You can think of a file system as an inverted tree. At the top of the structure is a single directory, called the root, or **/** (slash), directory. This is analogous to the trunk of a tree. All other directories in the file system branch out from the root directory, just as all the limbs of a tree branch out from the trunk. At the bottom of the structure are files, some of which are used by UNIX to set up the operating system and execute commands, and some of which are created by the users of the system. In between the root directory and the files are other directories. The directories of a UNIX file system can be thought of as the branches of the tree: They lead from the trunk to other directories and files. To continue the analogy, you can think of files as the leaves of the tree. If you follow a certain branch out as far as it will go, it probably ends in one or more leaves. Once you have reached a file, you have reached the tip of a particular branch of the file system tree.

Figure 4-1 shows the structure of a typical UNIX file system. The ellipses (. . .) under the names of directories indicate that that directory may branch out into other subdirectories that are not shown for reasons of space. Any directory that is inside another is called a *subdirectory*. In Figure 4-1, **usr** is a subdirectory of **/** (the root directory); **a, b,** and **public** are subdirectories of **usr,** and so on. Any directory that contains a file or subdirectory is called the *parent directory* of that file or subdirectory. In Figure 4-1, **/** is the parent directory of several directories, including **bin, dev, tmp,** and **usr; hayes** is the parent directory of **reports** and

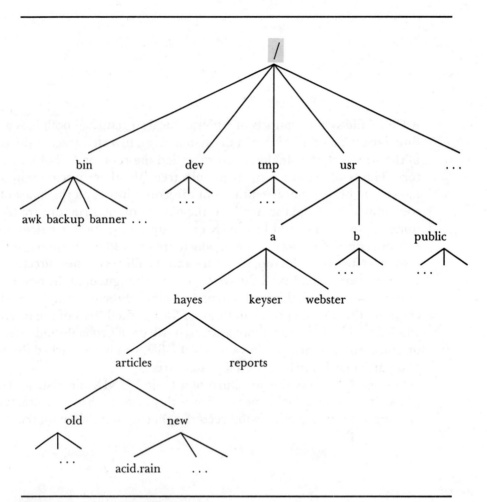

Figure 4-1. *A typical UNIX file system*

articles, and so on. (Note that in this context the words "directory" and "subdirectory" can be used interchangeably.) Finally, **acid.rain** is a file in the directory **new**.

At any level in the file system, you may find files, directories that branch into files, or directories that branch into other directories. Once you are familiar with the commands for creating and manipulating directories, you will be able to create in your UNIX account a system of directories and subdirectories in which to store your personal files.

Directories

Every file in a UNIX system is a part of some directory. This keeps files organized. If all of the files the system were simply stored in one place, it would take UNIX a very long time to search through all of the files and find a particular one. Directories provide a way of addressing files so UNIX can access them quickly and easily.

Even when you first log in to your account, you are in a subdirectory of the UNIX system, called your *home directory*. Unless you create some subdirectories in your account, all of your files will be stored in your home directory. In theory, you could do this, but it is much more efficient to maintain your own system of subdirectories. It is more efficient for you because it is easier to keep track of files if you group them in directories by subject or type. UNIX also searches smaller directories more efficiently than larger ones. A good rule of thumb is never to have more than 30 files or subdirectories in any one directory. The following sections will accquaint you with the commands you need to create directories, move and copy files between directories, list the contents of directories, move directories into other directories, and change the directory you are currently in.

Your Home Directory

As mentioned earlier in this chapter, your home directory is the directory you are placed in when you log in to your UNIX account. This directory has the same name as your login name. You can think of your account as a miniature version of a UNIX file system. At the top of your personal file system, instead of the root directory, is your home directory. Under that are subdirectories that you create, which may themselves branch into subdirectories and/or files.

Users' home directories look just like any other directory in a diagram of a file system. (In Figure 5-1, **hayes** is a user's home directory.) However, as the top directory in your account, your home directory has a special status. Every time you log in, UNIX sets up a variable called HOME that identifies your home directory. UNIX uses the value of the HOME variable as a point of reference for determining what files and directories in the file system you can access and where to move you when you change directories. The HOME variable will be discussed in more detail in the section about pathnames.

Certain files that determine your working environment are kept in your home directory. For example, the **.login** file in the C shell, or the **.profile** file in the Bourne shell, contains commands that are executed when you log in. These files determine such things as your prompt, your default terminal type, and your pathname, all of which will be discussed later in this chapter and in Chapters 9 and 10. Other files determine specialized aspects of your environment, such as how the **mail** program works for you. These files will be discussed in later chapters.

The Current Directory

The *current,* or *working, directory* is the directory you are in at any given time. For instance, when you first log in, the current directory is always your home directory. If you then move to one of your subdirectories, that subdirectory is the current directory.

At all times during a login session, UNIX keeps track of your current directory. Unless you specify alternate directories, commands will be executed relative to the current directory. For instance, any file you create will, by default, be a part of the current directory, as will any subdirectory you create. When you type **ls,** you will see a list of files and directories in the current directory.

Every UNIX directory contains a file called **.** (dot). This is a special file that stands for "the current directory." Whenever you want to refer to the current directory, you can use . to do so. Another file called .. (dot dot) stands for the parent directory of the current directory. When you need to refer to this directory, you can substitute .. for its name.

Pathnames

When you type a UNIX command that operates on a file or directory, you must specify the name of the desired file or directory. Every file and directory on a UNIX system really has two names. One is the name given by the person who creates it, for example, **accounts, figures,** or **sales.** This name will be referred to as the *short name* because it is actually an abbreviation for the file or directory's full name, or *pathname.* The pathname of a file or directory is the list of all the directories that form the connection between the root directory and the item in question. Every full pathname begins with **/** (slash), which is the name of the root directory. A **/** also separates the names of the directories in a pathname. Figure 4-2 shows a UNIX file system that has a user account called **edmond05** as one subdirectory. The directories that lie along the path of the subdirectory **edmond05** appear shaded. The pathname of this directory would be **/a/accounting/edmond05**. As shown in Figure 4-2, **edmond05** is a subdirectory of a directory called **accounting**, which is in turn a subdirectory of a directory called **a**. The directory **a** is a subdirectory of **/**, the root directory. If **edmond05** contained a subdirectory called **numbers**, its pathname would be **/a/accounting/edmond05/numbers**.

You can uniquely identify every file and directory on a UNIX system by its pathname, even if its short name is identical to the short name of another file or directory somewhere else on the system. For example, suppose two user accounts, **anderson** and **martino,** each contain a subdirectory called **sales.** UNIX can differentiate these two subdirectories by their pathnames. One would be **/. . ./anderson/sales** and the other would be **/. . ./martino/sales**, where the ellipses represent the intervening directories. Even though you can refer to a file or directory in your current directory by its short name, UNIX always interprets the name of a file or directory as its full pathname. UNIX can to do this because it keeps track of your current directory and can fill in that part of the pathname itself.

In addition to the full pathname, you can also use the *relative path-name,* of a file or directory. A relative pathname starts not with the root directory but with a directory closer to the directory whose path is being defined.

To specify a pathname relative to your home directory, you can begin the pathname with either **$HOME** or ~. UNIX will substitute the value of the HOME variable for **$HOME**. For instance, if your home directory is **keyser**, your HOME variable stands for **/. . ./keyser**, where the ellipses represent the directories between **/** and **keyser**. Whenever you type **$HOME** as part of a pathname, UNIX interprets it as the full pathname of your home directory. The HOME variable works in all shells. In the C shell, you can also use the single character ~ (tilde) in a pathname to stand for the home directory. The C shell sets up ~ just as UNIX sets up the HOME variable. If you are using the C shell, you can substitute ~ for **$HOME** whenever it appears in the examples. For example, suppose you had directories in your home directory called **sales** and **addresses**. If your current directory were **sales** and you wanted to refer to **addresses**, you couldn't just use the name **addresses** since it is not a

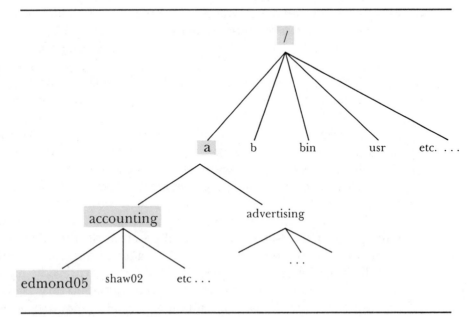

Figure 4-2.   *The path of user account **edmond05***

subdirectory of the current directory. Instead, you could use its pathname relative to the home directory, which would be either **$HOME /addresses** (in any shell) or **~/addresses** (in the C shell). In this case, the home directory is also the parent directory of the current directory, so you could refer to the subdirectory **addresses** by using **..** in the pathname to represent the home directory, as follows: **../addresses**. Figure 4-3 illustrates this situation.

To specify a pathname relative to the current directory, you can begin the pathname with either **.** (remember, this special file stands for the current directory) or the name of the first subdirectory in the path. Suppose that a subdirectory called **schedule** is in your current directory, and a file called **lectures** is in **schedule**. If you want to refer to the file in **schedule** without changing your current directory, you could refer to it as either **./schedule/lectures** or **schedule/lectures**. The **.** is optional in this case because if the pathname doesn't start with **/**, UNIX assumes you want it to start with the current directory.

If you've moved around between directories quite a bit, you may not be sure of your current directory. You could find this out by using **ls** and then remembering the name of the directory by the files that are in it. However, a simpler way to determine your current directory is to type **pwd** (for "print working directory"). The **pwd** command prints the full pathname of your current directory.

▶**NOTE**   Any time you type a UNIX command that operates on a file or directory, you can type either the short name of the file or directory if

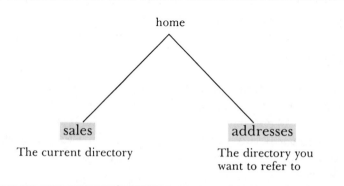

Figure 4-3.   *Referring to a directory outside the current directory*

it is in your current directory, or a full or relative pathname if it is not in your current directory.

Creating Directories

You can create a directory within your current directory with the command **mkdir** *dirname,* where you replace *dirname* with the name you want to give the directory. A directory or file name may consist of up to 14 characters, including upper- and lower-case letters, numbers, and all characters but the magic characters, which are characters that have special meaning to the shell, discussed in Chapter 5, the wildcard characters discussed later in this chapter, and **/** (slash). Since **/** is used to separate the names of directories in a pathname, short names of files or directories containing a **/** would be interpreted as pathnames.

▶**BERKELEY VERSION**   On Berkeley UNIX there is no limit to the number of characters in a directory name. Still, the shorter the name, the easier it is to type.

Some users give directories names beginning with, or consisting entirely of, uppercase letters to distinguish them from files, which are usually named with all lowercase letters. However, this is only a matter of preference. In this book, example files and directories will generally have all lowercase names. No two files or directories in the same subdirectory can have the exact same name. The two items would not then have unique pathnames, and UNIX could no longer identify which file or directory the pathname stood for.

   The following example shows how to create a directory called **letters**:

```
% mkdir letters
```

As with all commands that operate on directories, you can supply **mkdir** with a pathname instead of a short name if you want to create a directory outside of the current directory. For example, if your current directory, **sales**, were a subdirectory of your home directory and you wanted to make another subdirectory of your home directory called **profits**, you could type

```
% mkdir $HOME/profits
```

This would create a directory in your home directory rather than in your current directory.

The **mkdir** command does not print anything on the screen if it is successful: It just returns a prompt. If you want to verify that a directory you created is really there, you can use **ls**.

Listing the Contents of a Directory

In Chapter 3, you learned how to list the contents of the working directory with **ls**. On some systems, **ls** displays the contents of a directory in a one-column alphabetical list in which files and directories are not differentiated. However, **ls** has many options for displaying directory contents in different formats and orders. This section explains some of the more useful **ls** options.

If you have a large number of files in a directory, the list may take up more than one screen and you may not have a chance to read the whole list before some of it scrolls off the top. To keep this from happening, you can use the **-C** (uppercase C) option of **ls**, which displays the same list of contents, but in several columns instead of just one. The following examples show the contents of the same directory listed with **ls** and **ls -C**:

```
% ls
file.trans
letters
losses
mail1
mail2
mbox
printers
typescript
wastebasket
wp6
% ls -C
file.trans      losses   mail2    printers     wastebasket
letters         mail1    mbox     typescript   wp6
```

In some more recent versions of System V UNIX, the command **lc** functions just like **ls -C**.

▶**BERKELEY VERSION**   With no options, **ls** functions just like the **ls -C** or **lc** commands, producing multiple-column output.

The command **ls -t** lists the files and directories, not alphabetically, but in the order in which they were last modified, beginning with the most recently modified file or directory. This option is useful if, for instance, you have two different versions of the same file, with different names, and you want to know which one contains the most recent changes you made without having actually to look at the file.

There are some files in each directory that are not displayed with **ls**. These are called *dot files* because their names begin with a period (.), or dot. Some of these are special files that are part of your account when it is set up. The **.login** (dot login) file and the **.profile** (dot profile) file, mentioned before, are two such files. The . and .. files, which stand for the current directory and the parent directory, are also dot files. You can create your own dot files if you have files you don't want to see every time you list the contents of a directory. For example, some users like to back up important files as dot files. To list dot files, use the **-a** option of **ls**, which lists all files and directories, including dot files. The following example shows the contents of the sample directory as listed with **ls -a**:

```
% ls -a
.
..
file.trans
letters
losses
sales
file.trans
mail1
mail2
mbox
printers
typescript
wastebasket
wp6
```

Note that since there is no **.login** or **.profile** file in this directory, it cannot be the user's home directory.

The **-F** option lists the directory contents in alphabetical order, like **ls** without any options. In addition, it marks each directory with a slash (/) after the name and each executable file (a file that can be executed as a command) with an asterisk (*). Since directory and file names ordinarily look alike, this is an easy way to distinguish the two. The next example shows the preceding directory listed with **ls -F**:

```
% ls -F
file.trans*
letters/
losses/
mail1
mail2
mbox*
printers
typescript
wastebasket/
wp6/
```

The **-l** option of **ls** lists the directory contents alphabetically in long format. This means that not only the name of but also some information about each file and directory is listed. The following example shows the sample directory listed with **ls -l**.

```
% ls -l
total 20
-rwx------   1 sheila3  group        26 May 19 13:46 file.trans
drwxr-xr-x   2 sheila3  group       400 Jun  6 12:11 letters
drwxr-xr-x   2 sheila3  group        32 May 18 10:56 losses
-rw-r--r--   1 sheila3  group       140 Jun  1 09:49 mail1
-rw-r--r--   1 sheila3  group       564 Jun  1 09:57 mail2
-rw-rwxrwx   1 sheila3  group       215 Jun  1 10:57 mbox
-rw-r--r--   1 sheila3  group        32 May 19 14:01 printers
-rw-r--r--   1 sheila3  group       707 Jun  1 09:50 typescript
drwxr-xr-x   2 sheila3  group        32 May 18 10:56 wastebasket
drwxr-xr-x   3 sheila3  group        48 May 18 10:56 wp6
```

The first column consists of ten smaller columns. If the item is a directory, a **d** appears in the first column. The next nine columns show the permissions of the file or directory. (Permissions, codes stating which users are allowed to access the file, are discussed later in this chapter.) The long format also includes the number of links the item has (different names with which the item is associated), the owner of the file or directory (usually the person who created the file), the name of the group the owner is in, the size of the item in bytes (a unit equal to one character), the date it was created, and, in the last column, the name of the file or directory.

You can use each of the preceding five options (**-C, -t , -a, -F, -1**) either alone or in combination. For example, you could produce a multiple-column list that includes the dot files by using both the **-C** and the **-a** options. To use more than one option with **ls**, you can either type both of the options with separate dashes (**ls -C -a**) or both after one hyphen (**ls -Ca**). You can type the options in any order and the output will be the same. One combination of options that is not possible is **-l** with **-C**. Since a long format list takes up the whole width of a screen, you can't use multiple columns with it. If you try to use these options together, only **-l** will be invoked.

The **ls** command alone or with options and no directory specified lists the contents of the working directory. If you supply the name or pathname of a directory other than the current directory, **ls** will list the contents of that directory instead. For instance, to list the contents of **sales**, a subdirectory of the current directory, type

```
% ls sales
```

To list the contents of the parent directory of your working directory (identified by the dot file **..**), type

```
% ls ..
```

To list the contents of your home directory when your working directory is another directory, type

```
% ls $HOME
```

(Remember, if you are in the C shell you can replace **$HOME** with ~.)

Changing the Working Directory

To change your current directory, use **cd** (for "change directory"). If you use **cd** with no arguments, you will be placed in your home directory. If you want to move to one of your subdirectories, use **cd** *name,* where you replace *name* with the name of the subdirectory you want to change to. For example, to change to **letters**, a subdirectory of the current directory, you would type

```
% cd letters
```

Since **cd** returns only a prompt if successful, you can verify that you really have changed directories with **pwd**. You can also specify the pathname of the directory you want to change to if that directory is not an immediate subdirectory of the current directory. For example, suppose you had a directory called **letters** in your home directory, and within **letters** was a subdirectory called **business**. If you wanted to change to the subdirectory **business** and your current directory was neither **letters** nor your home directory, you would type

```
% cd $HOME/letters/business
```

Moving and Renaming Directories

The command **mv** has two functions concerning directories:

- You can use it to rename directories.
- On some systems, you can use it to move one directory into another.

You can use **mv** to rename a directory by typing **mv** *dirname1 dirname2*, where *dirname1* is the old name or pathname of the directory and *dirname2* is the new name you want to give it. Suppose you wanted to rename a directory called **sales** while keeping all the files the same. To change the name of the directory to **us.sales**, you could type

```
% mv sales us.sales
```

The **mv** utility can tell that the first item you named is a directory, not a file, so it will make **us.sales** a directory too; in fact, it is the same directory with a different name. If you now type **ls**, you will see that **us.sales** has replaced **sales**. If you type **ls us.sales,** you will see that it contains the same files and directories as **sales** used to.

On some systems, the **mv** utility can also move one of your directories into another. To do this, type **mv** *dirnameA dirnameB,* where both *dirnameA* and *dirnameB* are the names or pathnames of directories already existing in your account. Since **mv** can tell that you already have a directory called *dirnameB,* it will not rename *dirnameA* but will instead make it a subdirectory of the directory specified by *dirnameB.*

Suppose you had one directory called **bus.letters** and another called **letters** in your working directory. If you wanted to make **bus.letters** a subdirectory of **letters,** you would type

```
% mv bus.letters letters
```

Now typing **ls letters** will show that **bus.letters** is a subdirectory of letters.

Removing Directories

You may sometimes have directories that you no longer need. You can use the **rmdir** command to remove a directory. To do this, type **rmdir** *dirname,* where *dirname* is the name or pathname of the directory you want to remove. You can also remove more than one directory at a time by typing **rmdir** *dirname1 dirname2 . . . dirnameN,* where you replace each *dirname* with the name or pathname of a directory to remove. For example, to remove a directory called **graphs**, you would type

```
% rmdir graphs
```

To remove three directories—**accounts**, **sales**, and **insurance**—you would type

```
% rmdir accounts sales insurance
```

The **rmdir** command is designed so that you can only remove a directory if it is empty. This protects any files in a directory from being accidentally removed when you remove the directory. Only the files . and .., which cannot be removed, may remain in a directory to be deleted. If you attempt to remove a directory that contains any files or subdirectories besides . and .., an error message will indicate that the directory is not empty, and it will not be removed. Remember that a directory may contain dot files that will not show up when you list the contents with **ls**, so you could still get the error message when you try to remove a directory that appears to be empty. If listing the contents of a directory with **ls** just returns a prompt, try listing the contents with **ls -a** to see if there are any dot files in the directory.

Unlike some of the other commands discussed in this chapter, **rmdir** cannot operate on either the current directory or a parent directory. Therefore, if you type **rmdir .** to remove the working directory or **rmdir ..** to remove its parent directory, you will get an error message.

Files

A file is a collection of data, usually either text or machine code. All programs that run on UNIX are files of machine code. Whenever you give UNIX a command, you are in a sense telling the computer to execute the commands in a certain file or set of files. As a UNIX user, you will be able to create, edit, read, change, search, and remove your own files. Your files may be text files or they may be programs. In this chapter, you will learn how to create files with **cat**, and how to move, copy, rename, remove, and change the permissions on files. In short, you will learn most of what you need to know about files, except editing (covered in Chapter 6) and formatting (covered in Chapter 7).

Naming Files

The naming conventions that apply to directories also apply to files. File names may have up to 14 upper- and lowercase letters and characters, except for the magic characters described in Chapter 5. Since you may be typing certain file names a great deal, it is a good idea to keep them under the 14-letter limit.

▶**BERKELEY VERSION**   There is no limit on the number of characters in a file name.

If you name a file and later decide the name is too long or inappropriate, you can easily change it. Changing file names will be discussed later in this chapter.

Creating Files

One simple way to create a file is by using the **cat** command. When you type

cat > *filename*

where *filename* is the name of the file you want to create and press RETURN, everything you type on the following lines will be placed in that file. You must press RETURN at the end of each line of text so that everything you type won't be just one long line. When you finish the file, press RETURN and then, as the first character on a line, CTRL-D. The following example shows how you could create a file called **sample** by using **cat**:

```
% cat > sample
The quick, brown fox jumps over the lazy dog.
Do you know the way to San Jose?  What is the sound of
one hand clapping?
^D
%
```

After pressing CTRL-D, you are returned to a shell prompt. You can use **ls** to see that the file you've created is really there.
    If you want to look at a file you've created, you can type

cat *filename*

where *filename* is the name of the file you want to look at. The **cat** command will display the contents of the file. If the file is very long, it will scroll continuously across the screen, too fast for you to read. If you have a long file, you can stop the scrolling by pressing CTRL-S at any point, and then any key to resume the scrolling. In Chapter 5, you will learn other ways to view files.

So that you have some files on which to practice the commands in this chapter, you should now create a few short practice files with **cat**. Remember to give each file a different name. If you type **cat** > *filename*, where *filename* is an already existing file, whatever you type will replace the previous file contents.

Moving Files

The **mv** utility functions with files as it does with directories. You can use **mv** either to rename a file or to move it into another directory, depending on the input you give. To rename a file, type

mv *filename1 filename2*

where *filename1* is the file whose name you want to change and *filename2* is the new name you want to give the file. If *filename2* already exists in the working directory, **mv** first removes that already existing file and then renames your file. If you accidentally give an existing file name as the new name, you could write over that file and lose its contents. You can do two things to ensure that this doesn't happen:

■ Review the contents of a directory before you rename a file to check that there isn't already a file with the name you want to use.

■ Use the **-i** (for "interactive") option of **mv**. Typing **mv -i** will cause **mv** to check if there is already a file with the new name you've picked. If there is, **mv** will ask you if you want to remove it, as follows:

```
remove filename2 ?
```

If you do want to remove the old file, type **y** (for yes) and it will be removed. If you don't want to remove it, type **n** (for no) or any other character besides **y**, and the file will not be removed and **mv** will simply be aborted.

To move a file into another directory, type

mv *filename dirname*

where *filename* is the name of the file you want to move and *dirname* is the name or pathname of the directory to which you want to move it. For example, you could move a file called **lunches** into a directory called **expenses** by typing

```
% mv lunches expenses
```

If **expenses** were not in the current directory, you would need to type its pathname instead of its short name. Suppose it were in a subdirectory of your home directory called **budget**. You would type

```
% mv lunches $HOME/budget
```

When you use **mv** to move a file into a different directory, the file you move will have the same name in the new directory unless you specify a new name by appending it to the directory name after a slash. For example, suppose you had a file called **mom** in the working directory, which you wanted to move into a directory called **personal**. Instead of calling this file **mom** in the new directory, however, you wanted to call it **mom.n.dad**. To do this, you would type

```
% mv mom personal/mom.n.dad
```

Now **mom** will be gone from the working directory and **mom.n.dad** will be in **personal**. Note that you must use the same caution when moving files into different directories as when renaming a file in the current directory. If there is already a file in that directory with the name of the one you are moving (or with the new name you are giving it) that file will be removed before the new one is moved there. You can use the two precautions discussed earlier in this section to avoid this.

Copying Files

While **mv** renames or moves a file, **cp** (for "copy") makes a copy of a file with a new name or in a different directory and leaves the original file as it was. You can use this command to make backup copies of important files or to copy files that you want to change. If there are files that you want to have in more than one directory, you can also use **cp** to copy files to another directory. To make a copy of a file in the working directory, type

cp *filename1 filename2*

where *filename1* is the name of the file you want to copy and *filename2* is the name you want the copy to have. Remember, if you are making a copy of a file in the same directory, the copy cannot have the same name. Here again, you could accidentally lose a file you want if *filename2* is the name of a file that already exists in the working directory. The **cp** command writes the new file over the old one. The two precautions that apply to **mv** apply to **cp** as well.

To copy a file into another directory, type

cp *filename dirname*

where *filename* is the name of the file you want to move and *dirname* is the name or pathname of the directory you want to move it to. Once again, follow the two precautions mentioned earlier so that you don't overwrite an existing file in the new directory. By default, **cp** gives the copied file in the new directory the same name as the original. This is possible because the two files will not have the same pathname. If you want the copy in the new directory to have a *different* name, append the new name to the directory name with a **/**, as with **mv**.

Permissions

All files on a UNIX system are part of one large file system and could in principle be accessed by any user of the system. For this reason, there is a way to restrict access to files and directories so that only appropriate users can access them. Each file and directory has a set of *permissions* associated with it. These permissions determine which users can read, or look at, the file; write, or make changes to, the file; and, if the file is executable as a program, run that program. If a user has execute permission for a directory, he or she can search that directory, not execute it as a program.

When you type

ls -l

the first column in each row shows whether or not that item is a directory. The next nine columns in each row show the permissions associated with that file or directory. Figure 4-4 illustrates the permissions associated with the columns displayed with **ls -l**. Columns 2 through 4 show the permissions the owner of the file, or *user*, has. If the user has read permission, there is an **r** in the first column. If the user has write permission, there is a **w** in the second column. If the user can execute the file as a program, there is an **x** in the third column. In each of these columns, a - (dash) appears in place of the letter if the owner

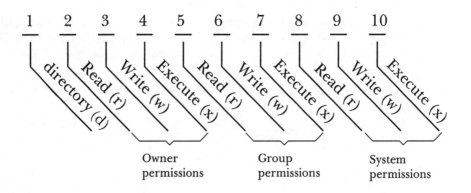

Figure 4-4. *Permissions as displayed by* **ls -l**

does not have this permission. The next three columns show the same permissions for other users in the same group as the owner, and the final three columns show the permissions for all other users on the system, except for the *superuser,* the person who logs in as **root**, who has all permissions on all files in the system. The following example is an entry for a sample file as displayed by **ls -l**:

```
-rw-r--r--   1 sheila3  group          32 May 19 14:01 printers
```

The dash in the first column indicates that **printers** is a file, not a directory. The next three columns show the permissions for the owner: The file is readable, as shown by the **r** in column 2, and writable, as shown by the **w** in column 3, but not executable, as shown by the **-** in column 4 (there would be an **x** in this column if the file were executable). Columns 5 through 7 show the permissions for the group. This file is readable by the group, but not writable or executable. The same is true for all other users on the system, whose permissions are shown in columns 8 through 10.

By default, your own files are usually readable and writable, but not executable, by you. The default permissions for other users may vary from system to system. Without editing this file, you can still change the permissions of any file or directory you own with **chmod** (for "change mode"). The **chmod** command recognizes the following three symbols that represent the three different user groups: u = user, g = group, and o = others. To add a permission to a file, type

chmod *user* **+** *permission filename*

where you replace *user* by the symbol for the user or group of users you want to give the permission to, you replace *permission* by the permission(s) you want to give them, and *filename* is the name or pathname of the file whose permissions you want to change. To take permissions away, do the same thing but replace the **+** by a **-**. The following examples show how you would add or take away various permissions for various users.

To give all users on the system permission to read a file called **charts**, type

```
% chmod go+r charts
```

This specifies that the other users in your group (**g**) and other users on the system (**o**) will have the read permission added to the file.

To make a file called **mk.chart** executable for yourself, type

```
% chmod u+x mk.chart
```

This gives you, the user (**u**), permission to execute the file as a program. Of course, the file must contain executable commands or it will not be executable, even if you do have execute permission. See Chapter 9, "The Bourne Shell," Chapter 10, "The C Shell," and Chapter 11, "Program Development with C," for discussion of creating executable files.

To take away execute permission on your home directory for users not in your group, type

```
% chmod o-x $HOME
```

This will prevent users not in your group from changing to your home directory with **cd**. However, if they still have read permission, they can list the contents of your home directory with **ls**. To take away this permission as well, type

```
% chmod o-r $HOME
```

Suppose you are in your home directory. If you want to add write permission for all users to a file called **memos** that is in one of your subdirectories, called **public**, type

```
% chmod go+w $HOME/public/memos
```

For a file in one of your directories to be writeable by other users, the file must be readable and the directory must be executable by those users.

Since all files on a UNIX system have these sets of permissions associated with them, there are probably many files and directories that you cannot access, unless you are the superuser. These include the files that contain the machine code for running UNIX programs, files used in system administration, and other users' personal files. You may have read but not write or execute permission on some files. You can look at these files with programs that view files, but you cannot make any changes to them. If you try to edit these files, a message will tell you that you have "read only" permission. If you attempt to access a file for which you have no permissions, an error message will tell you that permission is denied. If you think that you should have access to the file, you can talk to the file owner. Generally, however, if you don't have a given permission on the file, this is intended.

Removing Files

When you no longer need a file, you can remove it from your account with the command **rm**. Type

rm *filename*

where *filename* is the name of the file you want to remove. This works just as **rmdir** works on directories, except that **rm** works even on files that are not empty. Once you remove a file, you can only retrieve it if it was backed up when the system administrator did the last system backups. Even then, retrieving such a file is not a simple matter. Therefore, use **rm** with great caution, especially if you use a wildcard character like ∗ (see the next section for a discussion of wildcard characters).

If you want to give yourself one last chance to decide before you remove a file, you can use the **-i** (for "interactive") option of **rm**. When you type **rm -i** *filename*, where *filename* is the name of the file you want to remove, **rm** asks you whether you really want to delete the file (or files if you named more than one). For example, if you typed **rm -i sales**, you would see the following:

```
rm : remove sales ?
```

Type **y** (for yes) if you really want to remove the file, or **n** (for "no") or anything else besides **y** if you decide not to delete the file. If you use the C shell, you can later make **rm**, **mv**, and **cp** always use the interactive option for you by modifying your **.cshrc** file. The C shell will be discussed in Chapter 10.

Wildcard Characters

At times you may want to perform some operation on every file in a directory. For example, you might want to move all the files into another directory. If you had a large number of files in the directory, it would be very tedious to type

mv *filename dirname*

for each and every file. Fortunately, UNIX has *wildcard characters,* which allow you to refer to several files with one more general name. The two wildcard characters you can use to specify files for commands to operate on are * and ?. You can type these characters in place of or together with file names to make a command operate on more than one file or directory at a time.

The * alone stands for "any file name consisting of any number of characters." The only file names * does not encompass are those that start with . (dot). If no directory is named, UNIX assumes the current directory. You can type * alone in place of a file name when you want to perform some operation on all of the files in the current directory. To do this you would type

command *

where you replace *command* with the particular command you want to perform. For example, to remove all files from the current directory, type

% rm *

Remember that the preceding command will *not* remove any dot files in the directory, but that UNIX will attempt to remove any subdirectories the directory might contain. The wildcard characters always refer to directory names as well as file names. Thus, whenever you type a command with *, UNIX will attempt to perform the named operation on any directories as well as files that fit the pattern. In the preceding example, **rm** would attempt to remove any subdirectories of the current directory along with the files. Since you cannot remove directories with **rm**, you would get an error message for each directory **rm** attempted to remove.

When a command can operate on both files and directories, it will. For instance, to move every file and subdirectory in the current directory into another directory called **misc**, you could type

```
% mv * misc
```

Since **mv** can operate on both files and directories, this command would work just fine, with one exception: If *dirname* is the name of a subdirectory of the current directory, **mv** will attempt to move that directory into itself, which is, of course, impossible.

The * alone is useful for performing operations on all the files in a particular directory. Perhaps an even more useful function of the wildcard characters, however, is to perform operations on a certain set of files or directories. If you use * with a partial word, it still stands for "any number of characters, including none," but the file names it matches must contain the partial word as well. Here are some sample patterns with * and some file names they match:

■ *t means any number of characters followed by "t" and will match any word ending in "t." Examples: **t** (the number of characters before the "t" in this case is zero), **account, last, fact; accounts** would not be matched, since "t" is not the last character.

■ *t* will match any name with a "t" in it. Examples: **t, account, last, accounts, data**.

■ pr*t will match any name that begins with "pr" and ends with "t" and has any number of characters in between. Examples: **prt, product, profit.chart**.

The wildcard character ? matches any single character. The exception is a . as the first character in a name. In other words, ? cannot stand for the . in a dot file. It *does* match a . in the middle or end of a name. You can use ? alone, or with a partial name, just like *. You can also use ? in conjunction with *. Used alone, ? would match only file names that were one character long, ?? would match two-character names, and so on. Like *, ? is probably more useful when used with a partial name and/or in conjunction with *. Here are some patterns containing ?, sometimes in conjunction with *, and examples of the names they match:

■ **?s** means any one character followed by "s" and will match any two-letter word ending in "s." Examples: **ls, cs, ts.**

■ **?a?** will match any three-character name whose middle character is "a." Examples: **map, tax, 3ap.**

■ **account?** will match any name that begins with **account** and ends with one more character. Examples: **accounts, account1, account2.**

■ ***.?** will match any name which has some sequence of characters, a . (dot), and one character after the . (dot). Examples: **account.1, appts.c, funds.8.**

▶**TIP**   A common UNIX trick is to name files that have a similar purpose so that you can match them all by a single pattern with a wildcard character. For example, if you have several files containing information about different companies who have accounts with you, you might want to append **.a** to the name of each file, just to indicate to yourself what these files are about. Then whenever you want to do some operation on all files concerning accounts, you could refer to them as ***.a**.

Whenever you use a wildcard character in place of individual file names, you run the risk of doing the operation on a file you forgot about that coincidentally matches the name with the wildcard character. With commands like **rm**, this could be disastrous. Therefore, it is always a good idea to use the **-i** option with any commands that could cause you to unwittingly lose files or directories.

Learning how to create your own system of files and directories is one of the most important steps in starting your UNIX system. UNIX will become a really useful tool only when you are able to create and store files and directories in your account. You can use many of the most powerful functions of UNIX—including word processing, text formatting, and program development—only if you know the basics of creating a file. Having read this chapter, you now know how to create a system of directories and subdirectories which will be your "base of operations." In Chapter 5, you will learn more about some of the basics of UNIX operating system. In Chapter 6, you will learn how to use **vi**, the visual text editor, which you can use to create files in a more sophisticated way than with **cat**, thus putting your file system to the best possible use.

5 UNIX Command-Line Fundamentals

If you have read the preceding chapters, you have learned to execute simple UNIX commands. As you will soon find out, however, there is a lot more to a UNIX command line than just the command. UNIX provides many special symbols, which, when used in conjunction with UNIX utilities, enable you to issue much more complex commands. Some of these special symbols, such as redirection symbols and pipes, allow you to combine the effects of several utilities and to manipulate data in an unlimited number of ways. Later, you can even use the utilities and tools covered in this chapter to create simple programs of your own.

The Command Line

Since you have already used a number of UNIX commands, you should be familiar with the *command line*. The command line is the line that contains the command, the options (if any), and any *arguments* to the command. Arguments to a command are any words or numbers that follow the command and its options. Often these are file or directory names that tell the command what to operate on, but they may also be user names, dates, or other numbers, depending upon the command.

Each UNIX command has a certain *syntax*, that is, a certain format in which you type the options and arguments. The syntax of each command is discussed in detail in Chapter 13, "Command Reference." When a command is discussed in other chapters, many of the most useful components of its syntax are explained. However, to explicitly see the entire syntax of a command, refer to Chapter 13.

In addition to the options and arguments to individual commands, there are certain special symbols that you can add to a command line to execute commands consecutively, run programs in the background, and change the way the command behaves. This chapter explains the symbols that are used throughout UNIX. Chapters 9 and 10 discuss symbols that are specific to a particular shell.

Consecutive Execution of Commands

If you want to execute two commands consecutively, you can type them on the same command line, separated by a semicolon (;). For example, to change to a directory called **misc** and then list its contents, you could type

```
% cd misc ; ls
```

The list of contents of **misc** would appear immediately, and then you would be returned to a shell prompt. You can even execute more than two commands consecutively, as long as you include a semicolon after each one (except the last one). In fact, if you type so many commands that the command line is longer than a line on the screen, you can either let the line wrap around, or you can type a \ (backslash) at the end of the screen line, press RETURN, and continue typing commands on the next line. Typing a \ at the end of a line makes UNIX ignore the subsequent newline character. When you have finished typing, press a RETURN without a \ to execute all of the commands you typed.

Executing Commands in the Background

All of the commands you have learned so far execute very quickly. However, some utilities, like the formatting utilities discussed in Chapter 7, take some time to run. While these processes are running, you cannot type any more commands. Especially if you want to format a very long file, you could have to wait several minutes. Fortunately, UNIX can put jobs in the background. This means that the job continues running, but you are returned to a shell prompt and can continue working while it runs. To make a job run in the background, just type an **&** (ampersand) at the end of the command line. Because the commands you know at this point execute so quickly, there is no point in running them in the background. Just so that you can see how **&** works, however, you can try running a command such as **mkdir** or **rm** in the background. This is what will happen if you run **mkdir** in the background to create a directory called **forms**:

```
% mkdir forms &
1965
```

The number printed below the command line is the process number that UNIX has assigned to this job. See Chapter 12,"The UNIX Multiuser Environment," for more information about processes.

Input and Output

Almost all UNIX commands take some *input* and produce some *output*. The input to a command is the data upon which the command operates. This data may come from a file specified by the user, a UNIX system file, the terminal, or the output of another command. The output of a command is the result of the operation on the input. The output of a command may either be printed on the terminal screen, sent to a file, or fed to another command.

Standard Input

Some UNIX commands have only one possible source of input. For example, the **date** command always uses the built-in system clock to determine the date and time. Other commands require you to specify their input. Unless you specify a source of input along with a command name that requires input, UNIX assumes that the input for the command is to come from the keyboard—that is, from what you type. Input derived from what you type on the keyboard is called the *standard input file,* or simply standard input.

Information from the keyboard goes directly to the processing unit of the computer. As a convenience, UNIX also *echoes* (sends a copy of) what you type to the screen. This feature helps you to make sure you type commands correctly and makes using UNIX more friendly. When you type your password during execution of the login procedure or the **passwd** command, what you type must *not* appear on the screen, so the echo to the screen is turned off.

Standard Output

Almost all UNIX commands send their output to the user's terminal by default. The result of a command, which is sent by default to a user's terminal, is called the *standard output file,* or just standard output. As with input, you can redirect output to destinations other than the standard output, such as files or other commands.

Commands that change internal parameters, such as **rm, mv,** and **mkdir,** do not have output, which is why nothing prints on the screen if the command is successful. However, even commands with no output produce error messages on the screen if they are unsuccessful. This is because the terminal is also the *standard error file,* the place where error messages are sent. Don't confuse the error message of a command with output.

Filters

A *filter* is a UNIX utility that takes some input, performs some operation on it, and gives the results of the operation as output. Most filters take the standard input and give the standard output unless otherwise specified. It is important to understand that a filter does not make any changes to the input. In fact, a filter is somewhat like a change machine. You put in a dollar bill and a dollar's worth of change comes out. Your dollar bill itself is still intact inside the machine. It has not been physically converted into coins, yet the change is your dollar in a different form. UNIX filters work in a similar way, giving you the output that is a different form of the input without actually altering the input.

The following sections include explanations and examples of the kinds of operations various UNIX filters perform. Some filters can take either the standard input or a file whose name is given as an argument to the command. In general, the examples in this chapter show how filters behave when they take files as input.

cat

In Chapter 4, you learned how to use the **cat** utility to create and view a file. This section discusses some of the more basic **cat** functions. The **cat** utility (mnemonic for "catenate") takes as input one line at a time of text (ending with RETURN). Its output is that same line of text. Although this may seem trivial, **cat** has a multitude of uses, including creating and viewing files, joining several files, and getting input from the user during an interactive program. You can do all of these things only by specifying sources of input and output other than the default. First, however, you should see how **cat** operates in the standard input and output.

If you type **cat** alone and press RETURN, the cursor will be at the beginning of a blank line. You can now type whatever you want, pressing RETURN at the end of each line. After you press RETURN, the line you just typed will be printed on your screen. (Remember, the line appears because UNIX is echoing the standard input to the screen.) When you are finished typing, press RETURN and then CTRL-D as the first character on a line. You will be returned to a shell prompt. You may never actually need to use **cat** in this way, but this example shows just what **cat** does.

▶**NOTE**   In this and various other listings in this chapter that include input (beyond a single command) and ouput, input appears in boldface. The following example shows what happens when you type **cat** as a command.

```
% cat
There are several things we need to discuss at the next meeting.
There are several things we need to discuss at the next meeting.
Sherman will probably bring up that embarrassing matter of
Sherman will probably bring up that embarrassing matter of
the Fibster account.  Mr. Ellison will clear his throat and
the Fibster account.  Mr. Ellison will clear his throat and
move that the meeting will be adjourned until after lunch, and
move that the meeting will be adjourned until after lunch, and
everyone will hope that Sherman forgets.
everyone will hope that Sherman forgets.
^D
```

To make **cat** operate on a file instead of the standard input, just give the name of the file you want **cat** to operate on as an argument on the command line. Recall from Chapter 4 that you would type

```
% cat deeds
```

to display the contents of a file called **deeds** on the screen. When you see the file print on the screen, **cat** is copying one line at a time of the file and sending it to the standard output.

All of the filters in this chapter can take multiple file names as arguments. To view several files consecutively with **cat**, type all of the file names after **cat**, separated by spaces, in the order in which you want to see them. For example, to view files called **deeds**, **titles**, and **wills**, you would type

```
% cat deeds titles wills
```

head and tail

The **head** and **tail** commands are similar to **cat**. However, instead of printing out all lines of input, **head** prints out only the first ten. Likewise, **tail** prints out only the last ten. Both **head** and **tail** take the standard input and produce the standard output by default.

To use **head** or **tail** on a file, just type the file name or names as an argument to the command, as you did with **cat**. For example, to see the last ten lines of a file called **stocks**, you would type

```
% tail stocks
```

The last ten lines of the file will be printed on the screen, and you will be returned to a shell prompt.

Ten is the default number of lines printed by **head** and **tail**, but you can change this number. To do this, follow the command with a - (hyphen) and then whatever number of lines you want to be printed — just as you would type an option. To make **head** print 20 lines of a file called **brief**, for example, you would type

```
% head -20 brief
```

You can choose any number you want, and if the number is larger than the number of lines in the file (when you are using the command on a file), the whole file will be printed.

pg

The **pg** utility takes lines of input, arranges them in groups that will fit on one screen, and displays them one screen at a time. By default, **pg** takes the standard input, but its input may also be a file specified on the command line. To display a file with **pg**, you would type

pg *filename*

where *filename* is the name of the file you want to display. When one screenful of the file has been displayed, a colon will appear in the lower left corner of the screen. Now you simply press RETURN to see the next screen, and so on until you reach the end of the file. If you want to quit before viewing the entire file, type **q** (for quit) and then RETURN. You can also type **h** (for help) and then RETURN to display a list of other commands that you can type at this colon prompt.

The **pg** command also has several options that change the format in which the output is displayed. One useful option is **-c**, which makes **pg** draw each screen from the top of the page instead of scrolling. This way you can start to read the output before a whole screen is printed.

If you want **pg** to display a file in groups of lines smaller than the entire screen, you can specify the number of lines you want it to display at a time with the **-n** option, where *n* is replaced with the number of lines. To display a file called **taxes** ten lines at a time, you would type

```
% pg -10 taxes
```

To display the file starting at a line other than the first line of the file, you can type

pg +*linenumber*

where *linenumber* is the number of the line at which you want to begin. For example, to start displaying a file called **chung** at line 50, you would type

```
% pg +50 chung
```

To start displaying the file at the first occurrence of a certain pattern, you can type

pg +/*pattern*

where *pattern* is the pattern at which you want to start. To start displaying the file **chung** at the first occurrence of the word "product," you would type

```
% pg +/product chung
```

sort

The **sort** command is used to alphabetize lines of text.

▶ **NOTE**   Actually, lines are not so much alphabetized as ordered by byte according to the order in which the characters appear in machine or

ASCII code. This corresponds to the ordering of the English alphabet, although in machine code all uppercase letters precede lowercase letters, and numbers precede all letters.

By default, **sort** uses the standard input and output, though it is more often used on files than on the standard input. The following example shows how **sort** works on a file called **list**, which contains a list of words not in alphabetical order. The contents of **list** are first displayed with **cat**, and then the output of **sort** is displayed.

```
% cat list
Anderson
terms
Velasquez
Webster
1.quarter
dividends
interest
2.quarter
Engwall
estates
% sort list
1.quarter
2.quarter
Anderson
Engwall
Terms
Velasquez
Webster
dividends
estates
interest
terms
```

Notice that all words beginning with uppercase letters come before those beginning with lowercase letters, and items beginning with numbers occur before all those beginning with letters.

The **sort** command has several options that allow you to manipulate the order of the output. If you don't like the uppercase letters to appear before the lowercase letters, you can use the **-f** option, which causes the lowercase letters to be alphabetized with the uppercase letters. The next example shows how **sort -f** would work on the file **list**:

```
% sort -f list
1.quarter
2.quarter
Anderson
dividends
Engwall
estates
interest
Terms
terms
Velasquez
Webster
```

Notice that the words beginning with lowercase letters are integrated with those beginning with uppercase letters, but those beginning with numbers still appear first. In addition, when two words are the same, except that one begins with a lower- and one an uppercase letter (as in "Terms" and "terms"), the one beginning with the uppercase letter appears first.

To sort lines in reverse alphabetical order, you can use the **-r** option of **sort**. **sort -r** would sort the file **list** as follows:

```
% sort -r list
terms
interest
estates
dividends
Webster
Velasquez
Terms
Engwall
Anderson
2.quarter
1.quarter
```

Notice that lowercase letters appear before uppercase and numbers appear after all letters.

In addition to specifying how the output will be ordered, you can specify what part of the input lines **sort** will consider. By default, **sort** starts at the beginning of a line, but you may want it to start at a different point. The **sort** command looks at a line as being divided into *fields,* or sections, usually divided by a space. In the line, "1 2 3", there are three fields. You can refer to the fields with the *address labels* +*f1* and -*f2,* where *f1* is the field you want the comparison to start with and *f2* is the field that you want it to end with. Suppose that you wanted to sort some lines of numbers by the second number in each line. To do this, you would type

```
% sort +1 -2
```

(The first field on the line is 0.) The following example shows how this works on the file **figures,** which contains three unordered columns of numbers. The file **figures** is first displayed with **cat.**

```
% cat figures
1 3 256
0 99 23
3 1 45
% sort +1 -2 figures
3 1 45
0 3 256
1 99 23
```

In ordering this list, **sort** ignores the first field and orders the lines according to the second field.

Remember that when you use **sort** in a file, no changes will be made to the file itself, so you run no risk of ruining a file by running **sort** on it.

grep

The **grep** command is a filter that looks for a specified *pattern* (or sequence of characters) in a line of input, taken by default from the standard input. If the pattern is *matched* (found) in the line, that line is printed as output. Otherwise, the line is not printed. The **grep** command, the name of which comes from the words "get regular expression print," has two companion commands, **egrep** (from "extended grep") and **fgrep** (from "fixed grep string"), explained later in this chapter.

The difference between them is in the types of patterns they match, which will also be discussed in the section "Regular Expressions." To look for a pattern in a file with **grep**, type

grep *pattern filename*

where *pattern* is the word or other sequence of characters you want to search for and *filename* is the name of the file in which you want to search for the pattern. For example, to search the file **funds** for the word "cash," you would type

```
% grep cash funds
```

The **grep** utility will search each line in the file for the specified pattern, printing that line on the screen if the line contains the pattern. The following example shows how **grep** works on the file **funds**, which is first displayed with **cat**:

```
% cat funds
It's a cash flow problem.
There is no funding for this.
Cash this check immediately.
This check should be cashed immediately.
% grep cash funds
It's a cash flow problem.
This check should be cashed immediately
```

Since you are actually telling **grep** to look for a sequence of characters and not a word, it will find that sequence even if it is a part of a bigger word. For example, it will find "cashed" in the preceding example. It would also find the cash in "cashew," "cashier," and so on. To find only those occurrences of "cash" as a whole word, you must put spaces on either end and enclose the whole pattern in single quotes, as follows:

```
% grep ' cash '
```

This prevents the spaces around the word from being interpreted as superfluous spaces in the command line. The syntax for **egrep** and **fgrep** is the same as that of **grep**.

In the preceding example, the line **Cash this check immediately.** does not contain a matching pattern because **Cash** begins with an up-percase "C." If you wanted a word to be matched either at the beginning or at the end of a sentence, you could do two searches: **grep cash** and **grep Cash**. A simpler way to do this is to use the **-y** option of **grep**. This causes the case of letters to be ignored so that "cash" would match not only "cash", but also "Cash", "CASH", "cAsh", and all other possible combinations of upper- and lowercase letters. **grep** can also search for more than one word. However, to look for words separated by spaces, you cannot simply type

grep *word1 word2*

If there are two words specified after **grep** in a command line, the second of those words will be interpreted as the name of a file to be used as input. To make two (or more) words be interpreted as the pattern to be searched for, you can again enclose them in single quotes. For example, to search for the words "quality control" you would type

```
% grep 'quality control'
```

▶**TIP**   It is a good idea to get in the habit of always enclosing in single quotes the pattern you want to search for with **grep**. This way you have them automatically when you need them.

There are a few other **grep** options that you may find useful. For example, to see how many lines in the input contain the pattern, rather than the lines themselves, you can use the **-c** option. When you type

grep -c *pattern filename*

the output will be only a number, not lines of text.

▶**NOTE**   Since **grep** finds whole lines that contain matching patterns in the input, rather than individual occurrences of a pattern, a line containing two or three occurrences of the pattern will be counted only once.

The **-n** option displays the number of each input line containing a matching pattern at the beginning of that line. The following example shows how **grep -n** works on the file **funds**.

```
% grep -n 'cash' funds
1:It's a cash flow problem.
4:This check should be cashed immediately.
```

sed

The **sed** (for "stream editor") utility is a filter that takes as input lines of text, copies them, and performs some operation on specified lines. The operation **sed** performs on a line depends on the editing command you specify. Then it prints all lines, changed or not, as output. You could use **sed** to change all occurrences of a certain word in a file to another word, while keeping the rest of the file unchanged. Or you might want to use **sed** to delete all the lines that contained a certain word in every file in your home directory.

By default, **sed** takes the standard input and gives the standard output. It can also take as input a file specified on the command line. The syntax of **sed** is somewhat more complex than the other commands you've learned. **sed** has three options, two of which take arguments of their own. Unlike some commands, **sed** must have at least one option set in order to do anything. Just typing **sed** on a command line will return you to a shell prompt.

The **-e** option of **sed** takes as an argument an editing command (which will be discussed later in this section) and causes this command to be executed on the input.

The **-f** option of **sed** causes the commands contained in a specified file to be executed on the input. This file, called a *sed script,* is specified as the argument to the **-f** option.

The **-n** option suppresses the output of **sed**. This allows you to print only selected lines, as explained later in this section.

Unlike the options of other commands, the **sed** options can in general not be combined after a single hyphen. **-nf**, for example, is not interpreted as **-n -f**. However, you can use all of the options in conjunction with each other, as long as you precede each by a separate hyphen. For options that take their own arguments, the argument must come immediately after the option it goes with. That is, you would type

-e *editing command* **-f** *script*

and not

-e -f *editing command script*

Before you can use **sed**, you must be able to use some editing commands. An editing command has the following format:

[address[,address]] instruction [arguments]

sed addresses   The **sed** *addresses*, which are optional, specify certain lines to look for. These addresses can either be relative (line numbers) or contextual (marked by a pattern), and you can specify either one line or a range of lines, where the first line specified marks the beginning of the range and the second line marks the end of the range. For instance, if you wanted to do an operation to lines 1 and 2 of a file, the *relative addresses* would be **1,2**. If you wanted to do the operation on lines 1 through 10, the addresses would be **1,10**. Note that no space separates the addresses and the comma. If you want to change all the lines from a particular line to the last line in the input, you can use **$** to represent the last line; in other words, you don't have to know the line number of the last line. For example, to change all lines from lines 5 to the last line, use the addresses **5,$**. If you specify only one address, the operation is performed only on that line.

You specify *contextual addresses* in the same way as relative addresses. You can use either one or two patterns as markers. If you only specify one, changes are made only to lines containing that pattern. If you specify two patterns, changes are made to all lines starting with the first line containing the first pattern and ending with the next line containing the second pattern. If you wanted to make changes to all lines containing the word "paid", you would specify the address **/paid/**. The slashes (/) before and after the word are necessary to mark the beginning and end of the pattern. As with **grep**, if you want to change only those lines containing "paid" as a whole word, and not those containing "unpaid" or other words containing the sequence "paid", you must surround the word "paid" with spaces. In **sed**, the slashes protect the spaces like the single quotes used with **grep**. If you wanted to change all lines from the first occurrence of the word "account" to the next occurrence of the word "paid", you would specify the addresses **/account/,/paid/**.

You can also mix relative and contextual addresses. For example, you could change all lines from line 1 to the first line containing the word "market" by giving the addresses **1, /market/**. Likewise, you could change all lines from the first line containing the word "market" to line 10 by giving the addresses **/market/,10**.

sed Instructions   Once you have specified the addresses of the lines that you want to change, you must specify what changes you want to make. You do this with the **sed** instructions, which specify what changes are to be made to the selected lines. If you give no addresses, an instruction is applied to all lines of the input. Instructions are the only part of the **sed** commands that are not optional, since without an instruction, no changes would be made to the file. Instructions can do many things: append lines of text after certain lines, insert lines of text before certain lines, delete lines, substitute one pattern for another, and more. Some of the **sed** instructions are explained here. Examples appear in the next section, and a complete list of **sed** instructions can be found in Chapter 13.

a\ (append)   The **a** sed instruction appends subsequent text to the chosen lines. The text that follows it begins on the next line and must have a backslash at the end of each line except the last one, as in the following example:

```
a\
All those wishing to contribute to the Office Party Fund\
should make checks payable to Howard "Wildman" Jujube.\
Suggestions for party games and/or refreshments are also\
appreciated.
```

▶**NOTE**   You can specify only one address with this instruction.

i\ (insert)   The **i** instruction inserts lines of text before selected lines. Otherwise, it functions exactly like the **a** instruction.

c\ (change)   The **c** instruction changes lines of text by deleting them from the output and adding new lines specified as with the append (**a**) instruction. If you specify two addresses with this command, all lines in the range specified by the addresses will be replaced with the new text.

▶**NOTE**   Instructions that involve following text arguments can be used on the shell command line only if the command (including addresses and the text following the instruction) is enclosed in single quotes and the backslash at the end of each line is preceded by an extra two backslashes. As you learned, the backslash is a magic character to the shell. Thus, when a backslash on a command line is to be interpreted by the command (in this case **sed**) and not by the shell, you must precede it by another backslash to tell the shell not to interpret it. This means that two backslashes are necessary for **sed** to get the one it needs. You also know that a shell command can extend more than one line only if each line is followed by a backslash. This means that you need a third backslash for the shell to interpret. As you can see, it is easier to use the append (**a**), insert (**i**), and change (**c**) instructions if you place them in a **sed** script specified with the **-f** option (see the examples in the following section).

p (print)   The **p** instruction causes the selected line to be printed as output. This instruction overrides the **-n** option, so it is often used in conjunction with that option to print out *only* the selected lines as output. If you use the print instruction without the **-n** option, selected lines are printed as output twice, while nonselected lines are printed only once.

w (write)   The **w** instruction causes the selected lines to be written to a specified file. The file to which the lines are written must be specified by the name of a file separated from the write instruction by exactly one space, as in the following example:

```
w newfile
```

If the file named after the write instruction already exists, it will be overwritten by the new lines and the data in that file will be lost. For this reason, you should use the **w** instruction with caution.

r (read)   The **r** instruction causes a specified file to be read into the output after the selected lines. As with the append (**a**) instruction, you can only specify one address with the read instruction.

s (substitute)   The **s** instruction causes one pattern to be substituted for another. The format for the substitute instruction is

s/oldpattern/newpattern/flags

where *oldpattern* is the pattern you want to be replaced by *newpattern*. Note that the patterns, like the patterns in contextual addresses, must be surrounded by slashes. Like all of the instructions, the substitute instruction applies only to those occurrences of *oldpattern* on lines selected by the addresses, unless no addresses are specified.

   If you want *newpattern* to include *oldpattern*, *newpattern* can contain an **&** (ampersand), which will represent *oldpattern*. For example, suppose you want to change all occurrences of the word "interest" to "compound interest." Instead of typing

```
s/interest/compound interest/
```

you could just type

```
s/interest/compound &/
```

This becomes especially useful when you start using more complex patterns or *regular expressions,* patterns that match more than one specific pattern, as further discussed in the section on "Regular Expressions."

   There are three *flags,* **g**, **p**, and **w**, that you can specify at the end of a substitute command. The **g** (for "global") flag makes the substitution apply to every occurrence of *oldpattern* on the selected lines. Without the **g** flag, the substitution would apply only to the first occurrence of the pattern on any given line. The **p** (for "print") flag functions just like the print instruction—that is, it causes all lines on which substitutions were made to be printed as output. The **w** (for "write") flag functions like the write instruction. It causes the lines that are changed by the substitute instruction to be written to a specified file. The file to which they are written must be exactly one space after the **w** flag, as in the following example:

```
s/paid/& in full/w paid.accts
```

This instruction would cause the first occurrence of the word "paid" on each addressed line to be replaced with the words "paid in full", and all lines that had been changed would be written to the file **paid.accts**.

d (delete)   The **d** instruction deletes selected lines from the output.

! (not)   The exclamation mark stands for "not." When you use this instruction in front of any other instruction, it tells **sed** to carry out that instruction only on lines *not* selected by the specified addresses. For example, to delete all lines not containing the word "acquisition" you would use the following command:

```
/acquisition/ !d
```

The address here is specified with the pattern enclosed in slashes, and the instruction **d** is preceded by **!**, so it will be carried out on all lines not selected by the address.

q (quit)   The **q** instruction causes **sed** to stop processing, or "quit," when it reaches the selected line. All lines following a line addressed with the **q** command are not printed as output.

sed Arguments   The argument portion of a **sed** editing command varies depending on which instruction the command line contains. For example, when you use the append (**a**) instruction, the argument is the following text. When you use the write (**w**) or read (**r**) instructions, the argument is the file that you specify.

Examples   You are now ready to try some sample **sed** commands. The first example shows how **sed** operates on the input file **data**, which is displayed first with **cat**. First, try using sed with the **-e** option so that you can specify the command right on the command line.

```
% cat data
Here is the data you requested.
I am attempting to solve the problem, but
I need more data.
There is a lot of data to process,
so I expect this will take some time
```

Suppose you wanted to replace all occurrences of the word "data" with the word "information" in the file **data**. The following example illustrates the command line you would use to do this.

```
% sed -e 's/data/information/g' data
Here is the information you requested.
I am attempting to solve the problem, but
I need more information.
There is a lot of information to process,
so I expect this will take some time.
```

Since no address is specified, the substitute instruction will apply to all input lines that contain the word "data."

Now you can try creating a **sed** script and using **sed** with the **-f** option. The first step is to create a **sed** script by using **cat**. To do this, type

cat > *scriptfile,*

where *scriptfile* is the name you want the script to have. In the following example the script is named **changes**, but you can give it any legitimate file name. Now type some **sed** editing commands, as in the following example, pressing CTRL-D when you are finished:

```
% cat > changes
1,4 s/a/A/g
/distribution/ a\
NOTE: DISTRIBUTION IS NOW A SUB-DEPARTMENT \
OF DISTRIBUTION AND SALES.
^D
```

The first command in this example selects lines 1 through 5. On those lines, all occurrences of lowercase "a" are replaced with uppercase "A." The **g** flag instructs **sed** to make the substitution wherever "a" occurs on a line, and not just on the first occurrence. The second command selects all lines that contain the word "distribution" and appends to them the two lines of text that follow.

In the next example, **sed** uses the script just created to make changes to a file called **temp**. This file is first displayed with **cat**.

```
% cat temp
The transfer of equipment and hardware should be arranged
with the distribution department.
Should any unauthorized transfers be conducted,
the personnel supervisor will be alerted,
and the offending employees will be terminated.
% sed -f changes temp
The trAnsfer of equipment And hArdwAre should be ArrAnged
with the distribution depArtment.
NOTE: DISTRIBUTION IS NOW A SUB-DEPARTMENT
OF DISTRIBUTION AND SALES.
Should Any unAuthorized trAnsfers be conducted,
the personnel supervisor will be Alerted,
And the offending employees will be terminAted.
```

For more examples of **sed** editing commands, see Chapter 13, "Command Reference."

Other Filters

There are many more UNIX filters, which are explained in Chapter 13, "Command Reference." This section is a brief summary of some of the most commonly used filters.

uniq finds duplicate lines in the input. Only duplicate lines that are adjacent in the input count as duplicate. **uniq** outputs one occurrence of each line. By default, **uniq** takes the standard input and gives the standard output. However, both its input and output can be files specified as arguments on the command line.

diff is used to compare two files. It finds any lines that are different in the two files and displays those differences as output. You can use this filter to find duplicate files or to compare files to see which one contains the data you want.

split is used to divide input files into several smaller files. You specify the number of lines each file is to consist of as an option to the split command. By default, the output files are named **xaa**, **xab**, and so on.

wc (for "word count") takes lines of text as input and gives as output the number of words, lines, and characters in the input.

spell is a spelling checker that takes lines of text as input and scans those lines for any words not in the system dictionary. Any words in the input not found in the dictionary are printed as output. The **spell** command simply prints a list of unmatched words.

awk is similar to **sed**, but is more powerful. In addition to processing text, it can do mathematical operations and more.

Regular Expressions

As you saw, both **grep** and **sed** find a specified pattern in a line of text. Sometimes you may want to specify more than one pattern to look for. For example, suppose you wanted to find all occurrences of either the word "father" or the word "mother." You could do two separate searches for these two words, but notice that the last four letters of each word are the same. Likewise, suppose you wanted to find all occurrences of numbers following # (pound sign). To search for every possible number individually would be tedious indeed. Fortunately, UNIX provides a convention by which you can combine searches like these, and even more complex searches. By inserting special symbols into a string of letters or numbers, you can make that string a *regular expression:* a general pattern that includes some variables so that it matches several different particular patterns. You can think of a regular expression as a description of a pattern, rather than an actual pattern. A regular expression matches any pattern that fits its description. The special symbols, commonly called *magic* characters, used in a regular expression are explained here:

■ Enclosing several characters in square brackets ([]) means "match any one of the characters inside the brackets." For example, **[abc]** matches "a," "b," or "c." You can also specify a whole range of ASCII characters (letters or numbers) inside square brackets by separating the upper and lower limits of the range with a - (hyphen). To find any number from 1 to 9, you could use **[1-9]**. To find any lowercase letter, you could use **[a-z]**. The limits of a range of characters can only be specified with one character. For example, you could *not* find any number from 1 to 40 by using **[1-40]** in a regular expression. What this would match is any number from 1 to 4, or 0. If the first character in the range is actually ordered after the second in ASCII code, the pattern will match either the first character or the second one, as if the hyphen were not even there. So **[3-1]** will match only 3 or 1.

■ *(asterisk) means "match zero or more occurrences of the preceding character." For example, **a*** matches any number of a's, including none.

▶**NOTE**   * has a different meaning in regular expressions than it has as a wildcard character. Recall that as a wildcard character * stands for any number of characters. In regular expressions, it means any number of the character that precedes it. Thus, while you can use * alone as a wildcard character, it does not have its "magic" meaning in a regular expression unless it is preceded by another character.

■ . (period) matches any single character except the newline character, which is the character that represents the end of one line and the beginning of the next.

■ ^(caret) as the first character in a regular expression signifies the beginning of a line. If a regular expression begins with ^, only occurrences of the regular expression that are the first thing on a line will be matched.

■ ^(caret) as the first character in square brackets changes the expression to mean "match any character *except* those in the brackets." [^0-9] matches any character that is not a numeral.

■ Any expression enclosed between \(and \) matches the same patterns it would without the parentheses. This is useful because you can use it to refer to the expression later. Each time you set off an expression in this way, it is assigned a number, which you can refer to in a replacement pattern by preceding that number with a \. For example, the first part of the pattern that you enclose in backslashed parentheses can be referred to in the replacement pattern as \1. Then, whatever matches the expression in the parentheses will be printed as part of the replacement pattern.

■ \(backslash) "turns off" the magic of a subsequent magic character. This is useful if you want to find an actual occurrence of one of the magic characters in the input. For instance, if you wanted to find a period, you could use \. in a regular expression. Because of \'s power to turn off the special characters, it is itself a magic character. Thus, if you want to find an actual \ in a file, you need to precede it with another one in the regular expression (\\).

You can use regular expressions with **sed**, **grep**, and **egrep**, but not in **fgrep**. **fgrep** is faster to run than either **grep** or **egrep**, but you can only use it to match exact strings of characters. On the other hand, **egrep** matches most of the same regular expressions as does **grep**, and uses some additional magic characters that **grep** does not use. These are explained next.

■ ? means "match zero or one occurrence of the preceding character."

■ $ represents the end of a line. Any regular expression that ends with $ will only match a pattern if it is the last thing on the line. For example, **broccoli$** will only match the word "broccoli" if it occurs at the very end of the line. If there is even a period after "broccoli", it will not be matched.

■ | (pipe, which usually appears as a broken vertical line on the keyboard and screen) when between two regular expressions means "match either of the two regular expressions." For example father|mother

would match either "father" or "mother."

■ You can use parentheses to enclose some patterns or expressions you want to be grouped together. Parentheses do not have this special meaning when they are inside square brackets.

You can use several magic characters in a single regular expression, making it match even more patterns. What follow are some sample regular expressions that contain more than one magic character and examples of the patterns that they match:

■ **b[aieou]*d** matches a word or part of a word beginning with "b,"ending with "d," and with any number (including zero) of vowels in between. Examples: **bead, bad, bd.** The patterns **bond** or **ballad** would not be matched because they have characters that are not vowels between the "b" and the "d."

■ **^[0-9][0-9]\.** matches any two-digit number at the beginning of a line followed by a period. Examples: **29. , 33. , 08..**

■ **[aA]ccrual** matches either "Accrual" or "accrual." This is useful if you want to find a word either at the beginning or in the middle of a sentence.

■ **^[^A-Z]** matches the beginning of any line that does *not* begin with an uppercase letter.

Redirecting Input and Output

There are three basic ways in which the input or output of a command can be redirected — that is, taken from or sent to other files besides the standard input or standard output files. One is simply to supply the name of the file to be taken as input or output as an argument to the command. As you have seen, this works for the filters discussed in this chapter, but it does not work for all UNIX commands. For example, the **pwd** command cannot take a file name as an argument because it always gets its input from the same source. Even with filters, usually only the input source, and not the output destination, can be specified in this way.

Another way to redirect input or output to or from a file is to use the *redirection symbols*. Since many commands can take input files as arguments, the redirection symbols are most often used to specify the output destination, not the input source, for a command.

A third way to redirect input and output is to *pipe* the output of one command to another. This means that the output of one command becomes the input of another. Two different kinds of symbols are used for the two different types of redirection, redirection symbols to redirect to a file and pipes to redirect to a command. These are discussed in the following two sections.

Redirection Symbols

The symbol < (less than) is used to read a command's input from a file instead of the standard input. To do this, type

command < *filename*

where *command* is the name of the command and *filename* is the name of the file you want the command to take its input from. One of the most useful functions of < is to mail files to other users. Whereas **mail** normally takes its input from what you type, you can send a whole file to someone by typing

mail *user* < *filename*

where *user* is the name of the user or users you want to send the file to and *filename* is the name of the file you want to send. When you press RETURN, you will not see the "Subject:" prompt; instead, the file will be sent and you will be returned to a shell prompt. See Chapter 9, "Mail," for more information on mailing files.

In many cases, < is just like specifying the file name as an argument to a command. For example, typing

cat *filename*

would have exactly the same effect as typing

cat < *filename*

    The symbols > and >> redirect the output of a command into a file. > writes the output of a command to the named file regardless of whether that file already exists, overwriting any existing data in the file. >>, in contrast, appends the output of a command to the named file rather than overwriting what was already in the file. In the C shell, the file you name must already exist if you use >>; otherwise, you will get an error message and the output will not be appended.

▶**NOTE**   Since > will overwrite an existing file, you could lose an important file by accidentally redirecting output to it. Thus it is important to use > with caution. To prevent a file you want to keep from being lost this way, you can set an option called **noclobber** (really) in your **.login** file if you are using the C shell. See Chapter 10, "The C Shell," for instructions.

    The output redirection symbols work with all UNIX filters, as well as with many commands that produce output from something besides the standard input, such as **date**. In Chapter 4, you saw how to create a file using **cat**. When you give the command

cat > *filename*

cat reads the standard input (what you type at the keyboard) and directs the output, not to the standard output, but to the file represented by *filename*. This is a much more useful function of **cat** than simply echoing what you type back to the terminal. Other filters are also more useful when their output is sent to a file rather than printed on the screen because you can then save the changes the filter makes to the input.

    These redirection symbols also enable **cat** to combine several files. You have already learned how to display one or more files with **cat** and how to send the output of cat to another file. Now you can put the two functions of **cat** together. If **cat** takes one or more files as its input and sends the output to another file, the output file will contain all the lines contained in the input file or files. Thus to join two or more files into a new file, you can type

cat *filename1 filename2 . . . > newfilename*

where *filename1 filename2 . . .* represents the list of files you want to join and *newfilename* is the name for the new file containing the lines from all the other files. To join files called **s.carolina**, **n.carolina**, and **tennessee**, in that order, in a file called **south.us**, you would type

```
% cat s.carolina n.carolina tennessee > south.us
```

Remember that only copies of the lines from the input files, and not the files themselves, will be in the new file, **south.us**. The input files will all still exist as separate files.

Another way that you can use **cat** to join files is to append one or more files to another with the **>>** symbol. To do this, you would type

cat *filename1 . . .* **>>** *oldfilename*

where *filename1 . . .* represents the list of files you want to append and *oldfilename* is the file you want to append them to. To append files called **georgia** and **florida** to the file **south.us**, you would type

```
% cat georgia florida >> south.us
```

With the **>>** symbol, what was already in **south.us** will remain, and the lines from **georgia** and **florida** will be added to it. As with the previous example, the input files will still exist as separate, unchanged files.

Now that you have redirection symbols to work with, the range of operations you can do to a file is much larger. Without redirection symbols, you could perform only one operation on any given file, and the output of that operation would not be saved. In contrast, you can now save the output in a file and do additional operations on that output, thus effectively performing as many operations as you want on the same data. For example, suppose you have a file of accounts that you want to alphabetize and then look at with **pg**. Without redirection symbols, you could not do this. You would run **sort** on the file and the alphabetized output would be sent to the screen. You would never get a chance to look at it with **pg** because it would be gone after it scrolled off the screen. Using the output redirection symbols, you can first put the sorted output into a file and then look at that file with more, as follows

```
% sort accounts > temp
% pg temp
```

First you would send the output of the **sort** command to a file called **temp**. After sorting the file into another file, you could look at it with **pg**. You can save the output of any other filter in a file in the same way.

▶**TIP**   Users often give the name **temp** to files that they don't want to keep, but need temporarily. This makes it possible to clean up directories without checking each file.

Pipes

Redirection symbols offer one way to perform more than one operation on the same file. With just redirection symbols, you could accomplish everything you would ever want to do with UNIX commands. Suppose, however, that you want to do five different operations on a file. Each one would involve creating a new file, but the only purpose of the file would be to serve as input to another command. All you really want from the string of commands is the end result, not the intermediate files. In this case, using redirection symbols will clutter your account with files you will never use again and will just have to remove later. For situations such as this, UNIX offers another way of redirecting input and output that you may find more helpful: the pipe.

   The pipe key is the one labeled with a broken or solid vertical line. This key is used to send the output of one command to the input of another. You can use several pipes in a single command line, so you can combine as many commands as you want. The way to use a pipe is to type a command as you normally would, then a pipe, and then the command you want the output of the first command sent to:

command1 | command2

A line of commands separated by pipes is called a *pipeline*.

Suppose you wanted to find all the lines containing the word "leave" in a file called **benefits** and then you wanted to look at these lines with **pg**. Using redirection symbols, this would take two steps, as follows:

```
% grep 'leave' benefits > temp
% pg temp
```

Using the pipe, you can accomplish the same thing with one step, as follows:

```
% grep 'leave' benefits | pg
```

This tells UNIX that you don't want the output of **grep** to go either to the standard output or to a file, but to the **pg** command, which will display it a screenful at a time. Once you have finished looking at the output of **grep** with **pg**, that output is gone forever, whereas if you used >, you would be left with an extra file, **temp**.

Not all UNIX commands work successfully in all places in a pipeline. Which commands can be used in a pipeline varies with the spot in the pipeline. The requirements for the different positions are as follows:

■ The first element in a pipeline can be any UNIX command that generates some output. Some of the commands you have seen that generate output are **date, who, ls, pwd,** and all of the filters discussed in this chapter. Commands that adjust internal parameters—such as **mkdir, rm,** and **cd**—have no output, so they cannot be the first element in a pipeline, nor can interactive commands.

■ If the pipeline consists of more than two elements, the intermediate elements must be commands that take the standard input and give the standard output, namely filters. If the intermediate commands did not produce output, there would be nothing to send to the next command in the pipeline.

■ The intermediate or last element in a pipeline must be a command whose input you can specify. Commands that always take input from specific sources—such as **date** and **who**—cannot follow a pipe because no input can be sent to them.

Here are some example command lines that use pipes:

```
% cat temp1 temp2 | sort | uniq > newfile
```

This pipeline first catenates two files, **temp1** and **temp2**, and sends the output to **sort**, which alphabetizes both files together. That is, if **temp2** contains the line "aaaaa", and **temp1** contains the line "bbbbb", the line from **temp2** will appear before the line from **temp1** in the output of **sort**, even though **temp1** was catenated before **temp2**. The output of **sort** is piped to **uniq**, which gives as output one occurrence of each line in its input. The output of **uniq** is redirected to a file called **newfile**. If **temp1** and **temp2** contained identical lines, only one of those lines would appear in **newfile**.

```
% ls -t | head -1 >> latest
```

This next pipeline first lists the contents of the current directory and then pipes that list to **head**. Since a number, **1**, is specified with **head**, this pipeline gives only the first line of input as output, which in this case will be the name of the most recently modified file in the current directory. This name will then be appended to a file called **latest**.

```
% sort accts | split -10
```

This pipeline first alphabetizes a file called **accts** and then splits the alphabetized output into files named **xaa**, **xab**, and **xac**, each ten lines in length.

The preceding examples are relatively simple pipelines. They should give you an idea of the kinds of things you can do using pipes. Once you

have learned to use the UNIX filters and are familiar with their functions, you will probably find many occasions to create pipelines of your
own, perhaps more complex than these examples.

In this chapter, you learned about many useful UNIX tools. The semicolon (;) allows you to execute several commands consecutively. With the
ampersand (&), you can run programs in the background. Probably one
of the most important things to know about UNIX is how to manipulate
the input and output of commands. Now that you have gained a good
understanding of how various UNIX filters operate, you know many
simple ways of performing sometimes complex operations on data.
When you combine the power of filters with redirection symbols and
pipes, you will find that there is a way of doing almost anything you want
to a file or other input. In Chapter 9, "The Bourne Shell," and Chapter
10, "The C Shell," you will learn how to put complex command lines
with filters, redirection symbols, and pipes into shell scripts, so that you
can execute very complex and powerful commands by typing a single
command.

6 *The vi Editor*

The **vi** editor was developed at the University of California at Berkeley. The original text editor supplied with UNIX was **ed**, a *line-oriented editor*—it edited only one line at a time. However, the **ed** editor was rather unfriendly, so a new line editor, called **ex**, was developed. The **ex** editor encompassed the **ed** commands and added some new commands of its own. One of the new commands was the **vi** command, which allowed users to display a full-screen window of their file. The word "vi" stands for "visual" but is pronounced "vee eye." The **vi** editor is simply the **ex** editor with the full screen rather than a single line displayed. The **ex** editor was not abandoned altogether. All of the last line commands discussed later in this chapter are **ex** commands. You can still use **ex** and even switch back and forth between **vi** and **ex**.

The **vi** program is *not* a text formatter. That is, it does not handle line justification, line spacing, indentation, and so on. Thus text produced with **vi** is usually not very pretty. The lines will be long or short, depending on how you type them, and unless you type a blank line between each line of text, your document will be single spaced. The **vi** program is intended to be used with a text formatting program, which will arrange the text more aesthetically. Two of the most common UNIX text formatters are discussed in Chapter 7, "Text Formatting with nroff and troff."

While **vi**'s inability to format text may seem inconvenient, there are actually several advantages to editing text with **vi** and formatting it with a formatting program. For one, you can concentrate on composing your text and think about formatting later. In addition, since short and simple commands typed right in the file determine how the text will be formatted, a few changes is all it takes to format the text in a different way. Many seasoned **vi** users prefer **vi** to "fancier" word processors that incorporate formatting.

Once you are familiar with the more basic **vi** commands, you can quickly and easily look up particular commands in the "vi Quick Reference" at the end of this chapter.

The Three Modes of vi

The **vi** editor has three distinct modes of operation. While you are editing a file, **vi** is in either *insert mode, escape mode* (sometimes called *command mode*), or *last line mode*.

Insert mode is the mode in which you can do your typing. In insert mode, **vi** functions much like a typewriter except that you can backspace over text you have already typed to correct mistakes. Each character that you type appears on the screen as you type it. You can't move around on a line or between lines in insert mode.

In escape mode, ordinary characters (letters, numbers, and punctuation) have special meanings. Almost every character functions as an escape mode command, so there are many commands to learn; fortunately, most of them are fairly mnemonic. You use some escape mode commands—**a, A, i, I, o,** and **O**—to get into insert mode. You use others to move around in a file, change text, search for words, and more.

▶**NOTE** Unlike shell commands, you do not need to follow **vi** escape mode commands with a RETURN. The commands are executed as soon as you type them.

Because you execute the cursor-movement and editing commands in **vi** by pressing ordinary keys and not special function or control keys, it is especially easy to switch back and forth between insert mode and escape mode. Most people who use **vi** regularly move between modes almost unconsciously, inserting text and then moving around or making changes.

In last line mode, you type commands on a special last line on the screen that appears when you type a **:** (colon) in escape mode. Last line commands are generally used less often than escape mode commands, but they serve several important purposes. Using special commands typed after the colon, you can replace text, make global substitutions, write files or parts of files to the disk, read in other files, and execute shell commands without leaving **vi**.

The Buffer

While you are editing a file with **vi**, you are not really changing the file itself. The changes you make are written to the *buffer,* which is a copy of the file held in the system memory rather than on the disk storage system. When you want to make your changes a permanant part of the actual file, you must write the file to the disk. Using the **write** (**w**) command in last line mode, you can replace the old version of the file with the contents of the buffer, including any changes you have made. Since a file is not replaced with the buffer until you use the **write** command, you are safeguarded against losing the old version of the file. When you don't want to save the buffer, you can simply quit **vi** without writing to the disk to retain the old version of the file. Writing files to the disk is discussed in more detail in the sections, "Exiting vi" and "Writing Files and Partial Files to the disk" later in this chapter.

The Basics of vi

The **vi** editor provides a large number of commands that perform a wide variety of specialized editing, cursor-movement, and other tasks. In fact, it would be overwhelming to try to absorb all **vi** commands at once. Therefore, the following few sections cover only the most basic **vi** commands, those necessary to create a file, enter some text, and save that file on the disk. Later sections discuss the more advanced commands that will help you to become an expert **vi** user.

Creating a New File with vi

You can create a brand new file with **vi** by typing

vi *filename*

where *filename* is not the name of a file already in the current directory. The same naming restrictions (discussed in Chapter 4) apply to naming files created with **vi** as to files created with **cat** or any other utility. That is, file names must not exceed fourteen characters and cannot include spaces or magic characters. The following example shows how you would create a file called **practice**. Type

```
% vi practice
```

When you enter a new **vi** file, the screen will clear and you will see a screen similar to the one shown in Figure 6-1.

▶**NOTE**   Ordinarily, **vi** displays a full screen 23 lines long and 80 characters wide. The figures in this chapter contain slightly smaller screens.

The name of the file appears enclosed in quotation marks in the lower-left corner of the screen, followed by the message "[New file]." If this file had already been created, the number of lines and characters in the file would appear in place of "[New file]." Notice that there is a ~ (tilde) at the beginning of each line. This signifies that nothing has been typed on these lines yet. A line beginning with a tilde is *not* a blank line, but a null line. Actual blank lines in a file have nothing at the beginning.

Editing an Existing File

You can use **vi** not only to create new files, but also to edit any ordinary text file that you own, no matter how you created it. You can use **vi** to edit files created with **cat**, redirection symbols, or any other filter. You can also reedit any file created with **vi**. Figure 6-2 shows an already created sample file called **raise**. Notice that this file also does not fill up the screen — there are two null lines at the end. The file also contains one blank line above the word "Sincerely."

Getting into Insert Mode

When you enter a file with **vi**, you will be in escape mode. If you try to type normally at this point, **vi** will probably beep at you. This beep is the *error bell,* which rings whenever you type a nonexistent or inappropriate command. Since you are in escape mode and ordinary letters are interpreted as commands, to be able to enter text, you need to type one

```
~
 ~
 ~
 ~
 ~
 ~
 ~
 ~
 ~
 ~
 ~
 ~
 ~
 ~
 ~
"practice" [New file]
```

Figure 6-1. *A new vi file*

of the escape mode commands that put you in insert mode. Then you can type as you would on a typewriter, pressing RETURN at the end of each line. The cursor that you see in the shell also marks your place in **vi**. The line the cursor is on at any given time is called the *current line*. To correct mistakes on the current line, you can back up with whichever backspace key works for you (the same backspace key that works in the shell).

▶**NOTE**   Like the shell, **vi** is case sensitive. Therefore, the command **a** is different from **A**, **i** is different from **I**, and so on.

The escape mode commands that put you in insert mode are **a**, **A**, **i**, **I**, **o**, and **O**. When you first create a file, any of these commands will enable you to start typing on the first line. However, the commands all perform the following different functions if there is already text in the file:

■ The **a** (append) command appends text after the cursor.

■ The **A** (append) command appends text at the end of the current line, no matter where on the line the cursor is when you give the command.

■ The **i** (insert) command inserts text before the cursor.

■ The **I** (insert) command inserts text at the beginning of the current line, no matter where on the line the cursor is when you give the command.

■ The **o** (open) command opens a new line below the current line and puts the cursor at the beginning of that line.

■ The **O** (open) command opens a new line above the current line and puts the cursor at the beginning of that line.

Try using one of these commands to type a few lines of text, making sure to press RETURN at the end of each line. Assuming that you started with a new file, you should have a file that looks something like the one in Figure 6-3.

Dear Mr. McGillicutty, As you may be aware, I have now served in the
capacity of Chief Executive Officer in Charge of Excuses to
Creditors for well over ten years. Though I realize this
company's policy is never to give raises to any employee under 6'7"
in height, I feel that based on a) the fact that no employee of
this company has ever, according to my records, been over 6'3", and
b) my outstanding performance in the
aforementioned capacity, an exception should be made in my case.
Please consider my suggestion and get back to me.

Sincerely,
Evrath Bleitzer
Chief Executive Officer in Charge of Excuses to Creditors
~

~

"raise" 13 lines, 672 characters

Figure 6-2. *A vi file containing some text*

John: I talked to Susan about the Sutter account. She thinks that
we should act now in order to avoid losing it. What do you think?
I would like to hear from you very soon.
~
~
~
~
~
~
~
~
~
~
~

"practice" [New file]

Figure 6-3. *A new file entered with vi*

Getting Out of Insert Mode

While you are typing, you can press BACKSPACE to correct mistakes that you make on the current line, but what if you want to change something on a different line? Since the BACKSPACE key only works on the current line, you have to use an escape mode command if you want to change a previous line. To go from insert mode back to escape mode, simply press ESC, usually located in the upper-left corner of the keyboard. Some of the simpler cursor movements are up, down, forward, and backward. On many keyboards, you can use the arrow keys, labeled →, ←, ↑, and ↓ to move the cursor.

No matter what kind of keyboard you have, you can use the **vi** escape mode commands **h, j, k,** and **l** (all lowercase) to control cursor movement as follows:

■ The **l** command is the same as the SPACEBAR. You can use it to space forward on a line in escape mode.

■ The **h** command is similar to the BACKSPACE key. Use it to space backward on a line.

■ Use **j** to move down one line.

■ Use **k** to move up one line.

After you type a few lines, try pressing ESC and using these cursor-movement keys or the arrow keys to move around the screen. Now use one of the insert mode commands explained in the preceding section to add some text in one of the lines you've already typed. For example, to insert some text before the word "She" in the example file in Figure 6-3, you would move the cursor to the letter "S" and type the command **i**. This will put you back in insert mode. Nothing will look different, but whatever you type next will appear on the screen and will not be executed as an escape mode command.

Because **vi** does not automatically wrap text, if you add something to a line that is already as long as the screen is wide (usually 80 characters), the line will be too long to fit on the screen. It will appear to spread down on to the next line, although it is really only one line. Since you will probably run your file through a formatter eventually, your line length doesn't really matter. However, **vi** is not good at handling extremely long lines (lines that appear to fill up many lines on the screen). If inserting text makes a line too long, you should insert a RETURN some-where in the line by moving to an appropriate spot on the line (the beginning of a word) while in escape mode, typing **a** or **i**, and then pressing RETURN. When you are done inserting text, press ESC again to get back into escape mode.

Writing a File to the Disk

Remember, when you want to save the changes you've made to the buffer copy of a file, you must write the buffer to the disk to replace the original file with the new version. You do this with the last line command **write** (**w**). When in escape mode, type **:** (colon). This puts you in last line mode (discussed in greater detail later in this chapter). A colon will now appear in the lower-left corner of the screen. To write the file to the disk, simply type **w** and press RETURN. The name of the file and the number of lines and characters it contains will now be printed in the lower-left corner of the screen, as when you first enter a file. The cursor will also return to where it was before you entered last line mode. To decrease the risk of losing changes you've made to a file, you should write the file to the disk often.

Exiting vi

When you are done editing a file, you will want to exit **vi** and get back into the shell. There are several ways to do this. If you haven't changed the file since you last wrote it to the disk, you can use the last line command **quit** (**q**). If you have made changes since last writing the file to disk, you will get the error message

```
No write since last change (:quit! overrides).
```

If you really don't want to save your changes, or if you have already saved them to another file, type the last line command **:q!** as instructed. If you have made some changes that you want to save, you can do one of three things. First, you can type the last line command **wq** (shorthand for "write and then quit"). Second, you can use the last line command **x**, which writes the file only if changes have been made since the last write, and then exits **vi**. Finally, you can use the escape mode command **ZZ**, which does the same thing as **:x** without entering last line mode. This is a good way to exit **vi** when you are unsure if you've made any changes since the last write. Since **ZZ**, **:wq**, and **:x** all save your file if necessary and exit **vi**, you can try them all and then use the one you prefer.

More vi Commands

At this point, you are equipped to create a file with **vi** and to do simple editing. In the following two sections, you will learn how to use more escape mode commands to move around your documents and make changes with the fewest possible keystrokes.

Cursor-Movement Commands

You already learned how to use the simple cursor-movement commands **h, j, k**, and **l** to move around on and between lines. These commands are of limited usefulness when you want to move around rapidly. In this section, you will learn about some other commands for moving with precision between characters, words, sentences, lines, and screens. Just a few examples of each type of cursor movement are given here—for a complete list see the section "vi Quick Reference" at the end of this chapter.

You can precede a cursor-movement command with a number that indicates the number of times the cursor movement is to be repeated. For example, the command **3j** moves the cursor down three lines, and the command **12h** moves the cursor back twelve spaces. Unless stated otherwise, all of the cursor movement commands discussed in the following sections can be preceded by numbers.

Character-Related Cursor-Movement Commands Besides spacing backward and forward on a line, you can use commands to reach specific characters. The **f** (for find) command moves the cursor to the next occurrence on the current line of the character you type next. For example, the command **fB** moves the cursor to the next occurrence of uppercase "B." If none is found, the error bell rings.

The **F** (find) command moves the cursor backward on a line to the previous occurrence of the next character typed.

The **t** (to) command moves the cursor forward on a line to the character immediately before the next occurrence of the character that you type after the **t**. For example, the command **tC** moves the cursor to the character before the next occurrence of uppercase "C."

The **T** (to) command moves the cursor backward on a line to the character immediately before the character you type after the **T**. Since it is moving backward, however, the cursor is placed on what is logically the character *after* the named character.

▶**TIP** The four commands discussed in this section can come in very handy. If you want to move to a certain word in a line, it is often quicker to pick a letter unique to that word and move to it with **f**, **F**, **t**, or **T** than to move to the desired word space by space or word by word.

Word-Related Cursor-Movement Commands The **w** (word) command moves the cursor to the beginning of the next word, where a word is a sequence of letters or numbers bounded by either whitespace characters (spaces, tabs, or newlines) or punctuation marks. A sequence of punctuation marks is also counted as a word. Thus the sequence "don't" is actually three words as far as the **w** command is concerned: "don", " ' ", and "t".

When you want to move swiftly over words that contain punctuation, you can use the **W** command instead of **w**. This command works just like the **w** command, moving the cursor to the beginning of the next word, except that **W** counts as a word any sequence of characters, including punctuation marks, bounded by whitespace characters. Thus the **W** command treats "don't" as one word.

To move backwards on a line by words, use the **b** (back) command. This moves the cursor to the beginning of the preceding word, where a word is the same as what the **w** command considers a word. The **B** command works just like the **b** command, except that it counts words as the **W** command does, ignoring punctuation.

To move forward to the end of a word, use the **e** (**end**) command. The **e** command counts words as the **w** command does, while the **E** command counts them as the **W** command does.

Sentence-Related Cursor-Movement Commands   The (command moves the cursor to the beginning of the current sentence, or to the beginning of the previous sentence if the cursor is already at the beginning of a sentence. The) command moves the cursor to the beginning of the *next* sentence. Both of these commands find a sentence by looking for a period, exclamation point, or question mark followed by either two spaces or a newline. Make sure to type two spaces between sentences if you want to use the (or) command.

Line-Related Cursor-Movement Commands   You already know that **k** and **j** move the cursor up one line and down one line, respectively. You can also move easily to the beginning and end of the current line. The **0** (zero) command moves the cursor to the beginning of the current line. The ^ (caret) command moves the cursor to the first *nonwhitespace* (not a space or tab) character on the line. This is useful when the line is indented. The **$** command moves the cursor to the last character on the current line.

Since **vi** keeps track of the numbers of each line in a file, you can also move the cursor to specific lines in the file with the **G** (go) command. Used without a preceding number, **G** moves the cursor to the last line in the file. Used with a preceding number, **G** moves the cursor to the line with that number. For example, the command **78G** moves the cursor to line 78. If the number specified is greater than the number of lines in the file, the error bell will ring and the cursor will not move at all.

Screen Control Commands   If you want to move down by screenfuls rather than lines, you can use the **^D** (CTRL-D) command. Used alone, **^D** moves the cursor down half a screenful, also scrolling the text up the screen to keep the cursor in the same relative position on the screen. When you precede **^D** with a number, the cursor moves down that number of lines and the text scrolls up that number of lines. For example, the command **8^D** moves the cursor down, and scrolls the text up, eight lines. Figure 6-4 shows a screen before and after the execution of the **^D** command. The cursor appears shaded.

```
Memo:
To all employees.

As you have probably noticed, there has been quite a flurry of
activity around here the last few days. As you also know, the
workers have been installing our new Inter-Office Communication
System (IOCS). We feel that the added convenience this system
will give to inter-office communication is well worth the slight
inconvenience the installation may have caused. Below are
outlined some of the advantages we believe the new IOCS will have
over the old Inter-Office Messenger Service and Phone System
(IOMSPS).

Advantages of the new Inter-Office Communication System (IOCS):

1. Reduces elapsed time between sending and receiving a message.
```

```
worth the slight inconvenience the installation may have caused.
Below are outlined some of the advantages we believe the new IOCS
will have over the old Inter-Office Messenger Service and Phone
System (IOMSPS).

Advantages of the new Inter-Office Communication System (IOCS):

1. Reduces elapsed time between sending and receiving a message.
2. Does not require costly time and labor for delivery.
3. Uses a minimum number of envelopes.
4. Minimizes number of training hours.
5. Reserves telephone lines for important external business.
6. Reduces frequency of carpet replacement.
7. Eliminates "phone ear."
8. Records and logs every inter-office communication.
```

Figure 6-4. *A screen before and after executing the ^D command*

The **^U** (CTRL-U) command does just the opposite of the **^D** command. It scrolls the text down, and moves the cursor up, one screenful. Like **^D**, **^U** can be preceded by a number that specifies the number of lines you want the cursor to move.

Editing Commands

You have now learned how to use escape mode commands to insert and append text. Escape mode editing commands have many other functions as well. You can use them to change text, delete or copy text, and move pieces of text around in a file. Most editing commands operate by default on the current line, but some take addresses that allow you to specify a block of text on which to operate. Usually these addresses are cursor movements (such as those discussed in the preceding section), and the command operates from the current line, or the current cursor position on the line, to the place specified by the cursor-movement key. Editing commands that take addresses are indicated in the text and in the "vi Quick Reference." Like cursor-movement commands, most editing commands can also be preceded by numbers that indicate how many times to repeat the command.

Undoing Changes   Since escape mode commands do not appear on the screen, you can type a command by accident. You may also execute a command on purpose, but then decide that it was a mistake. Therefore, before you use any editing commands, you should know how to undo their effects. If you have typed only part of a command and want to cancel it before it is executed, you can press ESC without completing the command. If you have already executed the command, you can generally undo it with the **u** (**undo**) command. For **u** to work, you must type it immediately after the command you want to undo. That is, **u** undoes only the *last* command typed.

▶**NOTE**   Because **u** undoes only editing commands, not cursor movement commands, you can undo the latest change even if you subsequently moved elsewhere in the file. In this case, the cursor will move back to where the command was executed.

The **U** (**undo**) command undoes *all* of the changes made to the current line, no matter how many times you have changed it. Thus it restores the line to its unedited state. This can be useful if you decide you want to undo a change other than the last one. This command must be typed while the cursor is still on the line you want to restore. For example, if you make some changes to line 3 and then move to line 5, typing **U** will not undo the changes to line 3.

Marking Text You can mark sections, or *blocks* of text for subsequent reference with the **m** (**mark**) command. To mark one line, move the cursor to that line and type **m***x*, where *x* is any lowercase letter of your choice. That line can now be referred to with the address '*x*. For example, if you mark a line with the letter "a" by typing **ma**, that line can be referred to with the address '**a** after an editing command that takes a following address. You can also use the single quote (') as a cursor-movement command. For example, typing '**a** will move the cursor to the line marked with **a**.

Each time you mark a line of text, you also mark the exact cursor location on the line. Thus you can mark a section of text that is less than one line. In fact, the line and the spot on the line are marked simultaneously each time you use the **m** command. However, while you use a single quote (') to refer to a whole marked line, you use a *back quote* (`) to refer to the exact position on the marked line where the **m** command was issued. To use a marked spot on a line as an address to an editing command, you would refer to it as '*x*, where *x* is the letter you marked the spot with. Like the single quote, you can use the back quote as a cursor-movement command. For example, typing '**b** alone will move the cursor to the spot on the line marked with **b**.

To mark a whole block of text, move the cursor to the beginning of the block and mark that line with a letter. Then move to the end of the block and do the same thing, making sure that the two letters are not the same. The block can now be identified with the addresses '*x*, '*y*, where *x* is the letter you assigned to the first line in the block and *y* is the letter you assigned to the last line in the block. You can use the same letters each time you mark a block, but then the first block marked will no longer be identified with those letters.

▶**NOTE** When marking text for use with escape mode editing commands, you will only need to mark *either* the beginning *or* the end of the block since these commands usually take only one address. The delete command **d**, for instance, deletes from the current line to another specified line. So if the current line were the beginning of the block to delete, you would only need to specify the line marking the *end* of the block.

Delete Buffers While you are editing, **vi** maintains a buffer copy of the entire file. In addition, **vi** maintains *delete buffers*, which are copies in memory of the text you delete, copy, or change. Each time you delete a line or more of text, that text is placed on the top of a stack of delete buffers numbered 1 through 9. When you delete, copy, or change one line or more, what was in buffer number 1 is moved to buffer number 2, what was in buffer number 2 is moved to buffer number 3, and so on. These numbered buffers allow you to retrieve the last nine pieces of text you that you deleted, copied, or changed. To refer to a numbered buffer, precede it with double quotes. For example, to refer to buffer number 4, type "**4**. Text that is less than one line long is not placed in the numbered buffers unless it is also placed in a named buffer (see the following paragraph), but the most recently deleted text of any length (even just one character) is placed in a special buffer that can be accessed without a number.

You can also create *named buffers* to save deleted text of any length. These buffers are referred to with letters instead of numbers. You can refer to a named buffer by preceding it with double quotes. For example, to refer to a buffer "a," type "**a**. The next few sections will explain how to put deleted, copied, or changed text in named buffers and how to retrieve the text in both numbered and named buffers.

Deleting Text   You can use escape mode editing commands to delete characters, words, lines, or groups of lines. To delete the character the cursor is on, use the **x** command. Preceded by a number, **x** deletes that number of characters, starting with the one the cursor is on. The command **X** deletes the character *before* the cursor. Preceded by a number, **X** deletes that number of characters, ending with the character before the cursor.

To delete more than one character at a time, you can use either the **D** command or the **d** command. The **D** command does not take a following address. It operates only on the current line, deleting text from the current cursor position to the end of the line.

The **d** command must take a following address. If **d** is followed by another **d**, it will delete the current line. Like most editing commands, **d** can be preceded by a number. Thus the command **2dd** deletes two lines: the current line and the line below it. Since the second **d** acts like a cursor-movement key in this case, it too can be preceded by a number. The command **d2d** will accomplish the same thing as **2dd**. Furthermore, both the first and the second **d** can be preceded by numbers. The command **2d3d** will delete six lines (two sets of three lines). You can do the same thing with all escape mode editing commands that take addresses.

To delete anything besides just the current line, follow the **d** command with a cursor-movement address (any of the cursor-movement commands discussed in the section "Cursor-Movement Commands" or in the "Cursor Movements" section in the "vi Quick Reference"). When you specify a cursor-movement command as an address to the **d** command, you are telling **vi** to delete everything from the current cursor position to the place specified by the cursor movement command. The following examples illustrate how a cursor-movement address works with the **d** command:

■ The command **dw** deletes everything up until the beginning of the next word; in other words, it deletes the word the cursor is on.

■ The command **dt.** deletes everything from the cursor to the next period on the current line. This is a good way to delete words at the end of the sentence without deleting the period. Of course, you can substitute any character you like for the period.

■ The command **d(** deletes everything from the cursor to the beginning of the next sentence. After moving the cursor to the beginning of a sentence, you can use this command to quickly delete that sentence.

■ The command **dG** deletes everything from the cursor to the end of the file. **d89G** deletes everything from the current line to line 89. If the current line number is greater than 89, the command deletes backward to the specified line.

▶**NOTE**   When the address after the **d** command is an intraline command (such as **f** or **t**), the deletion starts from the cursor, leaving the preceding text intact. If the address specifies a whole line (as in **G**), the deletion affects the entire current line.

Of course, there are many more possible ways to use the **d** command. Experiment with different cursor-movement commands after **d**—you will probably discover some useful combinations.

As mentioned in the preceding section, text that you delete is automatically stored in numbered delete buffers. To put deleted text in a named buffer as well, precede any delete command with double quotes and the letter you want to assign to the buffer. For example, to delete the current line and put it in a buffer called **v**, you would type "**vdd**. You can precede the **d** command by *both* the name of a buffer *and* a number indicating how many lines or other units to delete. For example, to delete three lines, including the current line, and put them in a buffer called **v**, you would type **"v3dd**.

▶**TIP**   If you delete something accidentally and typing **u** does not restore it, try looking in the numbered buffers. You may have unknowingly deleted something else, in which case that text would have replaced the text you want in the first buffer.

Copying Text   To copy a section of text while leaving the original text unchanged, use the **y** (yank) command, which takes a following address. Just as the command **dd** deletes one line, the command **yy** copies one line. Like the **d** command, the **y** command can also take any cursor-movement command as an address and can be preceded by a number. Some sample **y** commands follow:

■ The command **yw** copies the word the cursor is on.

■ The command **y(** copies everything from the cursor to the beginning of the next sentence. If the cursor is at the beginning of a sentence, this command copies the entire sentence.

■ The command **y1G** copies everything from the cursor to the beginning of the file, copying backward from the cursor to line 1.

As with **d**, **y** commands copy either a partial line or whole lines, depending on the kind of address given.

When you yank text, it is stored in a delete buffer, either one of the numbered buffers or a named buffer that you designate. The text remains in the buffer until you retrieve it later, so you cannot use the **y** commands alone to move copied text elsewhere. To store yanked text in a named buffer, precede the **y** command with

"x

where *x* is the letter you want to assign to the buffer. For example, to copy the current line into a buffer called **f**, you would type **"fyy**.

Changing Text You can use escape mode editing commands to replace anything from one character to every line in the file. To replace one character, you can use either the **r** or the **s** command. The **r** (replace) command replaces the character the cursor is on with the *one* character that you type next. For example, the sequence **rS** replaces the character the cursor is on with "S". As soon as you type one character, you are automatically put back in escape mode.

The **s** (substitute) command replaces the character the cursor is on with whatever you type next until you press ESC. Since only one character is replaced, whatever was after that character on the line is pushed along after the replacement text. If you precede **s** by a number, that number of characters will be replaced with the replacement text. For instance, if you type **2s**, the subsequent text will replace two characters.

The **R** (replace) command replaces characters one at a time with new characters until you press ESC. For example, suppose the cursor is on the "n" in the word "new." If you issue the **R** command and then type **old**, the "n" will be replaced with "o," the "e" will be replaced with "l," and the "w" will be replaced with "d."

To change more than a character at a time, you can use the **c** command, which takes a following address. Following the same pattern as the **d** command, **cc** changes the current line to the text you type next until you press ESC. Like **d**, you can follow **c** with any cursor-movement key as an address, as in the following examples:

■ The command **cw** changes the word the cursor is on.

■ The command **cf**, changes everything from the cursor through the next comma on the line.

■ The command **c'a** changes everything from the cursor to the line you marked with **a**. If no line has been marked with this letter, the error bell rings and nothing is changed. This command works even if the current line is below the line marked **a** in the file. It simply makes the current line the last line changed instead of the first.

The **C** command replaces all characters from the cursor to the end of the current line with the text you type next. If you precede this command by a number, the rest of the current line, plus that number of lines minus one, is changed. For example, the command **3C** changes the current line from the cursor position to the end of the line, plus two more lines.

By default, pieces of text of one line or more that you replace with other text are stored in the numbered buffers, just like text that you delete or copy. You can also store the text that you replace in named buffers. To store changed text of any length in named buffers, follow the model used with the **d** and **y** commands and precede the **c** or **C** command with double quotes and the letter that you want to assign to the buffer. For example, to change from the cursor position to the end of the current line and save the text you are changing in a buffer called **m**, you would type **"mC**. To change ten lines and store the changed text in a buffer called **r**, you would type **"r10cc.**

Remember that the **c** and **C** commands put you in insert mode, so **vi** will accept new text until you press ESC. When the text you are changing with the **c** or **C** command is all on the current line, the last character of the text to be changed will be replaced with a **$**. This is just a placeholder that goes away as soon as you press ESC.

Recovering Text   Text that has been deleted with any deletion command, copied with the **y** command, or changed with any change or substitution command can be recovered with the **p** and **P** (put) commands. The **p** command puts the text after the cursor, while the **P** command puts the text before the cursor. If the text to be recovered is longer than one line, the **p** and **P** commands put the text on a new line above (**P**) or below (**p**) the current line. If the text to be recovered is less than one line long, it is placed immediately before (**P**) or after (**p**) the cursor on the current line. Putting text on a line that already fills the width of the screen sometimes causes the new text to meld with the old, forming some very strange words.

▶**NOTE**   Since pieces of text shorter than one line are not automatically placed in the numbered buffers, you must put them in named buffers if you want to save them.

By default, what is recovered with the **p** or **P** command is the last text deleted (or copied or changed), the text stored in the buffer number 1 and in the special, unnumbered buffer. Typing **p** or **P** alone will put that text back in the file. To recover text stored in one of the numbered or named buffers, type "*x***p** or "*x***P**, where *x* is the name or number of the buffer you want to recover. For example, the command "**gp** puts the text in the buffer called **g** after the cursor. The command "**3P** puts the text in buffer number 3 before the cursor.

▶**NOTE** There is no move command in escape mode. To move text using escape mode commands, you must first delete or copy it and then recover it. There is a last line **move** command that can do this in one step. See the section "Moving and Copying Text" later in this chapter.

Repeating Commands

Any editing command can be repeated by typing **.** (dot) as the next command. If the cursor position has changed since the last editing command was executed, **.** will cause the command to be executed relative to the new cursor position. Here are some examples of what **.** does in different situations:

■ If you delete a word with the **dw** command, the cursor will jump to the beginning of the next word. If you now type **.** (dot), the new word the cursor is on will be deleted.

■ If you insert some text with the **I** command, get back into escape mode, and move the cursor to another line, typing **.** will insert the same text you just inserted at the beginning of the new current line.

■ If you change two lines of text with the command **2cc** and then get back into escape mode and move to another line, typing **.** will change two more lines to the same text with which you replaced the previous two lines.

Remember, **.** repeats only escape mode editing commands, not cursor-movement commands or last line commands.

The only case in which **.** does not repeat the last command executed is when the last command replaced one of the numbered buffers. If you replace one of the numbered buffers with the **p** or **P** command, each time you type **.** the subsequent buffer will be replaced, until the last buffer on the stack is replaced.

Searching for a Pattern

The **vi** editor allows you to search a whole file for any pattern. One search command scans forward in a file (that is, from the current line to the end of the file); another scans backward (from the current line to the *beginning* of the file). However, **vi** has an environment option called **wrapscan** that causes **vi** to treat the file as a continuous loop rather than as an entity with a beginning and an end. If this option is set, when you search forward in a file, the scanning process will start again at the beginning once it reaches the end of the file. Usually this option is turned on, or set, when you use **vi**. If you don't like the **wrapscan** option, you will have to turn it off. See the section on "Environment Options" under "Last Line Mode" to learn how to do this.

To search a file for the next occurrence of a word or pattern, use the **/** and **?** commands. Typing **/** will cause a **/** to be printed at the bottom of the screen and will move the cursor there. This is the prompt to type the word or regular expression you want to search for. (For a discussion of regular expressions, see Chapter 5, "UNIX Command-Line Funda-mentals.") When you press RETURN, **vi** will search for that pattern in the file and move the cursor there. If the pattern is found far from the current line, **vi** will scroll the screen up until it reaches that pattern. Once you search for a particular pattern, that pattern is stored in memory. The next time you want to search for the same pattern, you just get into escape mode and type **n** (next), and **vi** will search for the next occurrence of the pattern. Notice that when you type **n**, a **/** prints at the bottom of the screen to show you that a search is being carried out.

To search backward in a file for a pattern, use the **?** command. A **?** will appear at the bottom of the screen, waiting for you to type the pattern to search for. Except that it searches backward, **?** functions exactly like **/**. If you initiate a search with **?**, typing **n** will continue the search backward. Now a **?** will print at the bottom of the screen to show that a backward search is being carried out.

To reverse the direction of either a forward or a backward search, type **N** instead of **n**. That is, if your last search was initiated with **/**, typing **N** will search *backward* for the same pattern, and a **?** will print at the bottom of the screen indicating the direction of the search.

Since **/** and **?** move the cursor to a new place in the file (as long as the pattern is found somewhere), you can use both of these commands as addresses for escape mode editing commands. The following examples show how search commands can be used as addresses.

■ The command **d/the** deletes everything from the current cursor position to the next occurrence in the file of the word "the."

■ The command **c?To** changes all text from the *previous* occurrence in the file of the word "To" to the current cursor position.

Last Line Mode

Last line commands have many functions. Some are editing commands that function like escape mode commands—deleting, copying, and replacing text, for example. Others, such as **w** and **q** (which you learned about in "The Basics of vi") let you write files or partial files to disk. You can also use last line commands to set certain parameters that determine how the **vi** program behaves.

Unlike escape mode commands, last line commands appear on the screen as you type them. This enables you to make sure you are typing correctly and to backspace and make corrections if you make mistakes. This feature can be especially important when you are making substitutions. Unlike escape mode commands, last line commands are not executed until you press either RETURN or ESC.

You can type many last line commands either in their full form or in an abbreviated form. For example, you can type the **write** command as **write** or as **w**. When this is the case for a command, both acceptable forms of the command name will be given, and the shorter form will be used in the examples. Since you must actually type the : to get into last line mode before any last line command can be executed, it is included in the examples. It is not included, however, in the command names.

Last Line Editing
Commands

In most cases, the format of last line editing commands is identical to that of **sed** commands discussed in Chapter 6. You can specify lines to be edited with addresses that are either regular expressions, line numbers, or marked blocks of text (see the section "Marking Text").

There are several additional symbols that you can use to represent certain addresses. You can use the symbol **.** in place of the address of the current line (the line the cursor is on when you enter last line mode). You can use the $ symbol in place of the address of the last line in the file. You can also use the **+** and **-** symbols with a following number to represent the line that number of lines from the current line. The **+** symbol specifies lines below the current line and the **-** symbol specifies lines above the current line.

One address before a command specifies one line to be edited. Two addresses separated by a comma delimit a block of text to be edited. Commands given with no address are executed on the current line. You can use the last line editing commands to delete, copy, and move pieces of text and to make global substitutions.

Like escape mode editing commands, last line editing commands can be undone with the escape mode **u** command. However, the **u** command must be the very next command you execute. The last line command **undo** does the same thing as the escape mode **u** command.

The Global Macro   The **g** (global) macro allows you to select for editing all lines in the file that contain a particular regular expression. You can use this macro with deletions, substitutions, and other editing commands. The syntax used with the **g** macro is

:g */pattern/command*

where *pattern* is the regular expression to be matched. Using the **g** macro with individual commands will be discussed under the relevant commands.

Deleting Text   Although you can delete lines with escape mode commands, there are certain types of deletions that you can perform more easily with the last line deletion command. With the last line **d** command, unlike the escape mode **d** command, you can specify lines to be deleted without the cursor having to be on one of those lines. For example, if the current line number were 12, you could delete lines 50 through 75 with the last line command:

:50,75 d

This would not be possible in escape mode unless the current line were either 50 or 75, since escape mode commands must start from the current cursor position.

With the global macro, you can use the **d** command to delete every line in a file containing a certain regular expression, something else that you cannot do with the escape mode **d** command. For example, suppose you wanted to delete every line that contained a sequence of two pound signs (##). To do this with escape mode commands, you would have to search for each such line with **/** or **?** and then delete it. With the last line **d** command, you can simply have the **g** macro select all lines containing this pattern. The following last line command would perform this global deletion:

:g /##/ d

Moving and Copying Text   With escape mode commands, the only way to move a piece of text to a different location is to delete it, store it in a buffer, and retrieve it from that delete buffer when you want to place it elsewhere. In last line mode, in contrast, the **move** (**m**) command can do this in one step. However, this command operates only on lines specified by addresses, so you will have to know either the line numbers, the identifying marks (for example **'a**), or an identifying pattern for both the lines you want to move and the line you want to move them to.

The syntax of the **m** command is

:address1 (*,address2*) **m** *address3*

where *address1* is the first line you want to move, the optional *address2* delimits the end of a block of text, and *address3* is the line under which you want the text placed. For example, to move line 5 to just below line 15, you would type

:5 m 15

This command does not include the optional second address, so only one line, not a block of text, is moved.

To move lines 1 through 5 to just below the line marked with **a**, you would type

```
:1,5 m 'a
```

To move a block delimited by the marks **a** and **b** to just below the current line, you would type

```
:'a,'b m  .
```

The **copy** (**co**) command does the same thing as the **m** command, but leaves the original text intact and moves a copy of the text. You could substitute the **co** command for the **m** command in each of the preceding examples. The effect would be the same except that a copy of the original text rather than the text itself would be moved to the location specified by *address3*.

You can use both the **m** and **co** commands with the **g** macro. Since the **g** macro picks out all lines containing a particular regular expression, all such lines would be moved or copied below the destination line. For example, suppose you wanted to copy under line 1 all lines containing the word "paid." To do this, you would type

```
:g/paid/ co 1
```

You could do the same thing with the **m** command.

Substitutions   The last line **s** (**substitute**) command is identical to the **sed s** command. The syntax of the command is

s/search pattern/replacement pattern/

where *search pattern* is the pattern you want to replace and *replacement pattern* is the pattern you want to replace it with. If you give no address, the substitution is done on the current line. The following command replaces the first occurrence of the word "signature" on the current line with the words "John Hancock":

```
:s/signature/John Hancock/
```

If you specify one or two addresses before the **s** command, the substitution is made on that line or the block delimited by the two addresses. For example, the following command makes the same substitution as in the previous example on line 10:

```
:10 s/signature/John Hancock/
```

The following command makes the same substitution on all lines from the one marked with **a** to the one marked with **b**.

```
:'a,'b s/signature/John Hancock/
```

The three previous examples will replace only the first occurrence of the search pattern on each specified line. If you want to replace every occurrence of the search pattern on the specified lines, you need to follow the **s** command with the **g** (global) flag, as in **sed**. For example, to replace *every* occurrence of the word "signature" on line 10 with the words "John Hancock," you would type

```
:10 s/signature/John Hancock/g
```

There are two ways to replace a pattern with another in every line of the current file. One is to use addresses denoting the first and last lines in the file. You can denote the last line either with its actual line number or with the variable $. You can also do the same substitution on every line in the file by using the **g** macro. A substitute command with the **g** macro has the syntax

:g/search pattern**/s//**replacement pattern**/**

To do the same substitution as in the previous examples on every line in the file using the **g** macro, you would type

```
:g/signature/s//John Hancock/
```

This instructs the **g** macro to do the following **s** command on all lines containing the word "signature." It also designates "signature" as the search pattern. Note that two slashes follow the **s** command. Ordinarily, you would type the search pattern between these slashes. In a global substitution, however, you have already specified the search pattern after the **g** macro. The empty slashes after the **s** indicate that the search pattern is the one already specified.

Using the **g** macro with the **s** command is not the same as following the **s** command with the **g** flag. While the **g** macro does cause the substitution to be made on every applicable line of the file, only the first occurrence of the pattern on a given line will be replaced. If you want every occurrence to be replaced, you have to type

`:g/signature/s//John Hancock/g`

You may not be sure that you want to change *every* occurrence of a pattern in the file with a global substitution. If so, you can follow the command with the **c** (confirm) flag, as in the following example. This will cause the substitute command to ask you to confirm each replacement.

`:g/signature/s//John Hancock/gc`

In any of the preceding examples, you could substitute a regular expression for the simple pattern "signature." Global substitutions are among the most useful last line commands, and their usefulness is increased when combined with the power of regular expressions. If you plan to use **vi** frequently, you should become familiar with both of these helpful features.

Writing Files and Partial Files to the Disk

You learned in a previous section how to write a file to the disk with the **w** command. You can also write just part of a file to the disk, either as a replacement for the original file or as a different file.

Suppose that you make some changes to a file and realize that you want to save both the changed version and the old version of the file. To do this, you just write the buffer to a file with a different name from the original. Follow the same procedure you would to write the file to disk, but after typing **w** type the name you want the new file to have. For example, if the original file was called **raise** and you want the changed version to be called **raise.new**, type

```
:w raise.new
```

Then you can quit **vi** without writing the buffer to the original file using the **q!** command.

To write certain lines of the current file to a new file, type

address,address **w** *filename*

where the *addresses* are either patterns, line numbers, or block markers that specify the first and last line to write to the disk. Some examples follow.

To write lines 1 through 12 to a file called **jargon**, type

```
:1,12 w jargon
```

To write all the lines from the first line after the current line containing the word "annual" to the next line containing the word "fiscal" to a file called **budget**, type

```
:/annual/,/fiscal/ w budget
```

For this command to work, the next occurrence in the file of the word "annual" must *precede* the next occurrence of the word "fiscal."

▶**NOTE** When you write lines from a file to the disk, these lines are *not* removed from the buffer. To remove them from the buffer, you must delete them.

To write only lines 1-100 to the disk, thus overwriting the entire original file, type

```
:1,100 w!
```

The exclamation point tells **vi** that you really want to replace the original file. If you want to write to a file that already exists, you need to use **w!** instead of **w**. If you try to overwrite a file that already exists with **w**, you will get an error message.

You can also append the current file or certain lines of the current file to another file. For example, to append the entire current file to a file called **insurance**, you would type

```
:w >> insurance
```

Reading in Other Files

You can integrate another file into the file you are editing with the **read(r)** command. This is called *reading* a file into another. The **read** command always inserts the new file just below the current line. It doesn't matter where the cursor is on the current line—the line will not be broken by the new file. To read a file called **plans** into the current file below the current line, you would type

```
:r plans
```

As the file is read in, its length in lines and characters is displayed on the last line. Like most last line commands, you can undo this command with the escape mode command **u**. If you read in a file and then change your mind, simply type **u**, but remember that no other escape mode or last line command can have been typed since.

vi Environment Options

As mentioned earlier in this chapter, there are several **vi** parameters that you can adjust to make **vi** operate differently. You can set these parameters, called *options*, either in last line mode using the **set** command or in your **.exrc** file (see the section "The .exrc File"). The syntax of the **set** command is

set *option*

where *option* is the option value you want to set.

   There are over forty options, but fortunately there are probably very few of them that you will actually need to set. Each option is assigned an initial value, and you only need to set a value for an option if you want to change it. To see a list of all the option values set for you, type the last line command

`:set all`

The list that now appears on the screen will show the default values of the options.

   Many of the environment options have binary values: on and off. For example, the **wrapscan** option has the values **wrapscan** (the option is turned on) and **nowrapscan** (the option is turned off). All options that have binary values follow this pattern. The on value is just the name of the option, and the off value is the word "no" prefixed to the name of the option. Other options have numerical values that you can change to any appropriate number. When an option takes a numerical value, you can set its value with a command of the syntax

:set *option* $=x$

where *option* is the name of the option whose value you want to set and *x* is the numerical value you want the option to have.

▶ **NOTE**   The option, equal sign, and number must not be separated by spaces.

Some of the more commonly set options with both binary and numerical values are discussed in the following sections. More of these options are discussed in the "vi Quick Reference" at the end of this chapter.

The wrapmargin Option   Ordinarily, **vi** is like the shell in that text does not wrap to the next line automatically. Instead, you must press RETURN yourself when you want a line broken. However, the **wrapmargin** option, when set, causes **vi** to automatically insert a newline character when the cursor gets to be a certain number of characters from the right edge of the screen. This option takes numerical values.

Initially the value of **wrapmargin** is set to 0, which means that the text is not wrapped at all. Essentially 0 is the off value for the **wrapmargin** option. If you set the value to 1, it will insert a newline as soon as the text you type is 1 character away from the right edge of the screen. If you are in the middle of a word when the limit is reached, the RETURN will be inserted *before* the word. To set the **wrapmargin**, type

```
:set wrapmargin=x
```

where *x* is the number of characters from the right side of the screen you want the margin to be. For example, to set the margin to five characters, you would type

```
:set wrapmargin=5
```

The larger the number, the wider the margin and the shorter the lines.

With the **wrapmargin** on (set to a value besides 0), **vi** appears on the screen a little more like some other word processors. However, it still does not format your text as a formatter would. The **wrapmargin** feature operates only on the text you are inserting at the moment and will not readjust lines when you add or remove text later.

▶**NOTE**   Since any text you type in **vi** will probably be formatted by a text formatting program, the margin you create with **wrapmargin** will be irrelevant to the finished version of the file.

The number Option   When the **number** option is set, line numbers appear to the left of each line on the screen while you are editing a file. These numbers do *not* appear in the file when you print it or when you view the file with any other utility. Initially this option is off (**nonumber** is set). To get line numbers, type

```
:set number
```

If you have the **number** option set, you can turn it off by typing

`:set nonumber`

You may like having the line numbers displayed to keep track of where you are in the file and to make sure you don't make your lines too long. (Two lines with only one number are really one long line.) However, some people find line numbers distracting. Whether or not you decide to have line numbers displayed, remember that lines are automatically numbered even if the numbers do not appear on the screen. You will still be able to use line-number addresses.

The wrapscan Option   The **wrapscan** option, discussed in the section on "Searching for a Pattern," determines whether, for the purpose of searches, the file is treated as a continuous loop or as a thing with a beginning and an end.

The report Option   The value of the **report** option determines how many lines you can delete, copy, change, or replace before that operation is reported on the last line of the screen. Initially, the value of this option is set to 5. Try yanking ten lines and you should see the message "10 lines yanked" at the bottom of the screen.

Abbreviations

As everyone knows, typing the same long word repeatedly can be tedious. Fortunately, **vi** provides a last line command called **abbreviate** (**ab**), with which you can designate abbreviations for long words or phrases. Then when you type the abbreviation in insert mode as a word (bounded by whitespace or punctuation), it will automatically expand to the entire word or phrase.

To designate an abbreviation for a word or phrase, type

:ab *abbreviation word*

where *abbreviation* is any abbreviation you choose and *word* is the word or phrase you want it to expand to. For example, to designate the abbreviation "cm" for the phrase "corporate merger," you would type

```
:ab cm corporate merger
```

Now every time you type the sequence **cm** as a word (in insert mode only), it will expand to say "corporate merger." The sequence **cm** will *not* expand if it is in the middle of a word, only if it is bounded on both ends by whitespace or punctuation. Remember that since **vi** is sensitive to case, the sequences **CM**, **Cm**, and **cM** would not expand.

▶**TIP**   The abbreviation you choose does not have to be a real abbreviation for the word or phrase it expands to, or even have any letters in common. For example, you could have the number 6 expand to the phrase "corporate merger." It is important, however, to choose abbreviations that are not real words that you might want to use. For example, the letter "a" is not a good abbreviation, because every time you type the word **a**, it will expand, whether you want it to or not.

You can designate abbreviations either on the last line for a particular editing session or in your **.exrc** file. If you decide you no longer want an abbreviation to take effect, you can use the **unabbreviate (unab)** command. For example, to unabbreviate the sequence **cm**, you would type

```
:unab cm
```

As you typed this command, **cm** would still expand, but for the last time. The next time you typed it, it would not. If an abbreviation is designated in your **.exrc** file, you can just delete that line from the **.exrc** file and it will no longer take effect.

Mapping

As you use **vi** more and more, you will probably find that you type certain sequences of escape mode or last line commands frequently. A convenient last line command called **map** allows you to designate one key to stand for a whole sequence of commands. Just as an abbreviation expands to a longer piece of text, you can map short commands of your choice to a sequence of commands. In this way, when you are in escape or last line mode, you can type just one key and all the commands in the sequence will be executed. You can do this either on the last line in a particular editing session or in your **.exrc** file.

You can map any ordinary key (letter, number, or punctuation) to a sequence of commands. If that key already functions as an escape mode command, your mapping will override its original function. For this reason, it is best to choose either keys that have no escape mode function or keys that you do not think you will need. For example, **v** does not function as an escape mode command, so it would be a good key to map. Uppercase **S** does function as an escape mode command, but it is identical in function to **cc**, so you could map it to some other sequence of functions.

The **map** command causes the mapping to work only in escape mode, while the **map!** command causes it to work in insert mode as well.

Some sample **map** commands follow:

■ The command **map g $** makes **g** function like the cursor-movement command **$**, which moves the cursor to the end of the current line. This command maps a key to only one command, but since **g** is handier to type than **$**, it makes this command more convenient.

■ The command **map v d)o** maps **v** to two commands. The first, **d)**, deletes everything from the current cursor postion to the beginning of the next sentence. The second, **o**, opens a new line below the cursor. Now just typing **v** while in escape mode will execute both of these commands.

■ The command **map # ct.** maps **#** to the command **ct.**, which changes everything from the current cursor position to the next period on the line.

■ The command **map S ISTOP** maps the character **S** to the command **I**, which inserts text at the beginning of the current line. Since **I** puts you in insert mode, the remaining characters in the mapping are simply typed as text. Thus the command **S** will now insert the word "STOP" at the beginning of the current line.

■ The command **map V xp** maps **V** to two commands. The first, **x**, deletes the character the cursor is on. The second, **p**, puts the last deleted text, which will be the character just deleted, after the cursor, which will have moved forward one character. In other words, this sequence of commands reverses the order of two characters.

Remember, these are just sample mappings. You could use different characters to map these same sequences of commands, or you could use the same characters to map any other command sequences you might find useful.

When you decide that you no longer want a particular mapping, you can use the **unmap** command to take away the special meaning of a mapped sequence. For example, to unmap the letter "S," you would type

```
:unmap S
```

If the mapping is set in your **.exrc** file, to unmap it just remove that line from the file. The **unmap** command will not work on a sequence mapped with **map!**. If you have a mapping set with **map!** for a particular editing session, you must exit **vi** to get rid of it.

The .exrc File

The **.exrc** file is a file in your home directory that contains commands that are executed each time you use **vi**. You can execute the last line commands **set**, **ab**, and **map** by placing them in your **.exrc** file. You can't do this with last line editing commands and shell escapes.

The **.exrc** file will probably not exist in your account when you first log in. If it does not, you will have to create one (if you want to use it) in your home directory.

▶**BERKELEY VERSION**   You can create a separate **.exrc** file in each directory, each containing a different set of commands that are executed only when you edit a file in that directory. The commands in the **.exrc** file in your home directory will still be executed when you use **vi** in these subdirectories, but the additional commands in the subdirectory's **.exrc** file will be executed as well.

You can create a **.exrc** file with **vi** or with **cat**. If you want a certain option to be set every time you use **vi**, it is better to set it in the **.exrc** file. If there are certain options that you want set only during particular editing sessions, you should set them in last line mode during those sessions.

Commands in **.exrc** look just like last line commands without the preceding colon. Figure 6-5 shows the contents of a typical **.exrc** file as viewed with **vi**. The commands in this sample file set the **wrapmargin** option to 10, turn off the **warn** option, designate three abbreviations, and map three characters to command sequences.

Executing Shell Commands from Within vi

While you are editing a file with **vi**, you can still access all the UNIX shell commands without exiting **vi**. You can also put the results of a shell command into the file you are editing, and even use a shell filter to change all or part of the file you are editing, replacing the original lines with the output of the filter.

```
set wrapmargin=10
set nowarn
ab lbg LeBlond group
ab di directory
ab co command
map g $
map S ISTOP
map # ct.
~
~
~
~
~
~
~
".exrc" 8 lines, 110 characters
```

Figure 6-5. *A typical .exrc file*

Shell Escapes   You can use a convenient feature of **vi** called the *shell escape* to execute shell commands while editing a file. This saves you from having to save your file, exit **vi**, get back into **vi**, and find your place again each time you want to execute a shell command. To execute a shell command from within **vi**, type

  :!*command*

where *command* is the name of the command you want to execute. For example, to execute the **date** command, you would type

  `:!date`

The date as displayed by the **date** command will now appear on the last line, and you will be instructed to press RETURN to continue. (Actually you can press *any* key to continue.) You can execute any shell command from within **vi**, even **vi**. That is, you can use **vi** to edit another file while still editing the first one. Unless the shell command you type mentions the file you are editing, no shell command you execute with a shell escape will have any effect on the buffer you are editing. That is, the results of the command do not appear in the buffer or change it in any way.

Unless you have the **warn** option turned off, **vi** will warn you each time you execute a shell escape if you made changes since last writing the current file. It will still execute the command, but will pause first. This warning is intended to protect your work, but it can be annoying. If you use shell escapes often, you should probably turn off the **warn** option by setting **nowarn**.

Putting the Results of a Shell Command in the File   When you execute a shell command with the last line ! command, the results of that command are displayed on the screen but do not become part of the file. However, there is a way to get the results of a command placed in the file. The **!!** (use without colon) command places results of the shell command whose name you type next in the file on the current line.

▶**NOTE**   Any text on the current line is replaced with the output of the shell command that you type, so the cursor should be on a blank line when you execute the **!!** command. If the output of the command is longer than one line, however, subsequent lines will be pushed along after the new text, not overwritten.

When you type **!!**, one **!** will appear at the bottom of the screen just as the **:** does when you type it. The **!** is the prompt for you to type the shell command of your choice. For example, if you type **!!date**, the output of the **date** command will be placed on the current line.

▶**NOTE**   Certain commands in your **.login** or **.cshrc** files may produce an error message of some sort (these vary from system to system) when you try to put the output of a command in a file. This error message will actually become a part of the file, like the output of the command. However, unless the error message tells you that it can't do the command, you can just ignore it and delete that line from the file.

Since the command output is placed in the file, you can include in a file only commands that produce some output.

Using Shell Filters on Part of a File   There are two ways to make a UNIX filter operate on all or part of a file without exiting **vi**. The first is similar to a last line editing command: You specify the lines the filter is to operate on as addresses, and instead of an editing command, you type the name of the filter after an **!**. For example, to run lines 1 through 10 through the **sort** program, you would type

`:1,10 !sort`

Lines 1 through 10 will now appear sorted in the file. Again, you may get an error message of some sort before the changed text, but you can simply delete this text.

The second way to filter part of a file is to use the command **!** (without a colon) followed by a cursor-movement command, and then the name of the shell filter you want to use. If you use this method, the filter operates on all lines from the current line to the line specified by the cursor movement address. For example, to sort all lines from the current line to line 34, you would type

`!34G`

Note that with this command, you do not type a preceding colon. The !! command puts the results of a shell command in a file. However, if you substitute a cursor-movement command for the second !, the specified lines are actually run through the shell filter whose name you type next.

Command-Line Options

Suppose you are editing a file and want to exit **vi** for a moment. When you return to **vi**, you will have to move the cursor to the place where you were editing, either with cursor-movement commands or by searching with **/**. There are convenient command-line options that make **vi** start up at a place other than the beginning of the file so you don't have to do this. The command **vi +** causes **vi** to start with the window at the end of the file. If you specify a number after the **+**, **vi** will start up with the cursor on the specified line, and that line in the center of the window.

Finally, if you specify a search pattern after the **+**, **vi** will start up with the cursor on the first line containing that pattern. The format to use when specifying a search pattern is

vi +*/expression file*

where *expression* is the regular expression at which you want **vi** to start up and *file* is the file you want to edit. For example, to start **vi** at the first line that contained the word "regret" in a file called **responses**, you would type

```
% vi +/regret responses
```

Notice that the shell can distinguish the regular expression from the file name by the intervening space. Therefore, if you include any spaces in the regular expression, you must either precede each one with a **** (backslash) or enclose the entire expression in double quotes. This tells the shell that these are not real spaces, but part of the regular expression. For example, if you wanted to start **vi** at the first line containing the phrase "unable to comply" in a file called **responses**, you could type either

```
% vi +/unable\ to\ comply forms
```

or

```
% vi +/"unable to comply" forms
```

▶**TIP** One way to take advantage of the **+/** command-line option is to always insert the same word (for example, the word "STOP") on a line just before you exit the editor. This way, even if you don't remember the context where you were last editing, you can simply type **vi +/STOP**. (Don't forget to delete the identifying word from the file.)

   Notice that the **/** used in the

+/ *expression*

option looks just like the **/** used in searches. In fact, it is the same. When you use this command-line option, a search is initiated as soon as you enter **vi**. If you now type the escape mode **n** command, the cursor will move to the next occurrence of the regular expression.

vi Quick Reference

You can use the **vi** quick reference in Table 6-1 once you have read at least the first few sections of this chapter and are familiar with the basic escape mode and last line commands. The following points will help you use the "vi Quick Reference" quickly and efficiently:

■ The commands are grouped by function and listed alphabetically within each section. In most cases, escape mode commands are listed separately from last line commands.

■ Unless otherwise stated, you can precede all escape mode cursor-movement and editing commands by a number specifying how many times the command is to be repeated. Only when a preceding number does something besides repeat the command will the preceding number be explained and indicated in the command syntax.

■ The variable *n* indicates a number as part of a command. Where this variable is enclosed in parentheses, it represents an optional number argument. For example (*n*)^D indicates that the ^D command may or may not be preceded by a number.

■ Unless otherwise stated, all escape mode cursor movements can be the address of any escape mode editing command that takes a following address.

Exiting vi	
:w	Writes the editing buffer to disk. If you specify a following file name, writes the buffer to a file with that name.
:q	Exits **vi** without writing to disk.
:wq	Writes the file to disk and then quits.
:x	Writes the buffer to disk only if changes have been made since the last **write**, and then quits.
ZZ	Same as **:x**.
Q	Puts you in **ex** command mode. Use the **ex** command **vi** to get back into visual mode.
Cursor Movements	
b	Moves back one word (bounded by punctuation or whitespace).
B	Moves back one word (bounded by whitespace).
e	Moves to end of current or next word.
E	Moves to end of word until whitespace character.
f	Moves to next occurrence on the current line of the character you type next.
F	Moves to previous occurrence on the current line of the character you type next.
(*n*)G	Moves to last line of file or line number *n*.
h	Moves back one space.
j	Moves down one line.
k	Moves up one line.
l	Moves forward one space.
(*n*)L	Moves to bottom of screen or *n* lines from bottom.
M	Moves to beginning of middle line of screen.
t*x*	Moves to the space before the next occurrence of character *x* on the current line.
T*x*	Same as **t**, but scans backward on the current line.

Table 6-1. *vi Quick Reference*

w	Moves to beginning of next word (bounded by punctuation or whitespace).
W	Moves to beginning of next word (bounded by whitespace).
$	Moves to last character of current line.
%	Moves to),], or } matching next occurrence of (, [, or {, respectively.
^	Moves to first nonwhitespace character on current line.
(	Moves to beginning of current or previous sentence.
)	Moves to beginning of next sentence.
&	Repeats last substitution (executed with last line command **s**) on current line.
{	Moves to beginning of current or previous paragraph, where a paragraph is marked with one of the **nroff** paragraph macros. Type **:set all** to see what these are.
}	Moves to beginning of next paragraph (see preceding command).
[[	Moves to beginning of current or preceding section, where a section is marked with one of the **nroff** section macros. Type **:set all** to see what these are.
]]	Moves to beginning of next section (see preceding command).
'x	Moves to line marked x (marked with the **m** command).
''	Moves to location where last major motion command was given.
`x	Moves to exact location on line marked x (marked with the **m** command).
``	Moves to exact location on line where last major motion command was given.
,	Repeats last search with **f**, **F**, **t**, or **T**, but reverses direction.
+	Moves up one line.
-	Moves down one line.
Screen Control Commands	
^F	Pages forward one screenful. Cannot be used as a cursor movement address.
^B	Pages back one screenful. Cannot be used as a cursor movement address.

Table 6-1. *vi Quick Reference* (continued)

(n)^D	Scrolls down half a screen or n lines. Cannot be used as a cursor-movement address
(n)^U	Scrolls up half a screen or n lines. Cannot be used as a cursor-movement address.
^R or ^L	Redraws the screen when it has been scrambled by a system message, a message from another user, or some other interruption.
(n)zsize	Redraws the screen with the current line or line n at the top of the screen. If *zsize* is specified, the screen is redrawn with that number of lines.
(n)zsize.	Redraws the screen with the current line or line n at the middle of the screen. If *zsize* is specified, the screen is redrawn with that number of lines.
(n)zsize-	Redraws the screen with the current line or line n at the bottom of the screen. If *zsize* is specified, the screen is redrawn with that number of lines.

Editing Commands

a	Appends text after the cursor.
A	Appends text at end of current line.
cc	Changes one line to the next text typed.
cx	Changes from cursor to place delimited by cursor movement x.
C	Changes current line from cursor to end.
dd	Deletes one line.
dx	Deletes from cursor to place delimited by cursor movement x.
D	Deletes from cursor to end of current line.
i	Inserts text before the cursor.
I	Inserts text at beginning of current line.
J	Joins current line and next line.
mx	Marks current line (and current cursor position) with letter x.
o	Opens new line below the current line.
O	Opens new line above the current line.
p	Replaces last deleted, copied, or changed text after the cursor.
"np	Places text in delete buffer number n after the cursor.
"xp	Places text in named delete buffer x after the cursor.
P	Replaces last deleted, copied, or changed text before the cursor.

Table 6-1. *vi Quick Reference* (continued)

"nP	Places text in delete buffer number *n* before the cursor.
"xP	Places text in named delete buffer *x* before the cursor.
r	Replaces character the cursor is on with next character typed.
R	Replaces one character at a time with characters typed next.
s	Substitutes character the cursor is on with text typed next.
S	Changes current line (identical to **cc**).
u	Undoes last editing command.
U	Undoes all editing changes to current line.
x	Deletes character the cursor is on.
X	Deletes character before the cursor.
yy	Copies current line.
Y	Copies current line (identical to **yy**).
"xyy	Copies current line into named delete buffer *x*.
&	Repeats last substitution (last line command) on current line (pattern must be matched).
~	Changes the case of the letter the cursor is on (upper- to lowercase, lower- to uppercase). Cannot be preceded by a number.
(*n*)>	Shifts *n* lines right by the value of the **shiftwidth** option.
(*n*)<	Shifts *n* lines left by the value of the **shiftwidth** option.
Searching	
f	Finds next occurrence on the current line of the character you type next.
F	Finds previous occurrence on the current line of the character you type next.
t*x*	Moves to the space before the next occurrence of character *x* on the current line.
T*x*	Same as **t**, but scans backward on the current line.
,	Repeats last search with **f**, **F**, **t**, or **T**, but reverses direction.
/*expression*	Searches for next occurrence of *expression* (any regular expression) in the file.
?*expression*	Searches for previous occurrence of *expression* (any regular expression) in the file.
n	Repeats last search with / or ?.
N	Repeats last search with / or ?, but reverses direction of search.

Table 6-1. *vi Quick Reference (continued)*

Miscellaneous Escape Mode Commands

"x	Names delete buffers. Puts next deleted, changed, or copied text in named buffer *x*.
^G	Displays at the bottom of the screen the current line number and information about the length of the file.
m*x*	Marks current line (and current cursor position) with letter *x*.

Last Line Editing Commands

x,y delete (d)	Deletes lines with addresses *x* through *y*.
x,y move (m) *z*	Moves lines with addresses *x* through *y* to below line with address *z*.
x,y copy (co) *z*	Copies lines with addresses *x* through *y* to below line with address *z*.
x,y s/*pat1*/*pat2*/(g)(c)	Replaces search pattern *pat1* with replacement pattern *pat2* on lines with addresses *x* through *y*. If **g** is set, substitutes for every occurrence of *pat1* on specified lines. If **c** is set, asks you to confirm each substitution.
g/*pat1*/s//*pat2*/(g)(c)	Same as above, but makes substitution on every line in the file containing *pat1*.

vi Environment Options

all	Displays a list of all the currently set option values.
autoindent (ai)	Used for writing structured programs where indentation is important for determining levels of embedded commands. When set, **vi** indents each line you type an appropriate amount dependent on the indentation of the previous line.
autoprint (ap)	Displays the current line after each **copy**, **move**, or substitute (**s**) command.
ignorecase	When set, the case of letters in regular expressions (in search patterns) is ignored except in ranges within square brackets.
magic	When **nomagic** is set, all magic characters (used in regular expressions) except ^ (beginning of line) and $ (end of line) lose their magic properties. By default **magic** is set, but even when **nomagic** is set, you can turn on the magic of individual characters by preceding them with \ (backslash).

Table 6-1.   *vi Quick Reference (continued)*

mesg	By default, **nomesg** is set. When set, **mesg** allows other users to write to your terminal with the **write** command, which can temporarily scramble your screen.
number	When set, the number of each line is displayed at the left of the screen.
report	**Report=5** is set by default. This option determines the threshhold at which the number of lines deleted, copied, moved, or changed is reported.
showmatch	When this option is set, each time a) or } is typed in insert mode, the cursor jumps quickly back to show the matching (or {.
showmode	Causes the message "INPUT MODE" to be displayed in the lower-right corner of the screen when you are in insert mode.
wrapmargin	By default, **wrapmargin=0** is set. When a different numerical value is set, causes a RETURN to be inserted that number of characters from the right edge of the screen in insert mode.
wrapscan	When set, **vi** treats a file as a continuous loop for searches with **/** and **?**. When **nowrapscan** is set, a search with **/** stops scanning when it reaches the end of the file, and a search with **?** stops scanning when it reaches the beginning of the file.

Miscellaneous Last Line Commands

=	Displays the current line number.
abbreviate (ab) *str1 str2*	Designates *str1* as an abbreviation that will expand to *str2* (any word or phrase) when typed in insert mode.
unabbreviate (unab) *str*	Unabbreviates (removes the special significance of) *str*, a string abbreviated with the **abbreviate** command.
map *str1 str2*	Maps *str1*, where *str1* is any sequence of characters, that will expand to *str2* when typed in escape mode.
unmap *str*	Unmaps *str*, a string mapped with the **map** command.
(*address1,address2*) w (*file*)	Writes lines with addresses *address1* through *address2* to a file called *file*.
(*address*) r *file*	Reads the file *file* into the current file below the current line. If an *address* is specified, reads the file in below the specified line.

Table 6-1.　*vi Quick Reference (continued)*

In this chapter, you learned how to use both basic and more advanced **vi** commands that will enable you to become an expert **vi** user. Not only ordinary text files, but also shell scripts and even advanced C programs are ordinarily created with the **vi** editor. (See Chapter 9, "The Bourne Shell," Chapter 10, "The C Shell," and Chapter 11, "Program Development with C" to learn about these types of files.) You can also use **vi** to edit the **.login** and **.profile** files, which determine certain aspects of your UNIX environment. The **vi** editor is therefore both a powerful text editor and one of the most basic UNIX tools. In Chapter 7, "Text Formatting with nroff and troff," you will learn how to use text formatting programs to give your finished text a polished and professional look.

7 Text Formatting with nroff and troff

The **nroff** and **troff** text formatters are part of the UNIX document preparation system designed to help you produce high-quality typeset documents. Macro packages, such as the **mm** and **ms** macros, add to **nroff** and **troff** a collection of commands that simplify typesetting by letting you concentrate on the structure of the text rather than on complex formatting commands. The **nroff** and **troff** formatters and their macros are simple to use, and allow you to turn your raw text into a professional, typeset document.

Text Formatting

The **nroff** and **troff** formatters offer features such as right-margin justification, automatic hyphenation, page titling and numbering, footnotes, and environments for quotations, displays, and figures. Additionally, **troff** allows you full control over fonts, sizes, and character positioning. For complicated formatting tasks, **nroff** and **troff** both provide macros, arithmetic operations and variables, and conditional testing, though these more complicated features are not covered in this book.

The **nroff** and **troff** formatters look at a file in which you have interspersed lines of text with lines of format control information. With this format control information, you may change how individual parts of your text will appear or how your entire document is to be formatted. You determine the format by including **nroff** and **troff** commands directly in your text. You enter both text and **nroff** and **troff** commands from an editor, such as **vi**, the visual editor, which is described in Chapter 6. When you finish entering the text, including formatting instructions, you ask **nroff** or **troff** to format it for you. When the formatting is done, you should have two files: your original text file and a new file containing the formatted version. The details of running your document through **nroff** or **troff** will be discussed later in this chapter in the section "Running nroff and troff."

▶**NOTE**   Formatting a document is a two-step process: First, you use an editor to create your text and place the format control information in a file. Second, you use one of the formatters—**nroff** or **troff**—to read the text and formatting commands, creating a typeset document. For example, typing the **nroff** command **.ce** for centering will not center your text immediately. Your text will center only after you've run the whole file through the formatting program.

The nroff and troff Formatters

The **nroff** and **troff** formatters are siblings from the same family of text formatters. You use the **nroff** formatter to format text for output to a line printer or letter-quality printer. You use the **troff** formatter to format text for a phototypesetter or laser printer. Although the output of the two formatters is different, the commands for **nroff** and **troff** are identical. Most files that can be formatted with **nroff** can be formatted with **troff**, and vice versa. Because of their similarities, the names "nroff" and "troff" are often used synonymously; in fact, the name "nroff" will often be used to mean "nroff or troff," as in "the *nroff* command **.ls.**" For simplicity, we will often just say "the formatter." The name "troff" will only be used to indicate those features that are unique to **troff**.

Although most features are shared by both **nroff** and **troff**, you can only see the effects of some commands (such as changes in font, point size, and variable spacing) on the phototypesetter by using **troff**. The **troff** formatter fully implements these commands on the typesetter, but **nroff** must ignore or approximate such commands on the line printer. All the examples in this chapter were produced by using **troff** and a laser printer.

Most **nroff** commands must begin with a period and be entered at the beginning of a line by themselves. For example, the **nroff** command **.na** stands for "no adjustment" (it turns right-margin justification off) and appears at the beginning of a line by itself:

```
.na
```

Some commands can take *arguments* that specify how much or how many times the command should take effect. Arguments can also specify text that will, in some way, be used by the command. The argument follows the command on the same line. For example, the **nroff** command **.ll** stands for "line length" and takes an argument that specifies the new length of a text line. To work, the **.ll** command needs some value for the new line length. The command

```
.ll 6i
```

tells **nroff** to set the new line length to 6 inches.

Some **nroff** and **troff** commands begin with a backslash (\) and may appear within the text. To italicize the book title in the following example, the **\fI** command (meaning "change font to italics") appears within the text, as follows:

```
The title \fIThe Little Prince\fR is on the reading list.
```

The **\fR** command restores the standard (usually Roman) font.

▶**TIP** The word "nroff" is a two-syllable word, read "n-roff" and pronounced *en rawf;* "troff" is read "t-roff." The -roff family of formatters originated from an older program named "roff," which stood for "runoff." The "t" in "troff" stands for "typesetting," as in "typesetting runoff." The "n" in "nroff," though, remains a mystery.

Macros

A macro package is a set of ready-made functions designed to simplify some rather complex procedures. Macros allow you to do in a few steps what would take a great deal of effort with **nroff** or **troff** commands. These macro packages meet most formatting needs. They define formatting rules and operations for specific styles of documents, such as memos and letters, as well as operations simplifying complex sequences of **nroff** commands, such as page formatting, lists, footnotes, and displays.

▶**NOTE** In many ways, **nroff** and **troff** resemble computer assembly languages: They are powerful and flexible but require many operations to be specified at a level of detail and complexity too difficult for most people to use effectively. For this reason, you should avoid using **nroff** and **troff** commands directly whenever possible. Instead, you should use a macro package, such as the **mm** or **ms** macros.

Many different **nroff** macro packages have been developed for special purposes, but only four have gained wide popularity. The **mm** (memorandum macros) package produces business letters and business memos. The **mm** macro package is the newest package. It is also the easiest to use and is especially suited for business communication. The **ms** (macros for science) package is used in engineering and computer science. The **me** (macros for education) package is used in universities for technical writing. Finally, the **man** (manual) macros are used to produce the UNIX reference manuals and to format the UNIX on-line manual. Only the **mm** macro package will be discussed in this book.

All macro commands, similar to most **nroff** commands, begin with a period and are placed at the beginning of a line all by themselves. Macro commands are usually all uppercase and one to two letters long. For example, to indicate the start of a paragraph, use

```
.P
```

at the beginning of a line by itself.

▶**TIP**   Because they work similarly, you can think of **mm** commands and **nroff** commands as the same thing. Actually, macros are collections of **nroff** commands. But since direct **nroff** commands can interfere with **mm** commands, there is an advantage to knowing which commands are which. When presenting each new command, this book tells you whether it is an **nroff** or **mm** command.

The **mm** macros have a special set of internal variables called *registers* to keep track of default settings such as heading levels and paragraph styles. You can manipulate the **mm** variables to get even more powerful results from **nroff**. The **mm** registers can be changed with the **nroff** number register command **.nr**.

The following sections describe the most fundamental and essential **nroff** operations. Whenever possible, commands from the **mm** macro set will be used instead of the direct **nroff** commands.

Fill and Justification

The ability to *fill* and *justify* lines is one of the most important features of a formatter. It is this process that gives the output text its finished appearance.

Filling

When it is in fill mode, the formatter scrunches all the input lines together in the output. The format of the output text does not depend on the format of the input file. To the formatter, the input file is only a stream of words. To produce a line of filled output text, the formatter takes words from the input file, regardless of the original line length, and adds them to the output line until it gets to a word that extends past the right margin. If the formatter can hyphenate and include part of this word on the line, it does. Otherwise, it saves this word for the next line of output and the new line is filled. For example, the input file, created with an editor, may look like this:

```
The geographical center of Boston is in Roxbury.
Due north of the center we find the South End.
This is not to be confused with South Boston which lies directly
east from the South End.
North of the South End is East Boston and southwest of East Boston
is the North End.
```

The filled output text would look like this:

The geographical center of Boston is in Roxbury. Due north of the center we find the South End. This is not to be confused with South Boston which lies directly east from the South End. North of the South End is East Boston and southwest of East Boston is the North End.

▶**TIP**   When you enter your text in **vi** (or another editor), you don't have to be concerned with the length of the lines. The formatter will ignore your line length, filling the text to fit within the margins. Conseqently, to make their text easier to change later, **nroff** users typically begin each sentence in their text on a new line.

Occasionally, you may not want the formatter to disregard the original line length in your input file—for a list or a poem, for example. To preserve the exact appearance of your input, you must set the formatter to no fill. You can turn off fill with the **nroff** no fill command **.nf** and turn it back on with the **nroff** fill command **.fi**. After a no fill command, subsequent output lines are neither filled nor justified; input lines are copied directly to output lines without regard to the current line length.

▶**NOTE** Unless you tell it otherwise, the formatter always fills text. Displays are an exception; text is not initially filled within a display (see the section "Displays").

Justification

When the formatter is in justify mode, all of the lines of the justified output text are flush with the right margin. An exception is the last line of a paragraph, which is never justified. Filled but unjustified text is said to have a *ragged* right margin, while justified text is said to have a *flush right* margin. A line must be filled before it can be justified; justification won't work if fill is off.

To justify text, the **nroff** formatter adds extra spaces between words in the filled line, one at a time, to bring the right end of the line to the right margin. The **troff** formatter, on the other hand, expands the space between letters, as well as between words, by fractions of spaces (a feature only available on typesetters and laser printers), making the justification less noticeable. For example, the input file may look like this:

```
Recently, Pacific Communication Center (CC) installed
the Maverick word processing program on the CC computers.
Unfortunately, it lacks the time and the resources to support
both the newer Maverick word processor and the older Colt
family of word processors.
Consequently, little support is currently available from the
CC for Maverick.
```

Filled and justified, the **troff** output text looks like this:

Recently Pacific Communication Center (CC) installed the Maverick word processing program on the CC computers. Unfortunately, it lacks the time and the resources to support both the newer Maverick word processor and the older Colt family of word processors. Consequently, little support is currently available from the CC for Maverick.

Some people like right-margin justification; others find a ragged right margin easier to read. You can use the **mm** set adjustment command **.SA** to turn right-margin justification off and on. It has the format

.SA *adjustment*

The single argument *adjustment* can be **1** or **0**. The command

```
.SA 1
```

turns on justification. The command

```
.SA 0
```

sets no justification. For instance, if you wanted to justify a paragraph but leave the following paragraph unjustified, you would precede the first with

```
.SA 1
```

and the second with

```
.SA 0
```

Initially, using the **mm** macros, **nroff** is set to no justification while **troff** is set to justify. In contrast, the **ms** macros always justify text by default. In any case, you can turn fill, justification, and hyphenation on or off. Turning fill mode off also turns off justification and hyphenation.

▶ **NOTE**   Since the output examples in this chapter were produced with **troff,** they are justified.

Paragraphs, Headings, and
Table of Contents

This section describes simple paragraphs, section headings, and the
table of contents.

Paragraphs are one of the basic building blocks of a document. You
can divide a document further into sectional units with section *headings*.
You can then use these to generate a *table of contents* that provides an
overview and map of the document.

Paragraphs

Describing a paragraph in **nroff** is simple. A paragraph command usually begins a paragraph, while one or more blank lines usually denote
the end of a paragraph. You can also format a paragraph manually.

The formatter gives you two types of paragraphs: left block and
standard. All lines in a *left-block* paragraph are flush with the left margin.
A *standard* paragraph is the usual indented paragraph; the first line is
indented while the following lines are flush with the left margin. With
the **mm** macros, the formatter by default fills but does not justify the
lines of the paragraph.

The **mm** paragraph command is **.P**. It has the format

.P [*type*]

The optional argument *type* specifies the type of the paragraph following
the command. If you specify **0**, the formatter produces a left-block
paragraph; a **1** produces a standard paragraph. For example, here is an
input file that creates first a left-block paragraph and then a standard
paragraph:

```
P 0
The Maverick documentation by Leslie Tremmons, Maverick's
author, is superlative, but does not address local
implementation concerns.
Instead, Tremmons references a series of implementation
```

```
dependent documents, called the Maverick Guide, in which is
detailed local concerns.
.P 1
Unfortunately, the CC has not produced a Maverick Guide for
its Maverick users, nor does it have an old version to modify.
Since the CC has no local documentation, there is a gap
between Tremmons's Maverick documentation and the Pacific
Communication Maverick users.
```

It produces the following output:

The Maverick documentation by Leslie Tremmons, Maverick's author, is superlative, but does not address local implementation concerns. Instead, Tremmons references a series of implementation dependent documents, called the Maverick Guide, in which is detailed local concerns.

Unfortunately, the CC has not produced a Maverick Guide for its Maverick users, nor does it have an old version to modify. Since the CC has no local documentation, there is a gap between Tremmons's Maverick documentation and the Pacific Communication Maverick users.

If you do not specify a *type* argument, the **.P** command initially produces left-block paragraphs. You can change this by changing the value of the **Pt** (paragraph-type) register. The **Pt** register controls the default paragraph style for all subsequent paragraph commands. Initially, the **Pt** register has a value of 0, causing **.P** commands to yield left-block paragraphs. To change the value of **Pt** to 1 and cause **.P** commands to produce standard paragraphs, include

```
.nr Pt 1
```

in your file. In the following example, **nroff** produces standard paragraphs without the use of an argument after each **.P** command.

```
.nr Pt 1
.P
```

```
The system uses a widely known sort technique known as the
```

```
Bubblesort.
To picture the Bubblesort, imagine that the records to be
sorted are kept in a vertical array.
The records with low sort values are "light" and slowly bubble
up to the top.
.P
The Bubblesort is simple and easy to implement and, on nearly
sorted files, takes little time to complete the sort.
However, on random files, it is the least efficient sorting
method available.
As we have exclusively random files, let's give the boys down
in the systems department a well-deserved round of applause.
```

This produces the following output:

_____

The system uses a widely known sort technique known as the Bubblesort. To picture the Bubblesort, imagine that the records to be sorted are kept in a vertical array. The records with low sort values are "light" and slowly bubble up to the top.

    The Bubblesort is simple and easy to implement and, on nearly sorted files, takes little time to complete the sort. However, on random files, it is the least efficient sorting method available. As we have exclusively random files, let's give the boys down in the systems department a well-deserved round of applause.

_____

It is convenient to set your default paragraph preference at the top of your input file and use **.P**, with no argument throughout. This way, if you decide to change the paragraph style in your document, you need only change the line that sets the default paragraph.

    You can manually format paragraphs in **nroff**. As long as you separate paragraphs by blank lines, the formatter will treat your paragraphs as integral blocks of text. However, since your paragraph is still only a block of text to the formatter (without the **.P** command, **nroff** does not really look at it as a paragraph), it cannot automatically be indented. Of course, you may indent it manually by inserting spaces or tabs in the first line, or you can leave it flush with the left margin. Manual formatting is okay for quick and dirty jobs but, for long documents, it does not provide the flexibility of the **.P** command.

Numbered Headings

A heading is a title within the text that sets apart sectional units such as chapters, sections, and subsections. Headings are set off from the surrounding text by their typeface and position. The **mm** macros give you up to seven levels of numbered and unnumbered headings.

A *numbered heading* is a sectional title that includes a number that describes the section's exact position in the hierarchical structure of the document. For instance, had the sections and subsections of this book been numbered, you would currently be reading subsection 7.5.2, entitled "Numbered Headings," which is part of Section 7.5, "Paragraphs, Headings, and Table of Contents," which in turn is part of Chapter 7, "Text Formatting with nroff and troff."

Use the **mm** heading command **.H** to create a numbered heading. With each **.H** command, you must specify the *heading level*. The heading level describes the depth of the sectional unit that follows the heading; for instance, a chapter is level one, a section is level two, a subsection is level three, and so on. The section number is automatically incremented. For instance, if the previous heading number were 7.5.2 and you specified a third-level heading, the new heading number would be 7.5.3; if you specified a second-level heading, the new number would be 7.6. The format of the heading command is

.H *level heading-text*

where *level* is the desired heading level, from one to seven, and the *heading-text* is the text of the section title. If *heading-text* includes any spaces, you must enclose the text in double quotation marks.

Unless told otherwise, **nroff** prints first- and second-level sectional titles in boldface followed by a blank line, while **troff** prints these (and all other) headings in italic. First-level sectional titles are usually entered in uppercase letters and second-level titles in lowercase letters with initial capital letters; thus these headings are distinguished by the way you enter them, as well as by their section numbers. Third- through seventh-level headings can have underlined or italicized titles that are run in to the text. These five levels are distinguished by the section numbers that precede them. Here is an example of the heading command and the first three heading levels produced by **troff**:

```
.H 1 "PROJECT PROPOSAL"
The following section describes a proposal that will bring the
diverse pieces of the sales growth problem together.
.H 2 "Assessment"
The objective is to narrow the gap between retailers and the
distributors.
If we cannot bring the product to the customer, we cannot
broaden the customer base.
The problem lies with distribution, value-added benefits, and
reliability.
.H 3 "Distribution"
Part of the problem is the archaic policy of distribution.
We cannot expect retailers to bear the entire responsibility
of shipping and handling.
This is outdated and calls for restructure.
```

It produces the output

---

9. PROJECT PROPOSAL

The following section describes a proposal that will bring the diverse pieces of the sales growth problem together.

9.1 Assessment

The objective is to narrow the gap between retailers and the distributors. If we cannot bring the product to the customer, we cannot broaden the customer base. The problem lies with distribution, value-added benefits, and reliability.

9.1.1 Distribution   Part of the problem is the archaic policy of distribution. We cannot expect retailers to bear the entire responsibility of shipping and handling. This is outdated and calls for restructure.

Unnumbered Headings

An *unnumbered heading* produces an unnumbered sectional title. It is similar to a numbered heading but is not preceded by the section number. Since unnumbered headings, like numbered headings, preserve the hierarchical structure of the document by automatically incrementing the corresponding level section number (even though this number is not printed), you can mix numbered and unnumbered headings. Unnumbered headings can be especially useful for setting up appendices and other sections that may not fit well into the numbering scheme of your document.

The **mm** unnumbered heading command is **.HU**. It has the format

.HU *heading-text*

As with a numbered heading, the *heading-text* is the text of the section title, enclosed in double quotation marks if it contains spaces. Unless the formatter is told otherwise, all unnumbered headings are second-level headings. What follows is an example of an input file that creates a numbered first-level heading and an unnumbered second-level heading:

```
.H 1 "UNDER PRESSURE"
In a business that "shoots first and asks questions later,"
there seems to be little time to stop and smell the roses.
The trick, it has been said over and over again, is Time
Management.
Easily said, but how does it really work?
.HU "Making a Deadline"
When up against a deadline, if you first muddle through what
must be done, then plan to do what should be done, saving for
```

```
last what would be fun to do, you will seldom get further than
the first category.
However, do those same things in reverse order, and somehow
they will all get done, often with time to spare.
```

It produces the output

---

3. UNDER PRESSURE

In a business that "shoots first and aks questions later," there seems to be little time to stops and smell the roses. The trick, it has been said over and over again, is Time Management. Easily said, but how does it really work?

Making a Deadline

When up against a deadline, if you first muddle through what must be done, then plan to do what should be done, saving for last what would be fun to do, you will seldom get further than the first category. However, do those same things in reverse order, and somehow they will all get done, often with time to spare.

Unless you tell the formatter otherwise, unnumbered headings exist at only one level: the level specified by the **Hu** (unnumbered-heading) register. Initially, the **Hu** register has a value of 2, causing **.HU** commands to yield second-level unnumbered headings. If you want unnumbered headings at a different level, you must change the value of the **Hu** register before issuing a **.HU** command. The following input illustrates the difference between a second-level and a third-level unnumbered heading. Remember, second-level unnumbered headings are the default.

```
.HU "Security"
The recent unauthorized entry by employees with low-level
security clearance into secured areas has led to a
```

```
reorganization of the security requirements of the company.
The changes that have been made and how they affect you are
outlined below.
.nr Hu 3
.HU "Key Code Locks"
The key code locks are the principal security clearance device
within the installation.
Each employee has his or her own key code.
Each key code has an associated security clearance.
Your key code identifies you; do not give your code to anyone
else.
```

It results in the following output:

Security

    The recent unauthorized entry by employees with low-level security clearance into secured areas, has led to a reorganization of the security requirements of the company. The changes that have been made and how they affect you are outlined below.

Key Code Locks   The key code locks are the principal security clearance device within the installation. Each employee has his or her own key code. Each key code has an associated security clearance. Your key code identifies you; do not give your code to anyone else.

Subsequent **.HU** commands will also produce third-level heads until you change the value of the **Hu** register. Typically, unnumbered headings, if they exist, are given the value of the lowest-level heading in a document.

Table of Contents

The table of contents gives an overview of the structure of your document and provides the page number to each section of the document.

A table of contents can be automatically generated from your numbered and unnumbered headings.

Place the **mm** table of contents command **.TC** at the end of the input file to print the table of contents. The table of contents is produced at the end of the output because the entire document must be processed before the table of contents can be generated. When it has printed, you can move the table of contents page to the front where it belongs.

The table of contents lists headings and the associated page numbers. It includes all headings lower than and including the heading level specified by the **Cl** (contents-level) register. Initially, the **Cl** register has a value of 2, causing first- and second-level headings to appear in the table of contents. If you want to change the depth of the table of contents, you must change **Cl** at the beginning of the input file, before the first header command. The following command changes the value of the **Cl** register to 3, causing the table of contents to include first-, second-, and third-level headings:

```
.nr Cl 3
```

Lists

In **nroff**, a *list* is a set of items, such as words, lines, or paragraphs, each one of which is preceded by some sort of mark, such as a number, dash, word, or phrase. This section describes the kinds of lists that you can obtain with the **mm** macros, including automatically numbered and alphabetized lists, bulleted lists, dashed lists, lists with arbitrary marks, and lists starting with arbitrary strings (with terms or phrases to be defined, for instance).

All **nroff** lists are composed of the following parts:

■ A *list-initialization* command that controls the appearance of the list— for example, line spacing, indentation, marking with special symbols, and numbering or alphabetizing

■ One or more *list item* commands, each followed by the actual text of the list item

■ The *list end* command that terminates the list

Lists can be *nested* (placed one inside another) up to five levels deep. For example, here is an input file that creates an automatically numbered list nested within a bulleted list:

```
Making a Presentation
.BL
.LI
Your idea comes across through what you say and how you say it.
Give yourself enough time to prepare your speech.
You will find that the shortest speech must have the
greatest content.
.AL
.LI
A good five-minute speech requires one month's advance notice and
preparation.
.LI
A fifteen-minute speech requires a week's notice and preparation.
.LI
A one-hour speech requires no advance notice.
.LE
.LI
The impression you give in the first ten seconds of your
presentation will set the mood of the audience for your entire
speech.  Appropriate dress helps.  Always dress one step better
than the best-dressed person in your audience.  If he or she is
wearing jeans, for example, you should wear a suit.
.LE
```

It produces the output

Making a Presentation

- Your idea comes across through what you say and how you say it. Give yourself enough time to prepare your speech. You will find that the shortest speech must have the greatest content.

    1. A good five-minute speech requires one month's advance notice and preparation.

   2. A fifteen-minute speech requires a week's notice and
      preparation.

   3. A one-hour speech requires no advance notice.

- The impression you give in the first ten seconds of your presentation
  will set the mood of the audience for your entire speech. Appropriate
  dress helps. Always dress one step better than the best-dressed person
  in your audience. If he or she is wearing jeans, for example, you
  should wear a suit.

List Item

The **mm** list item command **.LI** must precede each item in a list. The
format of the list item command is

.LI [*mark*] [*prefix*]

where *mark* specifies the mark that precedes the item and *prefix* controls
whether *mark* is used as a prefix. In most cases, you will use **.LI** with no
arguments. If no arguments are given, **.LI** labels its item with the
current mark, which is specified by the most recent list-initialization
command (a bullet in a bulleted list, a dash in a dashed list, and so on).
The optional argument *mark* specifies the mark used in a variable-item
list (explained in detail later). If you use *mark* with another type of list,
the *mark* argument will replace the current mark for the current item
only. If you give the optional argument *prefix* a value of 1, the *mark*
argument becomes a prefix to the current mark. The list item command
normally causes the output of a single blank line before its item, although this may be suppressed. Here is an input file that produces a
bulleted list and shows how the **.LI** command works with each of its
arguments:

```
Three Laws of the Universe:
.BL
.LI
```

```
Nothing in the known universe travels faster than a bad check.
.LI *
The fact that the label on a box claims that what's inside can be
assembled without tools has no bearing on whether you'll need
them.
.LI > 1
There are two types of dirt: the dark kind, which is attracted to
light objects, and the light kind, which is attracted to dark
objects.
.LE
```

It produces the following output:

Three Laws of the Universe:

- Nothing in the known universe travels faster than a bad check.

* The fact that the label on a box claims that what's inside can be assembled without tools has no bearing on whether you'll need them.

>• There are two types of dirt: the dark kind, which is attracted to light objects, and the light kind, which is attracted to dark objects.

▶**NOTE**   If the mark contains spaces, each space must be preceded by a backslash (\).

List End Command

The list end command tells the formatter to end a list. The **mm** list end command, **.LE**, must immediately follow all lists. It has the format

.LE [*separation*]

The optional argument *separation,* when set to 1, tells the formatter to output a blank line at the end of the list. You should use this option only when the list is followed by running text.

Automatic List

An *automatic list* is a sequentially numbered or alphabetized list. The **mm** automatic list command, **.AL**, generates lists in a variety of styles. It has the format

.AL [*type*] [*indentation*] [*separation*]

where *type* specifies the style of automatic list, *indentation* controls how far the list is indented, and *separation* controls the spacing around list items. The optional argument *type* gives the type of numbering of the list. You can use one of the following values:

1	Arabic numbers
A	Uppercase letters
a	Lowercase letters
I	Uppercase Roman numbers
i	Lowercase Roman numbers

If *type* is omitted or null (discussed in the next paragraph), the formatter will use Arabic numbers to label the list. The optional argument *indentation* gives the number of spaces that the text is to be indented. If it is omitted or null, the formatter uses the value of the **Li** (list-indent) register, initially six spaces. The optional argument *separation* controls blank lines around items in the list. It works with the **Ls** (list-spacing) register, discussed in a few paragraphs. If you omit *separation* or give it a value of 0, a blank line will separate each item in the list. If you give it a value of 1, no blank lines will separate items. However, a blank line will always occur before the first item.

To set an argument to null, use a pair of double quotes. You should explicitly set an argument to null if you need a placeholder. For instance, if you want to begin a list of the default *type* with an *indentation* of 10, you can use

.AL "" 10

Here is some input that creates a simple automatic list:

```
Rules for driving in New York:
.AL 1 "" 1
.LI
Anything done while honking your horn is legal.
.LI
You may park anywhere if you turn your four-way flashers on.
.LI
A red light means the next six cars may go through the
intersection.
.LE
```

It yields the output

Rules for driving in New York:

1. Anything done while honking your horn is legal.

2. You may park anywhere if you turn your four-way flashers on.

3. A red light means the next six cars may go through the intersection.

You can control the spacing above and below list items with the **Ls** register. As lists are nested, the **Ls** register specifies the deepest level list at which spacing is done. For instance, if you set **Ls** to 1, the formatter leaves blank lines only around items in the first-level list; setting **Ls** to 2 leaves blank lines only around items in the first- and second-level lists, and so on. The following command sets the value of the **Ls** register to 4, causing blank lines to appear only around items in lists nested one to four levels deep:

```
.nr Ls 4
```

Initially, **Ls** is set to 6, which means that the formatter leaves a blank line above and below each item in the first-through sixth-level lists. Note that if the *separation* argument of the **.AL** command is set to 1, spacing of items in that list is not done (regardless of the value of the **Ls** register).

The following input creates an automatic list that is nested to two levels. It also demonstrates the use of the **Ls** register and the *separation* argument of the .LE command.

```
.nr Ls 1
Preliminary Outline
.AL 1
.LI
The proposal has been broken down into the following parts:
.AL a
.LI
Project Assessment--What is the problem?
.LI
Objective--What are we trying to accomplish?
.LI
Significance--How important is the project?
.LE 1
Each topic must be covered in full detail in order to convince
the client that the project is even worthwhile.
.LI
The preliminary work for the report may be broken down
somewhat like the following:
.AL a
.LI
Audience--Who is this written for?
.LI
Goals--What are we trying to get across?
.LI
Content--What will the actual report contain?
.LE 1
These are some of the things we must think about when we set
out to create the report.
.LE
```

It produces the output

_____

Preliminary Outline
1. The proposal has been broken down into the following parts:
    a.` Project Assessment--What is the problem?
    b. Objective--What are we trying to accomplish?
    c. Significance--How important is the project?

    Each topic must be covered in full detail in order to convince the client that the project is even worthwhile.

2. The preliminary work for the report may be broken down somewhat like the following:
    a. Audience--Who is this written for?
    b. Goals--What are we trying to get across?
    c. Content--What will the actual report contain?

    These are some of the things we must think about when we set out to create the report.

_____

Bulleted List

Each item in a bulleted list is preceded by a bullet and a single space. The **mm** list-initialization command for a bulleted list is **.BL**, and has the format,

.BL [*indentation*] [*separation*]

The optional argument *indentation* specifies the number of spaces that the text is indented. If it is omitted or null, the formatter uses the value of the **Pi** (paragraph-indent) register so that the text lines up with the first line of an indented paragraph. The optional argument *separation* controls blank lines around items in the list. If you omit it or give it a value of 0, a blank line will separate each item in the list. If you give it a value of 1, no blank lines will separate items. However, there is always a blank line before the first item in a list. Here is an example of a bulleted list. The input

```
Business Communication
.BL "" 1
.LI
If you call in the morning rather than the afternoon, you are far
more likely to get what you called for.
.LI
Usually a telephone caller makes three points.  The third one is
the real reason for the call.
.LI
If you think that something goes without saying, it is probably
in the best interest of everyone involved to say it.
.LE
```

produces the list

Business Communication

- If you call in the morning rather than the afternoon, you are far more likely to get what you called for.

- Usually a telephone caller makes three points. The third one is the real reason for the call.

- If you think that something goes without saying, it is probably in the best interest of everyone involved to say it.

▶**TIP**   You can only produce the bullet character using **troff** and a typesetter or laser printer. The **nroff** bullet looks more like crosshairs (⊕). When using **nroff**, you may want to use a marked list and a well chosen mark, such as the asterisk or a lowercase "o".

Dashed List

Each item in a *dashed list* is preceded by a dash and a single space. The dashed list command is identical to the bulleted list command, except that you use a dash instead of a bullet. The **mm** list-initialization command for a dashed list is **.DL**. Like the bulleted list command, it has the format

.DL [*indentation*] [*separation*]

Here is an example of a dashed list:

_____

Famous last words:

—We won't need reservations.
—What happens if you touch these two wires tog--
—It's always sunny there this time of year.
—Don't worry, it's not loaded.

_____

Marked List

Each item in a marked list is preceded by an arbitrary mark, which may consist of one or more characters. The **mm** list-initialization command for a marked list is **.ML**, which has the format

.ML *mark* [*indentation*] [*separation*]

The *mark* argument specifies the element that is to appear before each item in the list. The *mark* may not contain ordinary spaces; each space in the mark (if any) must be preceded by a backslash (\ ). The optional argument *indentation* gives the number of spaces that the text is to be indented. If it is omitted or null, the formatter indents the text one space more than the number of characters in the mark. The optional argument *separation* controls blank lines around items in the list. If you omit it or give it a value of 0, a blank line will separate each item in the list. If you give it a value of 1, no blank lines will separate items. However, there is always a blank line before the first item in a list. For example, here is an input file that creates a marked list:

```
A Few Tips for Business Writers
.ML Important\ note: 16
.LI
Use the active voice.
.LI
Put statements in positive form.
.LI
Use definite, specific, concrete language.
.LI
Omit needless words.
.LE
```

It results in the output

A Few Tips for Business Writers

    Important note: Use the active voice.

    Important note: Put statements in positive form.

    Important note: Use definite, specific, concrete language.

    Important note: Omit needless words.

▶**NOTE**   Notice the position of the backslash within the mark. Marks that contain spaces must be enclosed in double quotes or each space within the mark must be preceded by a backslash.

Variable-Item List

A *variable-item list* allows you to put a different mark before each item in
the list. You specify the text that serves as the mark for a particular item
in each list item command. A variable-item list is typically used to display
definitions of terms or phrases.

The **mm** list-initialization command for a variable-item list is **.VL**. Its
format is

.**VL** *indentation* [*mark-indentation*] [*separation*]

The *indentation* argument gives the number of spaces that the text is
indented. The optional argument *mark-indentation* gives the number of
spaces that each mark is indented. If it is omitted or null, it defaults to
0 (the mark is left justified). The optional argument *separation* controls
blank lines around items in the list. If you omit it or give it a value of 0,
a blank line will separate each item in the list. If you give it a value of 1,
no blank lines will separate items. As with other lists, there is always a
blank line before the first item in a list. For example, here is an input file
that creates a variable-item list:

```
Day Two
.VL 20 2
.LI "12:30 pm"
Lunch in the Pheasant Room
.LI "1:30 pm"
Seminar: "Sales Management," R. R. Hopkins.
A sales management perspective from the executive offices.
.LI "3:00 pm"
Break
.LI "4:00 pm"
Lecture: "In Search of Mediocrity," J. Stanton.
A search for honest, non-excellence-oriented business.
A fair product at a good price.
America's lost commodity.
.LI "5:30 pm"
Dinner at the Flying Eel Banquet Room
.LE
```

It results in the following output:

Day Two

    12:30 pm   Lunch in the Pheasant Room

    1:30 pm   Seminar: "Sales Management," R. R. Hopkins. A sales
               management perspective from the executive offices.

    3:00 pm   Break

    4:00 pm   Lecture: "In Search of Mediocrity," J. Stanton. A search
               for honest, non-excellence-oriented business. A fair
               product at a good price. America's lost commodity.

    5:30 pm   Dinner at the Flying Eel Banquet Room

▶**NOTE**   Look at the quotes around the mark value. If there are spaces within a mark, the mark must be enclosed in quotes or each space must be preceded by a backslash. The mark is the argument of the **.LI** command—in this case, time.

Displays

A *display* is a block of text that the formatter treats as an integral unit, keeping it together rather than splitting it across a page. A display can be a chart, table, or paragraph that must appear intact. You can define a display by producing the appropriate commands before and after the block of text in the input file.

Unless you instruct the formatter otherwise, displays are not filled or indented in the output text; the formatter preserves the spacing and formatting of the text from the input file.

The **mm** macros provide two styles of displays: a static style and a floating style.

Static Displays

A *static display* stays exactly where you put it; it doesn't move. It appears in the same relative position in the output text as it does in the input file. When the formatter finds in the input file a block of text that you have specified as a static display, it places the display on the current page only if there is room for the entire block. If the display will not fit in the space remaining on the page, it will be shifted to the top of the next page. Of course, this may result in blank space at the bottom of some pages. Figure 7-1 illustrates a static display.

The text of a static display is preceded by the **mm** display-static command **.DS** and followed by the display-end command **.DE.** The format for the static display command is

.DS [*position*] [*fill*] [*right-indent*]
text
.DE

where *position* specifies how the static display is positioned, *fill* controls whether the display is filled, and *right-indent* specifies how much the right margin is to be indented. The optional argument *position* determines how the formatter positions the display. You can use one of the following values:

L	Left	Positions the display flush against the left margin
I	Indent	Indents the display by the value of the **Si** (static-indent) register, initially set to 5
C	Center	Centers each line between the left and right margins
CB	Center block	Centers the entire display as a block of text (a single unit), using the longest line for positioning

If you do not specify a *position* or if you use null, the formatter positions the display flush with the left margin. The optional argument *fill* controls whether the text in the display is filled. If you omit this argument, specify it as **N** (no fill), or use null, the formatter does not fill the text.

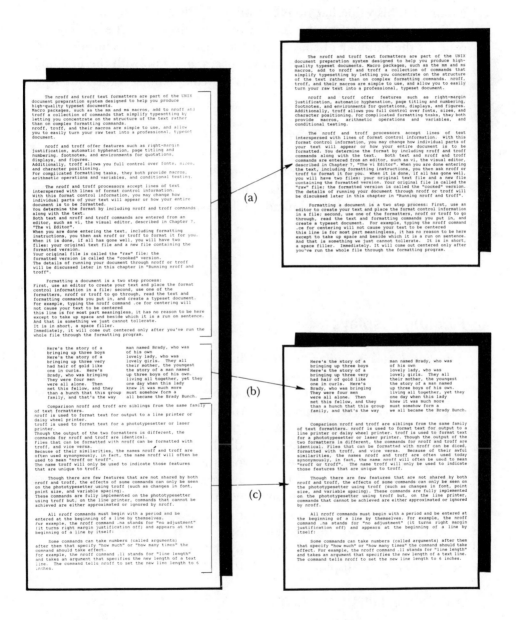

Figure 7-1. *Static display.(a) before display, text is placed as usual; (b) if display does not fit on page, it is moved to top of next page; (c) after display, text is placed as usual*

If you specify **F** (fill), the formatter fills the text. The optional argument *right-indent* specifies the number of spaces the right margin is to be indented. This value has no effect when the display is not being filled.

Two registers affect the format of static displays. The **Si** register controls the number of spaces that the formatter indents an indented static display. It is initially set to five spaces, lined up with the first line of an indented paragraph. The following command sets the indent to eight spaces:

```
.nr Si 8
```

The **Ds** (display-spacing) register controls spacing before and after the display; if you set it to 0, no blank line will appear before or after the display. The following command inhibits blank lines around displays:

```
.nr Ds 0
```

Floating Displays

A *floating display* is similar to a static display: It is a block of text that the formatter keeps on one page. However, floating displays will not leave blank space at the bottom of pages; if there is no room for a floating display on the current page, the formatter sets aside the display and finishes filling the page with the text that follows the display. When the page is full, the formatter places the display at the top of the next page and then continues with the text from the previous page. A floating display is useful when you are displaying a table or chart whose exact placement is flexible and you do not want blank space at the bottom of a page. Figure 7-2 illustrates a floating display.

The text of a floating display is preceded by the **mm** display-float command **.DF**. The text is followed by the display-end command **.DE**. Similar to a static display, the format of a floating display is

.DF [*position*] [*fill*] [*right-indent*]
text
.DE

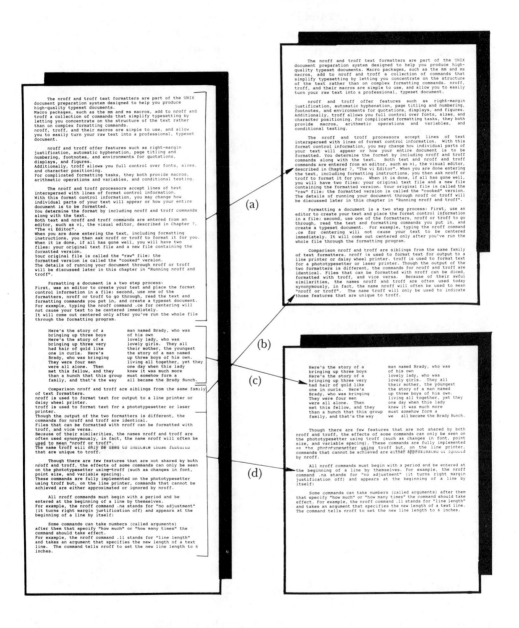

Figure 7-2. *Floating display. (a) before floating display, text is placed as usual; (b) if display does not fit on page, text following display in the input file is used to fill page; (c) display is placed at top of next page; (d) after display, text is continued from previous page*

where *position, fill,* and *right-indent* are all optional arguments identical to the arguments for static display.

Two registers affect the format of floating displays. The **De** (display-eject) register controls whether or not text will appear on the current page after a floating display has been produced. When you set **De** to 1, with

```
.nr De 1
```

a page eject will always follow the output of each floating display, so only one floating display will appear per page and no text will follow it. Initially, **De** is set to 0 and causes the formatter to continue printing text after a floating display.

The **Df** (display-float) register allows you to change the way the floating display is positioned in the document. You can use one of the following values:

0   Place all floating displays at the end of the document.
1   Place each floating display on the current page if there is room; otherwise, hold it until the end of the document.
2   Place only one floating display at the top of a new page.
3   Place only one floating display on the current page if there is room; otherwise, place it on the next page.
4   Place as many floating displays as will fit, starting at the top of a new page.
5   Place each new floating display on the current page if there is room; otherwise, place it at the top of the next page.

Initially, **Df** is set to 5, causing floating displays to float to the top of the next page only if there is no room on the current page.

Table Displays

You use the **mm** table start command **.TS** and table end command **.TE** to delimit text to be examined by the **tbl** processor (explained later in this chapter) as well as to set proper spacing around a table. The display function and the **tbl** delimiting function are independent of one another, however. In order to keep together blocks that contain a mixture of tables, equations, text, or caption lines, you should enclose these blocks within a display, as each display is treated as a single unit. Floating tables may be enclosed inside floating displays (**.DF**, **.DE**).

▶**NOTE** For more information on **tbl**, see the section "Tables with tbl," in this chapter.

Equation Displays

The equation formatters **eqn** and **neqn** use the **mm** equation start command **.EQ** and equation end command **.EN** as delimiters in the same way that **tbl** uses **.TS** and **.TE**. However, **.EQ** and **.EN** must occur within a display unless you use **.EQ** and **.EN** to delimit equations in the body of the text.

▶**NOTE** For more information on **eqn**, see the section "Equations with eqn," in this chapter.

Captions

You normally use the **mm** figure caption command **.FG**, table title command **.TB**, equation caption command **.EC**, and exhibit caption command **.EX** within a display to automatically number and title figures, tables, and equations. They have the formats

.FG [*title*]
.TB [*title*]
.EC [*title*]
.EX [*title*]

The output of a caption command consists of three parts: a single descriptive word, the caption number, and the caption title. Each command prints a single descriptive word: **.FG** prints "Figure," **.TB** prints

"TABLE" in all capitals, **.EC** prints "Equation," and **.EX** prints "Exhibit." A caption number follows the word and indicates which figure, table, equation, or exhibit is currently appearing. The formatter automatically assigns sequential numbers to captions. The optional argument *title* in the caption commands specifies the caption title that will follow the number.

▶**TIP**   As a matter of style, table titles are usually placed ahead of the corresponding tables, while figure, equation, and exhibit captions usually occur after the corresponding figures or equations.

Footnotes

In **nroff**, footnotes are embedded in the text immediately following their reference. That is, the footnote command comes immediately after the word or phrase the footnote is referencing. The formatter places a footnote at the bottom of the current page if there is room; otherwise, it moves the footnote (or part of it) to the next page. The formatter can automatically number footnotes, or you can label them yourself.

Footnotes are usually filled. As you might expect, other footnotes, headings, and displays are not allowed within footnotes.

There are two kinds of footnotes available with the **mm** macros: *automatically-numbered footnotes* and *labeled footnotes*. For both, the text of the footnote is preceded by the **mm** footnote-start command **.FS** and followed by the footnote-end command **.FE**. The difference is in the way you specify the footnote number or label.

The formatter sequentially numbers automatically numbered footnotes throughout the document. This is useful if you add and delete footnotes frequently because the formatter automatically renumbers the remaining footnotes. An automatically numbered footnote has the format

text**F
.FS
footnote
.FE
text

The formatter replaces the*F with the proper footnote number. You must place *F at the end of the text to be footnoted, just before the text of the footnote. Footnote numbers are usually displayed as *superscript,* a smaller type size located a half line above the text to be footnoted. If footnote numbers do not appear as superscript on your printer, you may want to use square brackets around footnote numbers; that is, use [*F] instead of *F. In this way, the footnote number will print in standard type, surrounded by brackets.

Labeled footnotes require you to specify your own label for each footnote, using an asterisk, a word, or whatever you like. A labeled footnote has the format

*text***
**.FS **
footnote
.FE
text

The ** is a label that you may replace with any label you like. You must put the label at the end of the text to be formatted, just before the text of the footnote, and also immediately following the **.FS** command.

Headers and Footers

Headers and footers are running titles that appear at the top and bottom of the page. Text that occurs at the top of the page is known as a *header.* Text printed at the bottom of the page is called a *footer.*

You can print headers on all pages, all odd-numbered pages, or all even-numbered pages. Headers that print on odd-numbered pages are often called *odd headers,* and headers that print on even-numbered pages are called *even headers.* There are also headers that print on *every* page; these are called *page headers.*

▶**TIP**   Since they are separate, you could potentially have page headers, even headers, and odd headers all at once. This would result in two lines at the top of each page: the page-header line that appears on every page and the header line for the even- or odd-numbered page.

All of the same choices are available for footers: odd footers, even footers, and page footers.

All running titles work the same way and have the same format. The **mm** macros provide three-part titles for headers and footers. For example, the **mm** *page header* command **.PH** has the format

.PH " '*left*'*center*'*right*' "

Left is text that the formatter places against the left margin at the top of each page. Similarly, *center* represents text that is centered at the top of each page and *right* represents text placed against the right margin.

The header and footer commands and their meanings are listed here:

.PH	Page header
.EH	Even header
.OH	Odd header
.PF	Page footer
.EF	Even footer
.OF	Odd footer

Page headers and page footers print on every page. Even and odd running titles print on even- and odd-numbered pages, respectively.

With the **mm** macros, the formatter initially prints the page number at the top of each page. To remove the page number, you can change the value of the center portion of the page header by setting the page header to null, with

```
.PH ""
```

You can put the page number somewhere else on the page by including the **P** (page-number) register in a title. For example, to place the page number against the right margin at the top of every page, use

```
.PH "´´´\\\nP´"
```

The sequence **\\\\nP** tells the formatter to include the page number in the header.

You can also place the date in a header or footer. The date is stored in the **DT** (date) register. For example, to center the date at the bottom of every page, use

```
.PF "´´\\\\*(DT´´"
```

The sequence ***(DT** instructs the formatter to put the date in the footer.

Page Formatting

For the most part, the **mm** macros take care of page formatting for you. They automatically set top, bottom, left, and right margins, spacing, and tab settings. You can change these from their initial values with direct **nroff** commands. As mentioned, it is generally a good idea to avoid mixing direct **nroff** commands with **mm** macros in your document, as some direct **nroff** commands interfere with **mm** macros. However, what follow are a few useful **nroff** commands that are safe to use with the **mm** macros.

Page Length

Page length is initially set to 11 inches (66 lines). Occasionally, you may want to change the page length if you use other than standard letter-size paper or if the initial length does not fit on one of your printer's pages. You can change the length of the page with the **nroff** page length command **.pl**. For example, to change the page length to 60 lines per page, place

```
.pl 60
```

near the top of your input file. To change the page length to 14 inches per page (legal size), insert

.pl 14i

at the top of your file.

When using **troff**, the maximum page length is about 75 inches. With **nroff**, the maximum page length is about 136 inches.

Line Length and the Left Margin

With the **mm** macros, the initial length of a text line is 6 inches (72 characters). If you prefer wider margins, you may want to shorten the line length. If you prefer more text on a page, you may want to lengthen it. You can change the length of the text line with the **nroff** line length command **.ll**. For example,

.ll 6.5i

sets the line length to 6.5 inches, and

.ll 60

sets the line length to 60 characters.

The maximum line length is about 7.5 inches, or 90 characters. To use the full length, however, you will have to reset the left margin as far left as it will go, that is, set the page offset to 0.

▶ **TIP** If you change the line length, you will need to adjust the left margin as well to keep the margins even. Here's a good way to make sure your right and left margins are even: Subtract the line length in inches from the page width in inches. Divide by 2 and use this result for your left margin.

With the **mm** macros, the left margin, or *page offset,* is initially set to 3/4 of an inch (nine characters) from the left edge of the page. You can change this with the **nroff** page offset command **.po**. To change the left margin to 1/2 inch, use

```
.po  .5i
```

To set it to 12 characters, use

```
.po 12
```

▶**NOTE**   When setting the line length, the left margin, or the page length in inches, you must put a letter "i" after the number. This tells the formatter that you mean inches rather than characters or lines.

Line Break

When in fill mode, unless told otherwise, the formatter joins one input line after another until it comes to a blank line that signals the end of a paragraph. Remember, the last line of the paragraph is ended (or *broken*) and is never filled or justified. You can also break a line that is not to be filled with the **nroff** break command or by putting spaces at the beginning of a line.

When you use the **nroff** break command, **.br**, the line currently being filled is ended. If justification is on, the line is unjustified. After the break, the text continues on a new line against the left margin.

If a line in the input file begins with *whitespace* characters (a space or a tab), the line currently being filled is ended. The new line begins with the whitespace characters against the left margin.

Double-Spacing

You can double- or triple-space your document by changing the line spacing in the output with the **nroff** line spacing command **.ls**. The following command creates double-spaced output:

```
.ls 2
```

The command

```
.ls 1
```

restores single-spacing. And, as you can guess,

```
.ls 3
```

sets triple-spacing.

Tab Settings

Tabs in **nroff** are similar to typewriter tabs. They define the horizontal positions for columns of information. Initially, the tab positions are set about every 1/2 inch (eight characters) from the current indent or left margin. Tabs are usually used only in unfilled text.

The **nroff** tab-adjust command **.ta** clears all previous tab positions and sets the new tabs. For example, to set tab stops every inch, use

```
.ta 1i 2i 3i 4i 5i 6i
```

Without any arguments, **.ta** clears all tab positions.

After you set your tabs, use the tab character (by pressing the TAB key) between columns to make each column appear at the next tab position to the right. The results will not appear right away when you are editing the file, but only in the output. The following input sets the tab positions and creates a small table inside an unfilled display:

```
.ta 1i 2i 3i
.DS
name TAB score TAB percent
Zoey TAB 35 TAB 98%
Drexal TAB 25 TAB 81%
Elyssia TAB 40 TAB 118%
.DE
```

It produces the output

---

name	score	percent
Zoey	35	98%
Drexal	25	81%
Elyssia	40	118%

▶**NOTE**   For complex tables, use the **tbl** program, which is described in "The tbl and eqn Preprocessors" in this chapter.

Centering

You can center one or more lines with the **nroff** center command **.ce.** To center one line, precede it with

```
.ce
```

To center the following five lines, use

```
.ce 5
```

▶**NOTE**   For centered displays use the **mm** display command **.DS C**.

Temporary Indent

If you want to indent a single line, use the **nroff** temporary indent command **.ti**. For example, to indent a single line 1 inch, use

```
.ti 1i
```

To indent one line by eight characters, use

```
.ti 8
```

▶**NOTE**   For indented displays use the **mm** display command **.DS I**.

It is useful to use the temporary indent with a negative argument to produce a one-line "reverse indent," as in bibliographies.

Here is an example of a one-line reverse indent in an indented display:

```
.DS I
.ti -5
Consideration:
Last, I must ask the board to consider the cost of this
project.
Looking at the project proposal and the project forecast, don't
the estimates seem blindly optimistic?
Unfortunately, we are presented with no worst-case analysis.
.DE
```

It produces the output

Consideration: Last, I must ask the board to consider the cost of this project. Looking at the project proposal and the project forecast, don't the estimates seem blindly optimistic? Unfortunately, we are presented with no worst-case analysis.

▶**NOTE**   Use the paragraph command, not the temporary indent, to indent the first line of a paragraph.

Fonts

This section discusses a number of **mm** and **nroff** features for controlling style, size, and the spacing of type fonts. As mentioned, you can only see the effects of some commands on a typesetter using **troff**. Features such as bold, point size changes, and changes in vertical spacing are either approximated or ignored by **nroff**. Fortunately, **nroff** output is usually fine for draft copies.

Underlining, Italic, and Bold

You can change the standard Roman font to italic, bold, or underline for emphasis in your document. Line printers and letter-quality printers, because they can't change fonts, represent italic as underlined text. The typesetter, however, with its superior quality, emphasizes text in italic.

There are at least two ways to produce italic, bold, and underline when using the **mm** macros. The first method is with the **mm** bold and italic commands, **.B** and **.I**. These, like other **mm** commands, are placed at the beginning of a line by themselves. The text on the lines that follow is either bold or italic until an **mm** Roman command **.R** is encountered. The second method is with the **nroff** in-line escape commands, \ **fB** and \ **fI**. You place these in the text within a line or word. The text that follows is bold or italic until another in-line command, such as \ **fR**, is found.

The **.B** command changes the font to bold and the **.I** command changes it to italic. The bold or italic text continues until it is restored to Roman font with the **.R** command. For example,

```
.I
You'll spend less time getting answers from people if you go
to their offices to ask them questions.
That way, you control when the conversation ends.
.R
```

yields emphasized text. If only one word is to be italicized, you can enter it alone on a line after a **.I** command, as in

```
.I word
```

In this case, no **.R** command is needed to restore the previous font. The previous font is automatically restored on the next line, as in this example:

```
Here, finally, is a solution that we can
.I work
with.
```

This produces the following output:

Here, finally, is a solution that we can *work* with.

Similarly, you can produce bold with

```
.B
If you want something done, give it to a busy person.
.R
```

As with the **.I** command, you can print a single word in bold by placing it alone on a line after a **.B** command.

You can also change fonts within a line or word with the in-line **nroff** command \ f. To produce italics, precede the text to be italicized with **\fI** and follow it with **\fR**. For example,

```
It is not the contract I want you to look at, it is \fIthe
authorization on the purchase order\fR and the open-ended way
the order was received.
```

produces

It is not the contract I want you to look at, it is *the authorization on the purchase order* and the open-ended way the order was received.

To produce bold, use the sequence **\fB** instead of **\fI**.

Point Size and Vertical Spacing

Point size is a measurement used by typesetters that describes the height of printed characters. One point is equal to 1/72 of an inch. Thus, 6-point characters are 1/12-inch high, and 36-point characters are 1/2-inch high. Legal point sizes range from 6-point to 36-point. The **troff** typesetter supports at least the following point sizes:

This is 6-point Roman type.
This is 7-point Roman type.
This is 8-point Roman type.
This is 9-point Roman type.
This is 10-point Roman type.
This is 11-point Roman type.
This is 12-point Roman type.
This is 14-point Roman type.
This is 16-point Roman type.
This is 20-point Roman type.
This is 24-point Roman type.
This is 28-point Roman.
This is 36-point.

If you use a value that does not correspond to a legal point size, your value is rounded up to the next valid size. The **troff** typesetter begins with 10-point characters and 12-point vertical spacing.

Vertical spacing is the spacing between lines. It is measured in points from the bottom of one line to the bottom of the next. You can set vertical spacing independently of the point size.

Point size and vertical spacing commands have no effect on **nroff** line printer output. They only take effect on **troff** output sent to the type-setter or laser printer.

As with type style, there are two ways to change the point size: with the **mm** size command **.S** and with the **nroff \s** in-line command. Since it does not automatically change vertical spacing, the **\s** command is best suited for temporary point size changes within the text. You should use the **.S** command for point size changes in longer blocks of text.

The **mm** size command **.S** changes both point size and vertical spacing. It has the format

.S [*point-size*] [*vertical-spacing*]

The optional *point-size* argument specifies the new point size of the text to follow. The optional *vertical-spacing* argument specifies the new vertical spacing. You can specify both *point size* and *vertical spacing* as either a legal point size or as one of the following special codes: **D** for default value, **C** for current value, or **P** for previous value. If you specify a point size, arguments may be signed or unsigned. Use an unsigned argument as the new value for either argument. A signed argument creates a *relative change* in point size or vertical spacing. If an argument is negative, the formatter subtracts the specified amount from the current value; if the argument is positive, the formatter adds the specified amount to the current value. If you omit both arguments, the previous (**P**) values are used. If you specify *point size* and omit *vertical spacing,* the default value (**D**) is used for the vertical spacing. The default vertical spacing is always 2 points greater than the current point size. The following example illustrates a few of your options:

```
.S +4
THE SLINKY RULE:
.br
.S
Never buy more than one Slinky
.br
.S 8
because they eventually will become intertwined.
.S P
```

It produces the following output:

THE SLINKY RULE:
Never buy more than one Slinky
because they eventually will become intertwined.

▶**NOTE**   Experimenting with the line spacing may produce strange results—overwritten letters or unwanted space, for example. If you omit
the second *line-spacing* argument, the formatter will take care of the
default spacing.

You can also change the point size in the middle of a line or even a
word with the **nroff** in-line size command **\s**. The **\s** should be followed
by a legal point size. A **\s**0 returns the size to its previous value. For
example,

```
The men of the farm would sit around at night.
Sometimes, they talked about \s16big things\s0;
sometimes, they talked about \s8little things\s0.
```

produces

The men of the farm would sit around at night. Sometimes, they talked
about big things; sometimes, they talked about little things.

As with the **.S** command, signed arguments for **\s** are treated as relative
size changes. For example, **\s+2** increases the current point size by two
points.

Running nroff and troff

After you have created your input file, you are ready to format it with **nroff** or **troff**. You use the **nroff** formatter to print on a line printer or letter-quality printer, and you use **troff** to print on a typesetter or laser printer.

You will run the formatter from the UNIX shell prompt (usually %
for the C shell and $ for the Bourne shell). To run **nroff** with the **mm** macros, use

% **nroff -mm** *filename* > *filename.n*

where *filename* is your input file. This creates a new file, *filename.n*, which you will send to the printer. For instance, to format a file named **report** by using **nroff** and the **mm** macros, and then have the formatted version placed in a file named **report.n**, type

```
nroff -mm report > report.n
```

at the UNIX shell prompt.

Similarly, to print a file with **troff** and the **mm** macros, use

troff -mm *filename*

at the UNIX shell prompt. The file will automatically be formatted and sent to the typesetter.

▶**NOTE**   Some systems use a formatter named **ditroff** instead of **troff**. The **ditroff** stands for "device independent troff." Often **ditroff** is set up to print files with a single command, as with **troff**. Sometimes, however, **ditroff** will involve a few more steps. The output of **ditroff** is different than the output of **troff**. A program called a *printer driver* is used to translate **ditroff** output to a language your printer understands. You may have to take care of this translation step or it may happen behind the scenes. If your system uses **ditroff**, ask your system administrator how to print **ditroff** output.

▶**TIP**   When you format your file with **nroff**, give the formatted version a **.n** extension; with **troff** give it a **.t** extension. This way, you know what kind of file it is when you see it in your directory.

You can preview an **nroff**-formatted file by typing the following command at the UNIX shell prompt:

more *filename.n*

where *filename.n* is the formatted file that you created with **nroff**.

Printing Your Formatted File

Now that you have created a formatted file, you need to print it. The steps involved in printing will vary depending on your system. Usually, you can send an **nroff**-formatted file directly to the printer with the following command:

lpr *filename.n*

The **troff** formatter, however, automatically formats your file and sends it to the typesetter, so there are no special printing considerations.

If you have any questions about printing, ask your system administrator.

The tbl and eqn Preprocessors

The **tbl** and **eqn** programs are parts of the UNIX document preparation system, distinct from, but closely tied to, the **nroff** and **troff** programs. They are specialized tools for meeting special formatting needs. The **tbl** program formats tables and other complicated multiple-column material. The **eqn** program sets mathematical equations. Although **tbl** and **eqn** use commands that are easy to learn and use, they can be quite complicated. Consequently, only the rudiments are covered in this section. If you need to create tables or equations in your documents, the effort of learning **tbl** and **eqn** will be well rewarded. You will be able to produce high-quality output with relatively little work.

Both **tbl** and **eqn** are *preprocessors* — that is, **tbl** and **eqn** commands are translated before they are fed to **nroff** and **troff**. As with **mm** and **nroff** commands, you insert **tbl** and **eqn** commands into your text as you are preparing it. These commands are translated by the **tbl** and **eqn** programs into sequences of direct **nroff** and **troff** commands, without altering your text or other formatting commands. The result is then processed by **nroff** or **troff**.

This section explains how to prepare your input file for **tbl** and **eqn** and how to run **tbl** and **eqn** with **nroff** and **troff**.

Tables with tbl

The **tbl** program is especially useful for preparing charts, multiple-column lists, and other tabular material. It allows you to control column alignment and will automatically calculate column widths when the elements are of varying lengths. It enables you to draw horizontal and vertical lines to emphasize your material. With a line printer, the effect may be somewhat limited, but with a typesetter, you will get high-quality tables.

As described under the section "Displays," tables in your document should be preceded by the **mm** table-start command **.TS** and followed by the **mm** table-end command **.TE**. To prevent tables from being broken across pages, you should enclose each table in a display by using the **mm** display-start command **.DS** and the **mm** display-end command **.DE**.

Each table is independent and must contain its own formatting information followed by the data to be entered in the table. The formatting information describes the individual columns and rows of the table, and may be preceded by options that affect the entire table.

Options   Immediately after the **.TS** command, you may place a single line of options that affect the whole table. It must contain a list of options separated by spaces and terminated by a single semicolon. Options you will find useful are

center	Centers the table
expand	Makes the table as wide as the current line length
box	Encloses the table in a box
allbox	Encloses each item in a box
doublebox	Encloses the table in a box with double lines
tab(*x*)	Uses the character *x* instead of tab to separate data items

Format   The format section of the table specifies the layout of the columns. Each line in this section corresponds to a line of the table. The last formatting line applies to all of the remaining lines in the table. Each formatting line contains a number of *keyletters;* each keyletter represents a column in the table. The keyletters describe how each entry in the column is to be formatted. Some useful choices are

L	Left justifies column entries
R	Right justifies column entries
C	Centers column entries
N	Lines up numerical data at the decimal
S	Entries from previous column continue across this column
|	(Vertical bar) A vertical bar between column keyletters creates a vertical line between the corresponding columns of the table. Two vertical bars between column keyletters produce a double vertical line. A vertical bar left of the first keyletter or right of the last keyletter produces a vertical line at the edge of the table.

▶**NOTE**   The default formatting for columns is left justified. Therefore, any columns that are not described by a column keyletter are automatically left justified.

To make your table formatting information more readable, you should separate with spaces the keyletters describing each column. The end of the format section is indicated with a period. For example, the format section of a simple table might look like

```
c c c
l n n.
```

and could determine the format of the following table:

Item	Qty	Price
snuff remover	6	29.95
smoke shifter	1	343.00

Data   You enter the text for the table after the format specification. Normally, each line of data represents a row in the table.You may break very long input lines by using a backslash (\) as the last character of the broken line; the formatter will combine the broken line with the line following it and the backslash will not appear. Table entries are separated by tabs.

An input line in the data section containing only an underscore (_) or an equal sign (=) creates a horizontal line that runs the entire width of the table. The underscore creates a single line across the table, while the equal sign makes a double line. If a single table entry contains an underscore or equal sign, it creates a single or double line extending the width of the column. These lines are extended to meet horizontal or vertical lines adjoining the column.

A table entry containing only the characters \^ indicates that the table entry immediately above spans downward over this row. It is similar to the keyletter **S**; but while **S** creates an entry that spans a column to the right, \^ creates an entry that spans a row downward.

The following table demonstrates typical table entries and single and double horizontal lines. The word "**TAB**" represents the tab character.

```
.TS
l|c s|
l|c|c|.
=
Word TAB Pronunciation
_
wind TAB wInd TAB waInd
tear TAB tir TAB ter
invalid TAB 'Inv@lId TAB In'vAlId
=
.TE
```

The resulting table looks like this:

Phonetic Spelling of Homographs		
Word	Pronunciations	
wind	wInd	waInd
tear	tir	ter
invalid	'Inv@lId	In'vAlId

Here is a more complicated table demonstrating table-width and column-width lines:

```
.TS
box tab(@);
c s s s
c|c|c|c
l|c|c|l.
Best Roads of Northern California
=
Road @Traffic @Patrol @Notes
_
Highway 1 @Moderate @Light @from SLO to SF: rugged coastal
 @ @ @_
 @ @ @from SF north: scenic coastal
_
Highway 35 @Light @Light @Skyline Blvd: Redwood forest
_
Highway 49 @Moderate @Light @Gold ctry: small towns, historic
.TE
```

produces the table

Best Roads of Northern California			
Road	Traffic	Patrol	Notes
Highway 1	Moderate	Light	from SLO to SF: rugged coastal
			from SF north: scenic coastal
Highway 35	Light	Light	Skyline Blvd: Redwood forest
Highway 49	Moderate	Light	Gold ctry: small towns, historic

Invoking tbl If you are using **tbl** or **eqn** to produce tables or mathe-matical equations, you must *pipe* the output of these specialized format-ters to **nroff** or **troff**. Chapter 5, "UNIX Command-Line Fun-damentals," explains how pipes work. Note that both **tbl** and **eqn** are designed to produce typeset output with **troff** on a typesetter or laser printer. You can use **tbl** and **eqn** with **nroff**, but the results are limited. Furthermore, to format equations for **nroff**, you need to use the **neqn** program instead of **eqn**.

If your file contains tables, use one of the following commands at the UNIX shell prompt to create a formatted file:

tbl | troff -mm *filename*
tbl | nroff -mm *filename* **>** *filename.n*

If your line printer or terminal acts strange when printing tables, your printer or terminal may not be able to produce the vertical line motions that **tbl** asks for. In this case, use the **eqn -TX** option, as in

tbl -TX | troff -mm *filename*

Equations with eqn

The **eqn** program simplifies the task of formatting complex mathemat-ical equations and printing special symbols. It is suited for formulas and subscripting and can produce special characters such as mathematical symbols and the Greek alphabet. The **eqn** program is relatively easy to learn. Wherever possible, formatting commands resemble ordinary En-glish words and the format is specified much as you might try to describe an equation in conversation.

As with **tbl**, **eqn** is designed to work with **troff** on a typesetter. You may achieve approximate, but somewhat limited, effects with **nroff** on a line printer by using the **neqn** program. Fortunately, **neqn** output is usually fine for drafts.

To tell **eqn** where a mathematical expression begins and ends, sur-round it with the **mm** begin-equation command **.EQ** and the **mm** end-equation command **.EN**, as mentioned in the "Displays" section of this chapter. If an equation will appear as a display, you must enclose it within the **.DS** and **.DE** commands. If the equation is to be centered or indented, you must also select the appropriate arguments for the display (C for center, I for indent, and so on).

You can give the **.EQ** command an argument that is treated as an arbitrary equation number and placed in the right margin. For example, the input

```
.EQ 4
A(1/2)=1/24 + C = 0
.EN
```

produces the output

$$A(1/2) = 1/24 + C = 0 \qquad\qquad\qquad\qquad 4$$

Subscripts and Superscripts   You can use subscript and superscript to create exponents and indices for variables. To produce subscripts and superscripts in your mathematical text, use the **sub** and **sup** commands. For example, the following

```
.EQ
F sub 1 = x sup 2 + y sup 2
.EN
```

produces

$$F_1 = x^2 + y^2$$

The commands **sub** and **sup** must be surrounded by spaces. The end of the text to be subscripted or superscripted must also be followed by a space. Otherwise, if you are not careful about spaces, the following expression

```
.EQ
(x sup 2 + y sup 2)
.EN
```

may turn out like this:

$$(x^2 + y^{2)}$$

It is a good idea to surround everything in your **eqn** equation by spaces.

Grouping You will often want to use more complicated expressions with commands such as subscript and superscript and the other commands that follow. You may group expressions together to be treated as a single unit with braces ({ }). Anywhere you can use a single item such as the variable x, you can also use any complicated expression, if you enclose it in braces.

For instance, you usually mark the end of a subscript or superscript by a blank. If you need to produce subscript or superscript with blanks in it, you can use braces to mark the beginning and end of the subscript or superscript. For example,

```
.EQ
n sup {x + y}
.EN
```

results in

$$n^{x+y}$$

If the braces were omitted from the previous example, the formatter would not know to superscript "x + y" but would only superscript "x."

You can use braces in the same way with other commands such as fractions and square roots, which are described next.

Fractions   Fractions are easy with **eqn**. To create a fraction, use the **over** command. The formatter makes the fraction line the proper length and positions it automatically. For example,

```
.EQ
x over r + y over r
.EN
```

produces

$$\frac{x}{r} + \frac{y}{r}$$

Use braces to clarify what goes over what. For example,

```
.EQ
{e sup x} over {sinh x}
.EN
```

creates the equation

$$\frac{e^x}{\sinh x}$$

Square Roots   You can easily create a square root with **eqn**. Simply precede the number or symbol with the **sqrt** command. For example,

```
.EQ
sqrt {1 + x sup 2}
.EN
```

results in

$$\sqrt{1+x^2}$$

Symbols and the Greek Alphabet   The **eqn** processor knows quite a few mathematical symbols, mathematical names, and the Greek alphabet. You must remember to separate symbols, names, and Greek characters with spaces or **eqn** will not recognize them.

The **eqn** processor knows the following mathematical words:

above	dotdot	italic	rcol	to
back	down	lcol	right	under
bar	dyad	left	roman	up
bold	fat	lineup	rpile	vec
ccol	font	lpile	size	~,^
col	from	mark	sqrt	{}
cpile	fwd	matrix	sub	
define	gfont	ndefine	sup	
delim	gsize	over	tdefine	
dot	hat	pile	tilde	

The following mathematical symbols print as shown:

>=	≥
<=	≤
==	≡
!=	≠
+-	±
->	→
<-	←
<<	≪
>>	≫
inf	∞
partial	∂
half	½
prime	′
approx	≈
nothing	
cdot	.
times	×
del	∇
grad	∇
,...,	, . . . ,
sum	Σ
int	∫
prod	Π
union	∪
inter	∩

Greek letters you can print by spelling them in the desired case:

DELTA	Δ	iota	ι
GAMMA	Γ	kappa	κ
LAMBDA	Λ	lambda	λ
OMEGA	Ω	mu	μ
PHI	Φ	nu	ν
PI	Π	omega	ω
PSI	Ψ	omicron	o
SIGMA	Σ	phi	φ
THETA	Θ	pi	π
UPSILON	Y	psi	ψ

XI	Ξ	rho	ρ
alpha	α	sigma	σ
beta	β	tau	τ
chi	χ	theta	θ
delta	δ	upsilon	υ
epsilon	ε	xi	ξ
eta	η	zeta	ζ
gamma	γ		

Invoking eqn   As mentioned, you must pipe the output of **eqn** to **nroff** or **troff**. Again, **eqn** is designed to produce typeset equations with **troff** on the typesetter. With **nroff** and the **neqn** program, you can produce approximate results on the line printer.

If your file contains equations, use one of the following commands at the UNIX shell prompt:

eqn | troff -mm *filename*
neqn | troff -mm *filename* > *filename.n*

If your file contains both tables and equations, use one of the following commands:

eqn | troff -mm *filename*
neqn | nroff -mm *filename* > *filename.n*

The **nroff** and **troff** formatters, with the help of the **mm** macros, provide you with powerful tools to produce professional-quality documents. With its complexities, subtleties, and idioscincracies, **nroff** can be quite a challenge. Mastering **nroff** may take some time, but it is well worth the effort.

8 *Mail*

One of UNIX's most convenient features is its ability to send electronic mail quickly and easily via the **mail** or **mailx** program. The UNIX mail system is sometimes called a mailbox system. Each user on the system has a *mailbox* to which other users can send mail.

Using the **mail** program is similar to sending real mail through the post office. When you send a letter, the **mail** program, like your letter carrier, delivers your letter directly to the recipient's mailbox. Naturally, to read your own mail you simply look in your own mailbox on the system.

The **mail** program provides you with tools for sending and receiving mail. This chapter describes how and why you use these tools and summarizes the most useful **mail** features. The first part of the chapter covers sending mail, and the second part of the chapter discusses receiving mail.

To differentiate between incoming mail and outgoing mail, this chapter will refer to mail that you receive as *messages* and mail that you send as *letters*. This is arbitrary but prevents confusion.

Variations on a Theme

There are numerous versions of the **mail** program, from very simple programs to quite complex ones, and each has different features and functions and, sometimes, different names. The various versions of UNIX provide mail tools that sometimes differ in subtle ways. For instance, on AT&T UNIX there are two versions of mail: **mail** and **mailx**. The **mail** program has few fancy features. The **mailx** program is more complex and offers many enhancements and convenience features. On some systems, the mail program is called **Mail** with a capital "M." On Berkeley UNIX, the **mail** program is called **mail** as well, but this version has more features and more flexibility than AT&T **mail**. In fact, AT&T **mailx** and other mail programs, such as SCO UNIX **mail**, are patterned after Berkeley **mail**.

The name "mail" is used throughout this chapter. If you use **Mail** or **mailx**, substitute the appropriate mail program for **mail**. For example, if you use **mailx**, you would use

```
% mailx smith
```

instead of

```
% mail smith
```

Commands

Before you plunge into the operation of **mail**, you should be aware of a few important details. Commands in **mail** are entered on a line by themselves at the **mail** prompt (usually **&** or **?**). Commands may be followed by arguments separated by spaces.

▶**TIP** You need not type entire **mail** commands. You can abbreviate most commands to one or two letters. For example, you can enter **t** instead of **type** for the **type** command and **ho** instead of **hold** for the

hold command. This chapter gives the abbreviation in parentheses after the name of each command.

An important **mail** concept is the *tilde escape,* which is a **mail** command consisting of a tilde ($\sim$) and a single-character code on a line by itself. For example, an important tilde escape is tilde-v ($\sim$**v**), which allows you to edit your letter with the visual editor. Tilde escape codes only work in the body of a letter in **mail**.

You know already that CTRL-C means "hold down the Control key and press C." These control codes are often represented on the computer screen with the *caret* (^). For example, CTRL-C may appear as **^C** on the screen.

Sending Mail

The **mail** program offers remarkable freedom and simplicity. From the UNIX shell prompt, you can send electronic mail at any time to anyone on the system, almost anywhere in the world. It is easy to send mail to someone across the room or across the nation. To send mail to someone else on the system, you must know their *account name,* sometimes referred to as a *login name, user name,* or simply *login.* You must differentiate between someone's real name and their account name (although in some cases they may be the same). You must also know the person's *system address,* or *network address.* To mail to someone on your own system, you do not need the system address, but to mail to someone on another system, perhaps in another part of the world, you need to know the system address. In **mail,** an account name and system address make up the complete mailing address, just as a real name and address make up the postal address of a letter.

Sending Mail to One
Person or to Several
People at the Same Time

Use the **mail** command to send mail from the UNIX shell. Every name you type after the **mail** command is an account to which you want to send mail. In UNIX parlance, the **mail** command takes one or more arguments that specify the user to whom mail is to be sent. For example, to send a letter to account **bartok** from the UNIX shell prompt (usually % or $), type

```
% mail bartok
```

You can mail identical copies to several users simultaneously. For example, to send a letter to two accounts at once, say accounts **enesco** and **liszt**, type

```
% mail enesco liszt
```

This tells **mail** that you are sending the same letter to both accounts.

After you type the command, **mail** may immediately ask

```
Subject:
```

Type a one-line summary of your letter and press RETURN. The subject will appear on the subject line within the letter and in the recipient's message list. (The subject line is described in the section "The mail Message," and the message list in the section "Listing Your Messages.")

Now, type the body of your letter, pressing RETURN at the end of each line. You may correct mistakes with BACKSPACE only in the current line. If you make a mistake and press RETURN before you correct it, it is too late. To correct those mistakes or make editing changes, you will need to use an editor (covered in the section "Writing a Letter Using an Editor.")

When your letter is ready to send, press CTRL-D on a line by itself (that is, hold down CTRL and press D simultaneously) to end your letter and send it. Older programs may allow you to end your letter with a single dot (.) on a line by itself, but this method does not work on newer releases of mail.

At this point on some systems, **mail** might ask

```
Cc:
```

The **mail** program is asking to whom you want "carbon copies" of your letter sent. If you want duplicate copies of your letter sent to any other accounts, type the account names, separated by spaces, and press RETURN. If you do not want any duplicate copies sent, just press RETURN.

Figure 8-1 demonstrates what is involved in sending a letter with **mail**. For example, to send a letter to account **jones**, type

```
% mail jones
```

at the UNIX shell prompt, type the subject and the body of the letter, and, finally, press CTRL-D to send it.

After you send your letter, the **mail** program will tell you if something went wrong. If UNIX does nothing after a command, everything is okay. If mail cannot be delivered to the user and address you specified, you will be notified either by a message or via return mail. The **mail** program may give you a message something like

```
bartok... User unknown
```

```
% mail jones
Subject: specifications
Mr. Jones:
     We need both the software and input-output specs as soon
as you are finished with them.  I trust that there were no
difficulties.
     There has been a little pressure from management about
the deadline, but I explained the situation.  They said, "Tell
that to the sales department."
     Anyway, looks like our deadline bought the farm.  I'll send
you the revised schedule.
^D
Cc:
(end of message)
%
```

Figure 8-1. *Sending a letter with* **mail**

The **mail** program (like your letter carrier) will return the mail to you. It saves the returned mail in a file named **dead.letter** in your home directory. If **dead.letter** is already there, the returned mail is appended to the file.

▶**NOTE**   Once you send a letter, there is no way to "unsend" it. For this reason, be careful of what you send. Because the editor allows you to carefully edit your letters, you should write your letters with an editor.

Sending Mail to Other Computers

If your system is part of a network, you can send mail to and receive mail from users on other systems. To send mail to people on other computers, just add the name of the recipient's computer to the account name, much as you would add the recipient's country to the address of an international letter.

   If you are part of the **uucp** network (often referred to as the **USE-NET**), you need only precede the user's name with the unique name of the remote system. The account name and system name are separated by an exclamation point (!). For example, to send mail to **rodrigo** at system **doc**, type

```
$ mail doc!rodrigo
```

   The **mail** program allows you to send mail from your system to other machines, even through a third (or fourth or fifth) machine. This is called *multihop mail*. For instance, to send multihop mail to account **vivaldi** through several systems in the network, you might use

```
$ mail ucbvax!ucsc!iris!sage!vivaldi
```

The mail you sent passes in turn through systems **ucbvax**, **ucsc**, **iris**, and **sage**. You are allowed up to 20 hops. The mail goes from one machine to the next machine that you specified in the path, finally ending on the **sage** system where the **vivaldi** account resides. Each intervening machine must know about the next machine in the path. If either the path through the network or the user is incorrect, **mail** will attempt to tell you and return your mail. Some machines will not return mail, so your mail may occasionally disappear off the face of the earth.

If you use the C shell, you must "escape" exclamation marks with the backslash (\). That is, the exclamation point in **ùucp** network addresses must be preceded by a backslash, as in

```
% mail lily\!bizet
```

If your system is connected to the **Internet**, sending mail to other systems is only slightly more complex. You must separate the account name from the computer name by the at sign (@). To send a letter to an account on the computer **chia**, you might type

```
% mail dvorak@chia
```

You may have to give the **Internet** network address in more detail. Each **Internet** system has a unique network address, each part of which is separated by a dot (.). **Internet** mail may look something like this:

```
% mail wagner@tarragon.leblond.COM
```

The **Internet** address has the format *user@host.subnet.domain*. In the previous example, **COM** is the *domain* and **leblond** is the *subnet* (**COM** stands for "commercial," while **GOV** and **EDU** stand for "government" and "educational," respectively). The host system **tarragon** puts the mail in the mailbox of account **wagner**.

▶**NOTE** On some systems, **Internet** addressing with the at sign is an outdated convention. If it doesn't work, try replacing the at sign with a dot.

There are many different conventions for many different networks. If your system is connected to another network, such as the **BITNET** or **CSNET**, you may have a completely different way of addressing remote mail. Sometimes you may need to go through one network to use another network; this may require even more complicated mail address-ing. If you have any questions about remote mail on your system, ask your system administrator.

▶**TIP**   Sometimes you may want to tell others *your* network address. If you do not know it, again, ask your system administrator.

Killing a Letter

Before long, you may want to abort a letter, perhaps to start the whole thing over. The easiest way to do this is with the interrupt key, usually CTRL-C. Press CTRL-C at any point in your letter, then again to confirm that you really want to kill the letter. For example,

```
% mail smith
Subject: Software specs
Mr. Smith -
     Enclosed are the software specifications that I promised
you. There is a lot more to it than I originally thought.
But, I guess that's how it goes ^C
(Interrupt -- one more to kill letter)
^C
Interrupt
%
```

Two CTRL-C's were used to kill the letter.

Another way to kill your letter is with a *tilde escape code,* tilde-q (~**q**) (for "quit"). To abort your letter, type ~**q** at the beginning of a line in the body of your letter. For example,

```
% mail smith
Subject: Software Specs
Mr. Smith -
     Here are the software specifications that I mentioned on
Tuesday. They are more extensive than we originally planned.
They sort of got away from me.
~ q
%
```

▶**NOTE**   With both methods of killing a letter, a copy of your letter is usually saved in your home directory in a file called **dead.letter**. Some systems will even tell you as much.

Reading Your Letter

As you write your letter, you may want to see what it looks like. To have **mail** show you your letter, type tilde-p (~**p**) (for print letter) at the beginning of a line in the body of your letter. For example, to show your letter so far:

```
% mail smith
Subject: Reminder
When you see Jones, don't forget to pick up the input/output
specs.
~p
------
Message contains:
To: smith
Subject: Reminder

When you see Jones, don't forget to pick up the input/output
specs.
(continue)
```

The mail program responds

```
(continue)
```

to tell you that you may continue writing your letter as usual. Again, if your letter is finished, you may now quit **mail** and send it.

Enclosing a File in Your Letter

It is useful to be able to include the contents of a file in your letter. Perhaps you want to put a report or table within a letter that you are writing. Use tilde-r (~**r**) to read in a file. For example, to enclose the file **fin.report** into your letter, type

```
~r report.fin
```

in the body of your letter. Of course, if the file is not there, **mail** will give you an error message. Enclosing a file in your letter may look something like this:

```
% mail jones
Subject: Route data
Mr. Jones:
     Here is the latest route data. To some degree, this may
influence the rest of the system.

~r route.data
"route.data" 7/390
~p
------
Message contains:
Subject: Route data
To: jones

Mr. Jones:
     Here is the latest route data. To some degree, this may
influence the rest of the system.

                    Current Route Traffic
                 1968  1972  1976  1980  1984  1988  1992
Rural route 1     25    21    19    13     8     4     4
Old highway 4     28    27    19    16     5     5     3
Interstate 401     3     5     6     9    14    22    28
Highway 46         6     6    12    13    23    24    26
(continue)
```

Writing a Letter Using an Editor

You may use an editor, such as **vi**, to write or edit your letters. This is useful for correcting mistakes that you missed on previous lines or for letters that require more than simple formatting. Knowing an editor, such as **vi**, allows you to make editing changes in letters sent by **mail**. You may get along fine without ever editing your letters, but for long letters an editor is a good idea. To find out more about the UNIX editors, read Chapter 6, "The vi Editor."

You may edit your letter with **vi** by entering the tilde escape code tilde-v (~**v**) (for "visual editor") at the beginning of a line in the body of your letter. For example, to edit a letter with **vi** after a typo on a previous line:

```
% mail smith
Subject:
Mr. Smith --
     If I de-emphasize the rural routes, am I also ot place a
cooresponding greater emphasis on the urban areas? This is not
really a problem, but it may take a little time. Is thta okay?
I know that time iis short, so ask your managers to decide how
important this change is. Ring me on the horn and tell me how it
goes.
~v
```

The **vi** editor will display your letter as illustrated in Figure 8-2. You may now edit the letter with **vi**.

When you finish editing, you must exit **vi** and return to **mail**. To exit **vi**, type **:wq** and press RETURN. Now **mail** will respond

```
(continue)
```

You may continue writing your letter using **mail** or, if your letter is finished, you can press CTRL-D and send it.

▶**NOTE** If you prefer a line editor to the visual editor, you can edit your letter with **ed** by typing tilde-e (~**e**) instead of tilde-v.

Sending a File with Mail

Sometimes you may want to send a file that has already been prepared elsewhere. With **mail**, you can send any text file. You just have to redirect the standard input of the **mail** command. For example, to send a file called **myfile** to account **bachjs**, at the UNIX shell prompt, type

```
% mail bachjs < myfile
```

```
Mr. Smith --
     If I de-emphasize the rural routes, am I also ot place a
cooresponding greater emphasis on the urban areas?  This is not
really a problem, but it may take a little time.  Is thta okay?
I know that time iis short, so ask your managers to decide how
important this change is.  Ring me on the horn and tell me how it
goes.

~

~

~

~

~

~

~

~

~

~
"/tmp/Re12139" 7 lines, 338 characters
```

Figure 8-2. *Editing a letter with vi*

The < character is the redirection symbol. It tells **mail** to look in **myfile** for its input instead of asking you to type your letter. Review Chapter 5, "UNIX Command-Line Fundamentals," for more about redirection. Of course, to send a different file to a different account, you would replace **myfile** with the name and path of the file you wanted to send and replace **bachjs** with the name of the account you wanted it sent to.

▶**TIP** Be careful when using redirection with **mail**. If you accidentally use the output redirection symbol (>) instead of the input redirection symbol (<), you will overwrite the file, destroying its contents.

After you have sent the file, UNIX doesn't issue a message if it has sent the file successfully; it tells you if anything goes wrong.

When you send a file with redirection, **mail** does not ask you for a subject. If you want the mail to have a subject line, you must use the **-s** option when you call **mail** from the command line. The text immediately following **-s** on the command line is the subject of the mail. If the subject contains spaces, you must surround it with double quotes. For example,

```
% mail -s "Third Quarter Earnings" schubert < report
```

mails a file named **report** to an account named **schubert** with a subject line that reads "Third Quarter Earnings".

Getting Help

To find out more about sending **mail**, type

```
% man mail
```

at the UNIX shell prompt. If the UNIX on-line manual is installed on your computer, **man** will give you a brief summary of all the functions and options of the **mail** program on your system. A good reference for all UNIX commands, including **mail**, is the *UNIX User's Guide* or the *UNIX User's Reference Manual* for your system.

Receiving Mail

Mail that is sent to you is collected and placed in your mailbox in the system post office. If you have mail waiting for you, UNIX tells you as soon as you log in with the message

```
You have mail.
```

or with the message

```
You have new mail.
```

You use the **mail** command both to send mail to other users and to retrieve mail sent to you. You may also save, manage, and reply to your incoming mail when you retrieve it. To retrieve your mail from the post office, type

```
% mail
```

at the UNIX shell prompt.

Some **mail** programs, especially the simpler ones, will automatically display message number 1. More complex **mail** programs will display a list of the messages in your mailbox and allow you to read them in any order. The list of messages may look something like this:

```
% mail
Mail version 5.2.  Type ? for help.
"/user/spool/mail/schumann": 3 messages 3 new
>N  1 mahler   Mon May 8 12:18  19/634    "romantics vs. classical"
 N  2 sibelius Mon May 8 13:23  46/2012   "Re: copyright"
 N  3 verdi    Tue May 9  1:02  22/937    "Concerto"
&
```

The **mail** program shows you the sender, time and date sent, size, and subject of each message that you have received. The section "Listing Your Messages" in this chapter tells you more about the message list.

▶**NOTE**   Some **mail** programs list your messages in reverse order, with the most recent at the top.

▶**TIP**   An important concept in **mail** is that of the *current message*. The current message is either the first new message in your mailbox or the last message read. As you can see from the example, some systems mark the current message with a greater than sign (>). When you use a read, reply, save, or delete command (all described in the following sections) not followed by a number, your command will refer to the current message. For example, if while in **mail** you type a lone **d** (for "delete") and press RETURN, mail will delete the last message you read.

If you have no messages, **mail** will tell you when you check your mailbox, as in

```
% mail
No mail for schumann
%
```

After the list of messages, **mail** displays a prompt. The **mail** prompt (like the UNIX shell prompt) indicates that **mail** is waiting for a command from you. It is usually an ampersand (**&**) or a question mark (**?**) or even another character.

Reading Your Messages

There are several ways to read the mail in your mailbox. By far the easiest way is simply to press RETURN after the **mail** prompt. The next message (or the first new one) in your mailbox will be displayed. To read your messages one by one, continue pressing RETURN after each message until the last message has been displayed. If you press RETURN when you have reached the end of the messages, **mail** will respond something like

```
At EOF
```

or

```
Can't go beyond last message.
```

This just means that **mail** could find no more mail in your mailbox.

▶**NOTE** With most **mail** programs, mail is displayed a page at a time. Thus, you don't have to worry about long mail scrolling off the screen. If your **mail** program does not paginate messages nicely, you may have to freeze the screen to read your message. Use CTRL-S to freeze the screen and CTRL-Q to unfreeze it.

Another way to read your messages is to type the actual message number at the **mail** prompt. When **mail** lists your messages, it numbers them sequentially, giving the earliest mail the lowest number. From the example in the previous section, you can see that the messages are numbered in a column on the left side of the message list. To read a message, type its message number at the **mail** prompt and press RETURN. For example, to read message 1, type **1**, to read message 2, type **2**, and so on.

▶**TIP**   Both methods—pressing RETURN or specifying a number—are shorthand for the **type** command (**t**). For instance, instead of typing **2** at the **mail** prompt, you might have typed **t 2** to have **mail** display message number 2 in the same way. If you typed **t** alone, **mail** would have displayed the next message just as if you had pressed RETURN alone. On some **mail** programs, you use **p** (for "print") instead of **t**.

Figure 8-3 illustrates several methods of displaying mail.

After reading a message, you will most likely want to either leave the message in your mailbox, save it in a file, reply to it, or delete it. These **mail** operations are described in the following sections.

The mail Message

Here is a sample of a message received through **mail**:

```
& 1
From smith Mon Jul 31 11:48:17
To: jones
Subject: Re: specs
Date: Mon Jul 31 11:48:17

Okay, everything looks fine. This has certainly been taken
uptown. Now, does this completely describe the system, or is
there some other companion document I will need to take this
through the next step?
&
```

The top line of the message is the *postmark* and was added by the **mail** program. If the message was from a user on the same machine, the message will have a one-line postmark. If the message was forwarded from another user or another machine, the postmark contains one line

```
% mail
Mail version 5.2.  Type ? for help.
"/usr/spool/mail/smith": 3 messages 3 new
>N  1 thomas   Mon Jul 31 11:39  5/210  "Input/Output Spec"
 N  2 williams Mon Jul 31 11:40  13/308 "about Using UNIX"
 N  3 jones    Mon Jul 31 11:40  4/190  "data-flow"
&
Message 1:
From thomas Mon Jul 31 11:39:38
To: smith
Subject: Input/Output Spec
Date: Mon Jul 31 11:39:38

John,
    You got most everything we needed from Jones.  You brought
back the software specs and the data-flow diagrams, but you
forgot the input/output specs.  Please return for them
immediately or have them Fed-Xed here today.

& 3
Message  3:
From jones Mon Jul 31 11:40:05
To: smith
Subject: data-flow
Date: Mon Jul 31 11:39:38

Mr. Smith --
Thanks for your input on the user doc.  I did not expect your
response so soon.  You really did your homework on this one.
This gives me a chance to talk to a few people here about it.
Thanks again.

&
At EOF
&
```

Figure 8-3. *Reading your messages with* **mail**

for each step that the message took on its way to your mailbox. Other
material below the postmark is called the *message header*. The message

header contains information, such as **To:**, **From**, **Date:**, and more. It can be just a few lines long or several pages long, depending on the system and the number of steps it took to reach you. Following the message header is the actual body of the message.

Exiting Mail

Eventually, you will want to leave the **mail** program. There are two commands for getting out: the **quit** command (**q**) and the **exit** command (**x**).

The **quit** command does two things: First, it removes the messages you have read and saves them in a file called **mbox** in your home directory. Second, it takes you out of the **mail** program. Since **quit** removes all of the messages you have looked at, leaving **mail** in this way prevents your mailbox from becoming too cluttered. This is the usual way to quit **mail**. For example, the following command quits **mail**, removes two messages from your mailbox, and returns to the UNIX shell prompt:

```
& q
Saved 2 messages in mbox
%
```

If you have held messages in your mailbox (see the section "Holding Messages"), **mail** may say something like

```
Held 2 messages in /usr/spool/mail/schumann
```

On the other hand, the **exit** command leaves the **mail** program and doesn't move or remove any of your messages. If you often exit **mail** this way and do not delete your messages (see the section "Deleting Messages"), your mailbox may become cluttered. The **exit** command is a hasty way to exit **mail**, useful if you want to take care of your mail at a later date. For example, the following command exits **mail**, does not touch any of the messages, and returns to the UNIX shell prompt:

```
& x
%
```

Listing Your Messages

After you have read and replied to a few messages, you may want to list
your messages to identify the current message or to see which messages
you have read. The **header** command (**h**) asks **mail** to list a summary of
your messages, as it may have done when you first entered **mail**. For
example, the list of message headers may look something like this:

```
& h
      1 smith      Thu May 18  2:18  19/634    "Re: final"
    * 2 jean       Thu May 18 13:23  46/2012   "House Swap"
  U 3 smith      Fri May 19  9:18  19/634    "Re: Yes, finis"
>P 4 wagner @doc.leblond.COM Fri May 19 13:23  46/2012 "Using UNIX"
  N 5 burger@mx.vanden.MIL Mon May 22  1:02  22/937  "clearance"
&
```

The message list includes a lot of information. As well as the sender,
date, time, size, and subject, **mail** tells you whether your mail is new, old,
unread, held, saved, or replied to. The code to the left of each message
number indicates that message's status. In the previous example, messages 1 and 2 have been read (they have no code), 2 has been saved or
replied to (hence the *), 3 is an old but unread message (the **U** stands
for "unread"), 4 has been held (the **P** stands for "preserved"), and 5 is
a new, unread message (**N** means "new message").

▶**NOTE**   The codes may be different on different systems. In fact, simpler **mail** programs may not offer status codes at all, but more complex
mail programs usually do.

Again, the greater-than sign marks the current message. The current
message is either the first new message in your mailbox or the last
message that you read.

▶**TIP**   If you have a lot of messages in your mailbox, the message list may not show all of your messages at once. Instead, it will display one screenful at a time. You can display the next screenful of messages with **h+** or the previous screenful of messages with **h-**. If you have a lot of messages in your mailbox, typing **h** alone will display a screenful of messages with the current message in the center.

Replying to Messages

As you read your messages, **mail** allows you to send a reply to the originator of any message. The **reply** command (**r**) sends mail to the original author of a message. The subject line of the reply will automatically hold the subject of the original message, often preceded by "Re:." To reply to the current message, type

    & r

at the **mail** prompt. To reply to message 3, type

    & r 3

For the most part, replying to mail is much like sending mail. The only difference is that **mail** does not ask for a subject when it is replying (unless no subject was given in the original message).

As with sending mail, you complete and send your reply letter by pressing a CTRL-D on a blank line in your letter. When the letter is completed, **mail** may ask

    Cc:

for accounts to send "carbon copies" of your letter. If you do not care to send duplicates of your letter to any other accounts, press RETURN.

▶**NOTE** You must treat the reply operation with care, especially when the original message is from another machine or is addressed to more than one person. On some systems, the **r** command is swapped with a similar command, **R**. On these systems, the **r** command will send your reply to every account that received the original message as well as every machine that played a part in getting your mail to your mailbox. Sometimes it is safer to just send new mail to the original author (described in the next section).

Originating Mail from Within mail

You can send a letter from within **mail** with the **m** command. Using **m** from the **mail** prompt is exactly like using the **mail** command at the command line. Follow the **m** command with one or more accounts to which you want to send mail. For example, to send a letter to two people simultaneously from inside **mail**, type

```
& m chopin stsaens
```

As with **mail** from the command line, type the subject and the body of your letter and then press CTRL-D.

```
& m smith
Subject:
Yes, the specifications as they stand right now are complete.
As far as I know, that'll fly.
^D
(end of message)
&
```

Deleting Messages

After you have read or replied to messages, you may want to delete them. Unless you indicate otherwise, each message that you read is automatically saved in a file named **mbox** in your home directory when you leave mail with **quit**. Often, however, you do not want to save messages that you have received. The **delete** command (**d**) deletes messages. To delete a message you have just read (the current message), type

& **d**

at the **mail** prompt. You can delete a specific message by referencing its message number. For example, to delete message 5, type

& **d 5**

You can delete several messages at once by separating their message numbers by spaces. For instance, to delete messages 1 and 3, type

& **d 1 3**

You can also delete a *range* of messages by specifying the first and last message to delete separated by a dash. To delete messages 2 through 7, type

& **d 2-7**

You may combine these ways of specifying messages. For instance,

& **d 1-3 5**

deletes messages 1, 2, 3, and 5. This method of specifying messages works with several other **mail** commands, such as the **hold** command introduced in the next section. As you would expect, trying to delete messages that don't exist produces an error message.

▶**TIP**   More ways to specify messages are provided by the caret, the dollar sign, the dot, and the asterisk. The caret (ˆ) specifies the *first* message in your mailbox, while the dollar sign (**$**) refers to the *last* message. The dot (**.**) refers to the current message and the asterisk (∗) refers to *all* the messages in your mailbox. For example, the command **tˆ-.** types all of the messages up to the current message. The command **ho3-$** holds all messages from message 3 to the last one. The command **d** ∗ deletes all messages in your mailbox.

▶**NOTE**   Messages that are "deleted" are not really removed from your mailbox until you use the **quit** command to leave mail. They are in limbo until you type the **q** command. You can bring them back to the land of the living with the **undelete** command (**u**). Use **undelete** as you use **delete**, but reference messages that you have deleted. Once you exit with **quit**, you cannot undelete deleted messages; they are permanently deleted.

Holding Mail

To prevent your messages from being removed from your mailbox when you use **quit** to leave **mail**, you may use the **hold** command (**ho**) to hold your messages in your mailbox. (Remember to use (**ho**) since **h** is the header command.)

    To hold a message you have just read, type

& ho

at the **mail** prompt. Like the **delete** command, **hold** has numerous ways to specify messages. You may hold a single message, several messages at the same time, a range of messages, or any combination of these.

Held messages are often indicated with a **P** (for "preserved") in the message list (see the section "Listing Your Messages"). If you have held messages in your mailbox, **mail** will say something like this when you use **quit** to leave **mail**:

```
Held 6 messages in /usr/spool/mail/mahler
```

Saving Messages

Occasionally, you may want to save a message as a file for future reference. Perhaps you want to edit or print the file separately. Or maybe someone sent you a shell script or a program that you want to compile. Use the **save** command (**s**) to save a message to a file. To save the message you have just read (the current message) to a file called **report**, type

```
& s report
```

at the **mail** prompt. To save message 4 to a file called **inventory**, type

```
& s 4 inventory
```

You can save several messages in the same file at the same time. For example, to save messages 2, 4, 5, and 6 in a file called **letters.home**, type

```
& s 2 4-6 letters.home
```

You can also save a message to a file with the **write** command (**w**). This command is virtually identical to **save**, but it does not put the message header (the block of text that identifies the sender, recipient, subject, and so on) in the file. The **write** command is useful for saving files—such as programs and scripts—in which the header is unnecessary.

▶**NOTE**   Saved messages are marked in the message list with an asterisk (∗). If you leave **mail** with the **quit** command, saved messages will be deleted from your mailbox.

Getting Help

On your system, the **mail** program may differ in the commands it uses and the way it uses them. You can get a succinct summary of the important commands on your version of **mail** by asking **mail** for help. At the **mail** prompt, ask **mail** for help by typing

```
& ?
```

or

```
& help
```

You can get a comprehensive list of the **mail** commands by typing

```
& list
```

at the **mail** prompt. Unfortunately, if you use this syntax no explanation for the commands is provided.

For further help in using **mail**, see the *UNIX User's Guide* or the *UNIX User's Reference Manual* that accompanies your system.

You use the **mail** command from the UNIX shell prompt to both send and receive mail. To send mail, use the **mail** command followed by one or more account names. When sending a letter, the tilde escapes allow you to print your letter, edit your letter with the visual editor, and much more. The **mail** command alone retrieves your mail from the system post office. When retrieving your mail, you may read, save, manage, and reply to your mail from the **mail** prompt.

The **mail** program offers simplicity, speed, and relative dependability. Neither rain, nor sleet, nor dead of night will keep **mail** from its appointed rounds.

9 *The Bourne Shell*

The shell acts as both a user interface and a programming language. As a user interface, the shell is a liaison between you and the UNIX kernel. The shell translates and executes your commands one by one as you enter them at the command line. As a programming language, the shell reads commands from a file and executes them one after another.

There are three principal shells on the UNIX system: the *Bourne shell*, the *C shell,* and the *Korn shell.* The Bourne shell is popular because it works with both AT&T and Berkeley UNIX and because it was developed first. The C shell offers more features than the Bourne shell but is not always supported by AT&T UNIX. The Korn shell is AT&T's response to U.C. Berkeley's C shell. It is compatible with the Bourne shell and encompasses many features of the C shell and more. It is one of the newest UNIX shells and has not yet gained wide acceptance. Only the Bourne shell and the C shell are discussed in this book. At the command line, the Bourne shell is often distinguished by the dollar sign prompt, while the C shell typically uses the percent sign prompt.

To enter the Bourne shell from the C shell, type the command **sh** on the command line, as the following example demonstrates.

```
% sh
$
```

If your login shell is the C shell, but you want this login session to use the Bourne shell, use the **exec** command. The following example demonstrates that the C shell is exchanged for the Bourne shell with **exec**.

```
% ps
   PID TTY  TIME COMMAND
  4032 i1a  0:07 csh
  4260 i1a  0:00 ps
% exec sh
$ ps
   PID TTY  TIME COMMAND
  4032 i1a  0:07 sh
  4261 i1a  0:00 ps
```

The **exec** command runs the specified command in place of the current shell.

Shell Scripts

When the shell is used as a programming language, it reads and executes commands from a file called a *shell script*. A shell script is identical to a bunch of commands entered interactively at the keyboard. Commands in the shell script can be any commands that you can enter at the command line: UNIX utilities, compiled programs, or other shell scripts. As with commands that you give on the command line, commands in shell scripts can use wildcard file references and input and output redirection or piping. In addition to the usual commands you use on the command line, shell scripts offer *flow control commands*. These commands allow you to change the order of execution of commands in the shell script, much as with high-level programming languages, such as C or Pascal.

Creating a Shell Script

A shell script is nothing more than an executable text file that contains shell commands. Creating a shell script involves making the text file and setting the permissions to make it executable. You may create the text file with an editor such as **vi**, or by simply redirecting to a file the output of the **cat** command. The text file you create will not have execute permission set. You must use the **chmod** command (see Chapter 4) to change the access permissions of your shell script.

The first line of a Bourne shell script should contain a single colon (:) on a line by itself. This tells the shell that the script is indeed a Bourne shell script. If you are running the script from the Bourne shell, the Bourne shell assumes that *any* script is a Bourne shell script and the colon is not essential. If you are running your script from the C shell, the colon tells the shell to interpret the shell script as a Bourne shell script. From the C shell, a Bourne shell script without the colon may not work. Another more explicit method of identifying a script as a Bourne shell script is to place **:/bin/sh** on the first line of the script.

For example, create a shell script called **mkreminder**. This shell script will maintain in your home directory a hidden file, **.reminder**, in which you may compile notes to yourself. Later, you will create another shell script that retrieves these notes. Use an editor to create the text file or simply redirect the standard output of **cat** to the file **mkreminder**, pressing CTRL-D when you are finished, as shown here.

```
$ cat > mkreminder
:
# mkreminder
#    Enter a one-line reminder
#
echo "Enter reminder (end w/CTRL-D):"
cat >> $HOME/.reminder
^D
```

▶**NOTE** Lines beginning with the pound sign (#) are comments and are ignored by the shell.

If you tried to execute the script now, the shell would not recognize **mkreminder** as an executable file, and would give you an error message, such as

```
$ mkreminder
mkreminder: execute permission denied
```

You need to set the proper permissions to make the **mkreminder** shell script executable. Use the **chmod** command to give the owner execute permission. The **ls** command with the **-l** option shows the access privileges for the **mkreminder** file.

```
$ ls -l mkreminder
-rw-r--r--    1 modes     group          69 Aug 19 13:46 mkreminder
$ chmod u+x mkreminder
$ ls -l mkreminder
-rwxr--r--    1 modes     group          69 Aug 19 13:46 mkreminder
```

At this point, the **mkreminder** file is executable.

Executing a Shell Script

To run a shell script, simply type its file name at the command line. The shell executes the commands in the script, one after another. You can run the **mkreminder** script by typing **mkreminder** at the command line. Then you can type a note to yourself.

```
$ mkreminder
Enter reminder (end w/CTRL-D):
Don't forget to turn off the coffee pot!
^D
```

Here is another useful shell script. As promised, this script retrieves the reminders from the **.reminder** file. You already have the script **mkreminder** that allows you to enter a reminder. The new script will be called **reminder** and will allow you to see the notes you have entered. The following example creates the text file **reminder**, sets the proper permissions, and runs the script:

```
$ cat > reminder
:
# reminder
#    Display reminders
#
echo "Notes:"
more -10 $HOME/.reminder
^D
$ chmod u+x reminder
```

```
$ reminder
Notes:
Don't forget to turn off the coffee pot!
```

Variables

A *variable* is a symbol to which you may assign a value. The value can be a number, a word, or a string of words. The shell has variables that you create and assign, as well as variables that are set by the shell itself.

Variables that you create and assign values to are called *user variables*. You can change their values or make them *read-only*, so that they cannot subsequently be changed. A user variable is usually only available within the shell in which it was created. However, you can *export* user variables so that they will be accessible to subshells you may enter during your login session.

Variables that are set by the shell are called *shell variables*. One group of shell variables are the *environment variables*, whose names have special meanings to the shell. Some of the environment variables, such as **HOME** and **PATH**, are inherited from the environment when you enter a shell. Other environment variables are automatically created and assigned default values when you enter the shell, while others do not exist until you set them.

Another group of shell variables are the *read-only shell variables*. These are set by the shell and cannot be changed. The read-only shell variables have two-character labels (such as **$?** and **$#**) and allow you to access information about your interaction with the shell, such as parameters from the command line, process numbers, and exit status.

User Variables

You may create user variables from any sequence of letters and digits, as long as the first character is a letter. Use the equal sign (**=**) to assign a value to your variable. In the following example, the *value* **summary** is assigned to the *variable* **TARGET**:

```
$ TARGET=summary
```

Do not put any spaces before or after the equal sign. To print the contents of a variable, use the **echo** command. Whenever you reference a variable, you must precede the variable name with a dollar sign ($). Without the dollar sign, the shell does not recognize a variable as a variable, as here:

```
$ TARGET=summary
$ echo $TARGET
summary
$ echo TARGET
TARGET
```

Because of the leading dollar sign, the shell recognizes **$target** as a variable. Whenever the shell finds a reference to a variable, it immediately substitutes a variable reference with the value of the variable, and passes this value to the command line.

▶**TIP**   Be careful not to confuse the Bourne shell dollar sign prompt with the dollar sign preceding a variable reference.

   To display a dollar sign and prevent shell variable substitution, use backslash to "quote" the dollar sign or enclose the text within single quotes. Without a backslash or single quotes, the shell attempts to substitute the value of a variable when it finds a dollar sign.
   When you assign a variable, put double quotes around values that contain spaces or tabs. Without double quotes, the shell will assume that the first word is the variable's value and that succeeding words are commands.

```
$ TARGET=summary report
report: not found
$ TARGET="summary report"
$ echo $TARGET
summary report
```

Furthermore, put double quotes around *references* to variables whose values might contain multiple spaces or tabs. If not, multiple spaces or tabs on the command line are usually treated as single spaces.

```
$ TARGET="summary      report"
$ echo $TARGET
summary report
$ echo "$TARGET"
summary      report
```

Put double quotes around references to variables that contain the special characters * and ?. If you do not, the shell interprets these special characters as wildcard characters when you reference the variable. For example, if you place a * in the value of a variable and echo the value without quotes, the shell will substitute the value and the **echo** command will interpret the * as an ambiguous file reference. Thus, instead of the expected value, **echo** prints a list of the matching files.

```
$ DOCUMENT=memo*
$ echo $DOCUMENT
memo1.txt memo2.txt
$ ls memo*
memo1.txt
memo2.txt
$ echo "$DOCUMENT"
memo*
```

Clearing Variables   Occasionally, you may want to get rid of a variable that you created. To clear the value of a variable, set the variable to null. A null is an empty or blank value. For example,

```
$ echo $TARGET
summary
$ TARGET=
$ echo $TARGET

$
```

Giving the variable a value of null does not remove the variable itself, only its value. To actually remove the variable, use the **unset** command, as in

```
$ unset TARGET
```

▶**BERKELEY VERSION** In Berkeley UNIX, the **unset** command only removes the variable's value.

The readonly Command With the **readonly** command, you can ensure that the value of a variable cannot be changed. This can prevent a variable from being accidentally changed. You must assign a value to a variable before you declare it to be read-only, since it cannot be changed afterward. For example,

```
$ MANUAL=coatings
$ readonly MANUAL
$ MANUAL=transport
MANUAL: is read only
```

▶**TIP** With multiple arguments, the **readonly** command, like many UNIX commands, acts on each of the arguments. For instance, the command

```
$ readonly CLIENT MANUAL
```

makes both variables read-only.

The **readonly** command without arguments displays a list of all read-only user variables.

```
$ readonly
readonly CLIENT
readonly MANUAL
```

▶**NOTE** Read-only *environment* variables are also displayed by the **readonly** command, but the special read-only shell variables are not.

The export Command User variables are ordinarily accessible only within the shell in which they were created. They are not accessible to subshells you enter unless you tell UNIX to make them available. Use the **export** command to make variables available outside of the shell in which they were created. The **export** command passes a copy of the variable to the environment of the new subshell.

```
$ MODEL=luxury
$ echo $MODEL
luxury
$ sh
$ echo $MODEL

$
```

When you attempt to display the value of a variable that has not been declared, it displays nothing; the value of an undeclared variable is a null string. If you use the **export** command, you can reference the variable from a subshell.

```
$ MODEL=luxury
$ export MODEL
$ echo $MODEL
luxury
$ sh
$ echo $MODEL
luxury
```

You would not often run one shell from another as in the example. However, when you execute a shell script, a new shell is started that interprets the commands in the script one after another. Therefore, a variable assigned in a shell may not be accessible from within a shell script. In fact, a variable assigned in one shell script may not be accessible from another shell script. The following example demonstrates the use of the **export** command with the shell script **getcity**:

```
$ cat getcity
:
echo "City is: $CITY"

$ CITY=Chicago
$ getcity
City is:
$ export CITY
$ getcity
City is: Chicago
```

Since the old shell passes a copy of the variable to the environment of the new shell (the shell interpreting the shell script), reassignment of the variable within the new shell will not affect the variable within the old shell, since only the copy is modified. For example, the shell script **newcity** changes the value of the variable **CITY** created outside the shell script (and proves it by printing the new value), but the change has no effect outside of the script.

```
$ cat newcity
:
CITY="New Orleans"
echo "New city is: $CITY"

$ CITY=Chicago
$ echo $CITY
Chicago
$ export CITY
$ newcity
New city is: New Orleans
$ echo $CITY
Chicago
```

The read Command   With the **read** command, the script can prompt the user for information and store the input in a user variable. The **read** command reads one line from standard input and assigns the line to one or more variables. The next example illustrates user input with the **read** command:

```
$ read STATE
California
$ echo $STATE
California
```

You can use **read** in a shell script, as in the following shell script **getstate**:

```
$ cat getstate
:
echo "Enter state: \c"
read STATE
```

```
echo "State: $STATE"

$ getstate
Enter state: Montana
State: Montana
```

▶**NOTE** The variable reference is in quotes because you cannot antici-
pate what the user will type (even if you did ask specifically for a state).
The user may type a *, a ?, or multiple spaces. Without the quotes
around the variable reference, the results might surprise the unsuspect-
ing user. The **\c** prevents the **echo** command from generating a new
line.

You can read words into more than one variable by supplying the
read command with multiple arguments. The **read** command assigns
one word to each variable, except the last variable, which is assigned the
remaining words. In the following example, the shell script **readaddr**
reads user input, assigns it to several variables, and prints the result:

```
$ cat getaddr
echo "Input street address: \c"
read HOUSE STREET
echo "House number: $HOUSE"
echo "Street name: $STREET"

$ getaddr
Input street address: 12485 Walnut
House number: 12485
Street name: Walnut
$ getaddr
Input street address: 447 East Santa Barbara Ave
House number: 447
Street name: East Santa Barbara Ave
```

Shell Variables

The shell variables are automatically set by the shell; they include
command-line arguments, process numbers, exit status, and environment variables.

Command-Line Arguments   The shell stores each word of the command line in variables **$0** to **$9**. Since these variables specify the position of the word on the command line, they are called *positional parameters*. The variable **$0** typically holds the name of the calling program, since it is usually the first word of the command line. Variables **$1** through **$9** hold up to nine arguments of the calling program. The following example uses a shell script **getargs** to demonstrate the positional parameters:

```
$ cat getargs
:
echo Calling program: $0
echo Argument 1: $1
echo Argument 2: $2
echo Argument 3: $3

$ getargs where art thou Romeo
Calling program: getargs
Argument 1: where
Argument 2: art
Argument 3: thou
$ getargs intractable situation
Calling program: getargs
Argument 1: intractable
Argument 2: situation
Argument 3:
```

Another positional parameter you may find useful is the **$*** variable. It gives all of the command-line arguments, not just the first nine. Its best use is to pass the parameters of a shell script to another command, as the script **lookat** demonstrates:

```
$ cat lookat
:
echo Looking at $*:
cat $*

$ lookat file1 file2
Looking at file1 file2:
contents of file one
contents of file two
```

The variable **$#** is not really a positional parameter, but is related. It gives the number of parameters on the command line, as follows:

```
$ cat argnum
:
echo has $# arguments.

$ argnum one two three
has 3 arguments.
```

▶**NOTE**   The **set** command allows you to set the values of the positional parameters from within a script. The arguments that follow the **set** command set the command-line argument variables (**$1** to **$9**). For example, the line

```
set one two
```

sets the positional parameters **$1** and **$2** to one and two, respectively, regardless of their previous values.

Process Identification Numbers   The **$$** variable holds the process identification number of the current shell. For example,

```
$ echo $$
5071
$ ps
  PID TTY  TIME COMMAND
 5071 i1a  0:00 sh
 5072 i1a  0:00 ps
```

The **$$** variable is often used by shell scripts to create unique temporary file names. Since no other process can share the same process number, using the process number as part of a file name ensures that there will be no file name conflicts. The shell script in the following example uses a temporary file to append a file **report** to text from the standard input. The script creates a temporary file from the standard input, combines it with **report**, and sends it to the standard output. Finally, it deletes the temporary file it created.

```
$ cat add2top
:
# add2top
#   Appends "report" to top of the standard input
#   using temporary file
#
cat >> tmp$$
cat report tmp$$
rm tmp$$
```

The **$!** variable holds the process identification number of the last process that you ran in the background. The following example runs **sleep** as a background process, prints the process number, and kills the process using the **$!** variable:

```
$ sleep 60 &
5160
$ echo $!
5160
$ kill -9 $!
5160 Killed
```

Exit Status   The **$?** variable holds the exit status of the last command executed. When a process ends, naturally or otherwise, it returns an *exit status* (sometimes called a *condition code* or *return code*) to the parent process. Typically, a nonzero exit code indicates that the command failed and a zero indicates that the command was successful. You can return an exit status from your shell scripts with the **exit** command. The exit status is covered in detail in the section "Shell Programming."

Environment Variables   Most of the environment variables are either inherited with the environment or assigned by the shell when it is started. You can change these values from the command line or in your **.profile** file, as described in the section "Modifying Your Environment."

Since you want these variables to apply to all the subshells you enter, the environment variables are almost always exported with the **export** command.

■ **HOME**   Stores the location of home directory. You are placed in your home directory when you first log in. It is originally set by the system administrator when your account is created. The following example displays the **HOME** variable:

```
$ echo $HOME
/usr/schumann
```

■ **PATH**   Determines the *search path* that the shell uses to find a file or command you have given. The search path is a list of directories in which the shell will search sequentially in an attempt to find your file or command.

When you log in, the shell assigns a default value to the **PATH** variable. On most systems, **/bin** and **/usr/bin** are the standard directories for holding utilities and must, therefore, be included in the search path.

Reset the search path by changing the value of the **PATH** variable. The following example tells the shell to look for files first in **/bin**, then in **/usr/bin**, in **/usr/schumann/bin**, and finally in the current directory where each directory in the search path is followed by a colon:

```
$ PATH=/bin:/usr/bin:/usr/schumann/bin:
```

■ **PS1**   Specifies the Bourne shell prompt. Changing the value of this variable changes the appearance of the prompt, which is initially set to a dollar sign followed by a space.

If you are working on more than one machine from the same terminal, it is sometimes difficult to remember which machine you are currently logged onto. You can change the prompt to help keep track of which machine you are connected to. For example, to change the prompt to the machine name "violet," use

```
$ PS1="violet$ "
violet$
```

■ **PS2**   Defines the secondary prompt (the default is >).

■ **MAIL**   Specifies the name of the file in which your mail is stored (the default is **/usr/mail/***login* or **/usr/spool/mail/***login*).

■ **MAILCHECK**   Specifies how often (in seconds) the shell will check for the arrival of mail in the files specified by **MAIL** and **MAILPATH** (the default is 600 seconds, or 10 minutes).

■ **MAILPATH**   Contains a list of file names. The shell informs you if mail arrives in any of the specified files. The file names in the list are separated by colons. If you follow any file name in the list with a percent sign and a message, the shell will print that message if mail arrives in that file.

■ **SHELL**   Specifies the default shell in your environment. This must be set before you configure your terminal with the **tset** command. See the section "Setting Terminal Options."

■ **TERM**   Identifies your terminal type. You must set this variable if you are editing with the **vi** editor. This variable also must be set before you configure your terminal with **tset**.

■ **TERMCAP**   Contains information about your terminal. It is usually set by **tset** in your **.profile**.

■ **TERMINFO**   Specifies the directory that contains information about your terminal.

■ **TZ**   Defines the time zone (default is **EST5EDT**).

Shell Programming

The shell programming language offers the following features:

■ Comments allow you to document your shell scripts.

■ The here document allows you to include within the shell script lines to be redirected to the input of a command in the script.

■ The **exit** command lets you terminate a script and return an exit status to the calling program.

■ The conditional commands, **if** and **case**, execute a set of commands only if particular conditions are met.

■ The looping commands, **for** and **while**, repeatedly execute a set of commands in a loop.

■ The **break** command allows a script to exit unconditionally from a loop, while the **continue** command allows the script to skip to the top of a loop.

Comments

You can enter a comment in your shell script with the pound sign (**#**). Put the pound sign at the beginning of a line to have the line ignored by the shell. Put the pound sign after a command and the remainder of the line will be ignored. For example, the comments in the following shell script are preceded by the pound sign:

```
$ cat mkreminder
:
# mkreminder
#   This script allows you to enter a reminder
#   created:    Rodger Lee      12 April 1988
#   modified:   Karri Lamport   26 March 1990
#
echo "Enter reminder (end w/CTRL-D):"   # prompt for reminder
cat >> $HOME/.reminder  # gets input
```

This simple script may not need such elaborate documentation. However, as a script grows in size and complexity, it becomes more and more important to know who created it, who modified it, what the script does, and how it does it. Comments are essential to good programming. The scripts you write will often be modified and maintained by other people, who will need your comments to understand your script.

▶**NOTE** Most of the useful shell scripts in this chapter are commented, although for simplicity's sake the commenting is sparse.

The Here Document

A *here document* allows you to redirect the input of a command in a shell script to lines that you place within the shell script itself. Thus, you can provide input to a command without having to use a separate file. It is called the here document because the input is *here,* within the shell script, not *there,* in another file.

The beginning of a here document consists of the redirection symbol << followed by a delimiter. The delimiter can be one or more characters and tells the shell where the here document begins and ends. The delimeter follows the text of the here document on a line by itself. The following shell script redirects the here document to the **grep** command, and uses **+++** as the delimiter:

```
$ cat phone
:
# phone
#    Lookup phone number
#
grep -i "$1" <<+++
Dave Crockett      342 4279
Pacific Data       425 3821   contact: Bill West
Ross Olivera       425 4279
Mike Chon          448 2455   until April
Garage Barbecue    458 4003   hours: 10-8 M-F 10-12 F-S
Jessica Sedois     338 4647   or 338 2432
+++
$ phone jess
Jessica Sedois     338 4647   or 338 2432
```

Note that within a here document, the shell continues to perform variable substitution and substitution for commands in backquotes.

Exit Status

Most shell commands return an exit status (sometimes called a condition code or return code) to the shell when they finish. It tells the shell whether the command failed or succeeded. A nonzero exit status usually indicates that the command failed and a zero indicates that the command succeeded. The exit status will become increasingly important as you learn about conditional commands and looping commands.

The $? Variable   You can determine the exit status of the last command executed with the $? variable. The following example uses the $? variable to display both a successful and an unsuccessful exit status:

```
$ cat test
I am a test file.
I may be dull, but I do my job
if I am successful.

$ grep "successful" test
if I am successful.
$ echo $?
0
$ grep "failed" test
$ echo $?
1
```

The exit Command   You can use the **exit** command either to terminate a shell script before the end and to make your shell scripts return exit codes.

When the shell encounters an **exit** command in a shell script, the script is terminated.

Normally, a shell script returns the exit status of the last command executed in the shell script. When the **exit** command followed by a number appears in a shell script, the shell script is terminated and the number is returned as the exit status. The following example illustrates the **exit** command:

```
$ cat err
echo "err: general failure."
exit 1

$ err
err: general failure.
$ echo $?
1
```

▶**NOTE** The **exit** command is especially useful with the **if..then** construction, discussed under "Conditional Commands." You can use the **if..then** construction in a script to check that conditions are met. If the conditions are not met, the **exit** command can terminate the script and return an unsuccessful exit code.

The test Command The **test** command tests certain conditions and returns the results in the form of an exit status. If the condition is true, the **test** command returns a zero exit status. If the condition is false, it returns a nonzero value. The **test** command is used primarily with the **if..then**, **while..do**, and **until..do** constructions. For example, the **test** command is used here to test the equality of two strings:

```
$ test "one" = "two"
$ echo $?
1
```

Here are the options for the **test** command:

Parentheses

( )   Change the order of operation. Also for
                                 grouping

Logical Operators

!   Negation
-a   AND
-o   OR

Strings

-z *s1*	True if the length of string *s1* is zero
-n *s1*	True if the length of string *s1* is nonzero
s1 = *s2*	True if strings *s1* and *s2* are identical
s1 != *s2*	True if strings *s1* and *s2* are *not* identical

Numbers

n1 **-eq** *n2*	True if the integers *n1* and *n2* are algebraically equal. The following operators may be substituted for **-eq**
n1 **-ne** *n2*	Not equal
n1 **-gt** *n2*	Greater than
n1 **-ge** *n2*	Greater than or equal
n1 **-lt** *n2*	Less than
n1 **-le** *n2*	Less than or equal

Files

-r *file*	True if *file* exists and is readable
-w *file*	True if *file* exists and is writable
-x *file*	True if *file* exists and is executable
-f *file*	True if *file* exists and is a regular *file*
-d *file*	True if *file* exists and is a directory
-s *file*	True if *file* exists and is not empty

When used in a conditional or looping construction, the **test** command can be abbreviated with square brackets ([ ]). Place square brackets around what would be the options or arguments to the **test** command. Leave spaces between the arguments and the brackets or **test** will not work. For example, the following line from a shell script

```
if test -s .reminder
```

might appear as

```
if [ -s .reminder ]
```

Conditional Commands

The idea behind a *conditional command* is that it only executes if a certain condition is met. The **if..then** construction is the simplest of these commands, while the **if..then..else**, **if..then..elif**, and **case..esac** constructions are more complicated.

The if..then Construction   The **if..then** construction works like this: *if* some condition is met, *then* execute the following commands. It has this format:

```
if test-command
  then
      commands
fi
```

The *if* and *then* statements must appear on separate lines. The **fi** statement marks the end of the **if..then** construction ("fi" is "if" spelled backward).

The shell will execute the commands following **then** only if the last command following **if** returns a true or nonzero exit status.

▶**NOTE**   You can use the **test** command with the **if..then** construction, as well as with other conditional commands, to return an exit status based on the results of a test. You can employ the square brackets ([ ]) as a synonym for the **test** command (each bracket preceded and followed by a space).

The following shell script illustrates the **if..then** construction by using **test** (implicitly with the square brackets) to check that an argument was specified:

```
$ cat format
:
# format
#   nroff a file with the mm macros
```

```
#
# -z option true if string is length zero
if [ -z $1 ]
    then
        echo "format: No filename specified." 1>&2
        echo "Usage: format [file]" 1>&2
        exit 1
fi
nroff -mm $*
```

▶**NOTE** The symbol **1 > &2** redirects the *standard output* to the *standard error.* If you redirected the standard output of the **format** script to a file, the error message would also be redirected and would not print on your terminal. Therefore, you need to redirect the error message to the standard error, which is not affected by output redirection. See the section "Redirecting Standard Error."

The if..then..else Construction The **if..then..else** construction is simply this: *if* some condition is met, *then* execute one set of commands, or *else,* if the condition is not met, execute another set of commands. It has the following format:

if *test-command*
   then
      commands
   else
      commands
fi

The **fi** statement ends the **if..then..else** construction.

    The following shell script illustrates the **if..then..else** construction, using **test** to check if the user's system mail box contains mail:

```
$ cat mailchk
:
# mailchk
#   check if mail has arrived
#
# -s option true if file not empty
if [ -s "$MAIL" ]
    then
```

```
        echo "You have mail, and here it is!"
        mail
    else
        echo "So sorry, maybe later we'll have something for you."
fi
```

The if..then..elif Construction The **if..then..elif** construction is like the **if..then..else** construction, but it combines the **else** and another **if..then** into a single statement: *if* some condition is met, *then* execute one set of commands, or *else,* if the condition is not met, consider another *if* statement with another condition. The statement **elif** is a combination of **else** and **if**. This structure allows you to create a nested set of **if..then..else** constructions. It has the following format:

if *test-command*
   then
      commands
   elif
      test-commands
   then
      commands
fi

The shell script **copy** demonstrates **if..then..elif**:

```
$ cat copy
:
# copy
#    copy a file to directory
#
# -f option true if file is regular file
# -d option true if file is directory
#  ! option negates expression
if [ ! -f $1 ]
    then
        echo "copy: $1 is not a regular file."
    elif [ ! -d $2 ]
    then
        echo "copy: $2 is not a directory."
```

```
    else
        cp $1 $2
fi
```

The case..esac Construction The **case..esac** construction has a multiple-choice format that matches one of several patterns and executes a corresponding set of commands. It has the format

case *word* **in**
    pattern1)
       commands

    ;;
    pattern2)
       commands

    ;;
    pattern3)
       commands

    ;;
esac

Each pattern must be followed by a right parenthesis. The ;; symbol marks the end of a set of commands for a particular branch of the **case..esac** structure. The **esac** statement marks the end of the **case..esac** construction ("esac" is "case" spelled backward).

The asterisk (*) matches any string of characters. It is often used as the last pattern in the **case..esac** structure, to match input that does not match any other pattern. This provides a useful way to detect erroneous or unexpected input.

Other patterns that you can specify are the characters ?, [], and l. The question mark matches any single character. The square brackets match any single character contained within the brackets. A hyphen between two characters within the brackets specifies a range of characters. The vertical bar (l) separates alternate choices of the **case..esac** construction. The input may match either of the patterns separated by the vertical bar.

The following shell script **hint** illustrates the **case..esac** construction and the available patterns:

```
$ cat hint
:
# hint
```

```
#   Print a hint on directory command usage
#
case $1 in
    pwd|PWD)
        echo "PWD - Print Working Directory Name"
        echo "usage: pwd" ;;
    cd|CD)
        echo "CD - Change Directory"
        echo "usage: cd [directory]" ;;
    mkdir|MKDIR)
        echo "MKDIR - Create Specified Directories"
        echo "usage: mkdir dirnames" ;;
    rmdir|RMDIR)
        echo "RMDIR - Remove Empty Directories"
        echo "usage: rmdir directories" ;;
    *)
        echo "HINT - Explain a Message or Command"
        echo "usage: hint [command]" ;;
esac
```

Looping Commands

Normally, commands will execute one after another from the top to the bottom of a shell script. The conditional commands are one way of altering the shell's path through the script; the *looping commands* are another. The **for, while,** and **until** loops allow a shell script to execute a command or set of commands several times.

The for..in Loop   The **for..in** loop executes a set of commands once for each member of a list. It has the format

for *variable*
    in *argument-list*
do
    commands
done

For each repetition of the loop, the next member of the list is assigned to the variable given after the **for** statement. You can use this variable within the commands of the loop, as in the following example:

```
$ cat receipts
:
# receipts
#   record day's cash receipts in databases
#
echo "Input today's cash totals:"
read cash
for DATABASE
   in `ls *db`
do
   echo `date +"%a %d %h"` "cash receipts: $cash" >> $DATABASE
done
```

The for Loop   The **for** loop, similar to the **for..in** loop, executes a set of commands once for each argument of the command line. It has the format

for *variable*
do
   commands
done

For each repetition of the loop, the next argument of the command line is assigned to the variable after the **for** statement. This variable can be used anywhere within the commands of the loop. The following example shows the use of the **for** loop:

```
$ cat vis
:
# vis
#   edit several files with the visual editor
#
for FILE
do
   edit "Editing $file"
   vi $FILE
done
```

The while..do Loop   Another looping command, the **while..do** loop, repeatedly executes a set of commands *while* some particular condition is met. It has the following format:

```
while test-command
    do
        commands
done
```

The shell will execute the commands following **do** as long as the last command following **while** returns a true or nonzero exit status.

▶ **NOTE**   You can use the **test** command with the **while..do** loop to return an exit status based on the results of a test. You can use the square brackets ([ ]) as a synonym for the **test** command (again, surround each bracket by spaces).

The following shell script illustrates the **while..do** loop by using **test** (specified implicitly with the square brackets) to test whether the user entered an empty line:

```
$ cat add
:
# add
#    Add text to a file
#
echo "Enter addendum (end w/empty line):"
INPUT=" "
while [ -n "$INPUT" ]
    do
        read INPUT
        echo $INPUT >> $1
done
```

The until..do Loop   The **until..do** and **while..do** loops are very similar. Whereas the **while..do** loop repeats its commands *while* some particular condition is met, the **until..do** loop repeats its commands *until* some particular condition is met. The difference is in what causes **until** and **while** loops to stop looping. The conditions specified in a **while** loop indicate the conditions under which the loop is to repeat. The conditions specified in an **until** loop indicate the conditions at which the loop is to stop. The **until..do** loop has the following format:

until *test-command*
   do
      commands
done

The shell will execute the commands following **do** until the last command following **until** returns a true or nonzero exit status.

    The following shell script illustrates the **until..do** loop. Before executing a potentially dangerous command, the script verifies the action with the user. Using **until..do**, it repeats the verification until it gets a definitive **y** or **n**.

```
$ cat deldir
:
# deldir
#   delete a directory (full or not)
#
IN=""
until [ "$IN" = "y" -o "$IN" = "n" ]
    do
        echo "Deldir: $1"
        echo "Are you sure? \c"
        read IN
done
if [ $IN = "y" ]
    then
        rm -r $1
fi
```

Unconditional Commands:
break and continue

You can interrupt a **for, while,** or **until** loop with a **break** or **continue** command. The **break** command exits the loop completely, transferring control to the command after the **done** statement. The **continue** command immediately begins the next execution of the loop, transferring control to the **done** statement, which continues the loop.

The **break** command is useful for exiting a loop when something comes up that was not originally in the loop condition. For example, if you create a loop that repeats a number of times, you may want to exit the loop prematurely if certain input is received (a script that asks for a password, perhaps). You can exit the loop prematurely with **break**.

The **continue** command is useful for skipping to the top of a loop when you do not want the remainder of the loop executed. For example, you might have a loop that executes once for each file in an argument list, and one of the files in the list is not found. Since you do not want to execute the remainder of the loop for a nonexistent file, you can skip to the top of the loop and process the next file. Use **continue** to immediately jump to the top of the loop.

Redirecting Standard Error

In Chapter 5, "UNIX Command-Line Fundamentals," you learned how to redirect the standard input and output. To redirect the standard output of a command such as **head**, use the output redirection symbol **>**, as in

```
$ head news > headline
```

In the Bourne shell, you can also use **1>** to redirect the standard output. The next example does the same thing as the previous example:

```
$ head news 1> headline
```

In addition to the standard output, many commands produce output to what is called the standard error—by default, your terminal screen. A command can send error messages to the standard error to prevent them from becoming mixed up with the text it sends to the standard output. As with the standard output, the shell sends the standard error to your terminal unless you redirect it. If you redirect the standard output with >, commands will still send their error messages to your terminal. For example, if you redirect the standard output of **cat**, as in

```
$ cat a b > file1
```

and the file **b** doesn't exist, you will see an error message, although the output of **cat** (that is, the contents of file **a**) has been redirected to **file1**:

```
$ cat a b > file1
cat: cannot open b
$ cat file1
The contents of a
$
```

To capture the standard error output, use **2 >**. For example, to send the standard error of the **cat** command to a file named **file2**, use

```
$ cat a b 2> file2
The contents of a
$ cat file2
cat: cannot open b
$
```

For example, to send the standard output of **cat** to **file1** and the standard error to **file2**, use

```
$ cat a b 1> file1 2> file2
$ cat file1
The contents of a
$ cat file2
cat: cannot open b
$
```

You may sometimes want to redirect the standard output to the standard error. This is useful if you create shell scripts that are used as filters or whose output is commonly redirected. You can redirect standard output to the standard error with the sequence **1>&2**. The following shell script redirects to the standard error the output of the **echo** command:

```
$ cat prep
:
# prep -- format a file, filename.txt
#
if [ $1 = "" ]
   then
       echo "prep: No filename specified." 1>&2
       exit 1
fi
nroff -mm $1.txt

$ prep > report.n
prep: No filename specified.
```

Although the standard output of the script is redirected to the file **report.n**, **prep** can still display an error message. The error message has been sent to the standard error, which is displayed at the terminal even if the standard output has been redirected.

Modifying Your Environment

If the Bourne shell is your login shell, a shell script in your home directory called **.profile** runs each time you log in. The **.profile** file is responsible for setting much of your environment, such as your terminal type, home directory, and search path. You can modify your **.profile** to customize your environment or alter the actions taken when you log in.

Modifying Your .profile

Because **.profile** is a regular shell script (a text file), you should have no problem changing it with an editor such as **vi**. On some systems, you can edit this file yourself; on others, the system administrator must do it for you. Since the **.profile** is a dot file, it does not ordinarily appear when you type **ls**. To move to your home directory and see **.profile**, type

```
$ cd
$ ls -l .profile
```

For example, you might like your **.profile** to print a list of personal reminders (see the shell scripts **reminder** and **reminders** earlier in this chapter). If you keep the personal reminders in a file named **.reminder** in your home directory, you might want to append the following lines to your **.profile**:

```
# check for .reminder file and display it if there.
if [ -s $HOME/.reminder ]
    then
        reminder
fi
```

▶**TIP**   Before you change your **.profile**, you should make a copy of it for safekeeping.

Environment Variables

The *shell environment variables* determine your environment and are often set in your **.profile** file. (Environment variables were discussed in detail earlier in this chapter.) You can change various aspects of your environment by editing the values assigned to them in the **.profile** file. The following example shows a **.profile** in which various environment variables are set:

```
:
# .profile
#    Set environment variables
#
# set default shell
SHELL=/bin/sh
# set terminal type
```

```
TERM=tvi920
# set home directory
HOME=/u/schumann
# set search path
PATH=.$HOME:$HOME/bin:/bin:/usr/bin:/etc
# set mail file
MAIL=/usr/spool/mail/schumann
# set mail check
MAILCHECK=0
# set prompt
PS1="BETA $ "
# set timezone
TZ=PST8PDT
# export all environment variables
export SHELL HOME PATH MAIL MAILCHECK PS1 TZ
```

You can change these environment variables with an editor.

Setting Terminal Options

If you plan to use a full-screen program, such as the **vi** editor, the system must know what type of terminal you are using. Since the system needs to know this each time you log in, you should set your terminal type in your **.profile**.

For example, the following lines in your **.profile** automatically set your terminal type when you log in:

```
SHELL=/bin/sh
TERM=wy50
eval `tset -s`
```

In place of **wy50**, set the **TERM** variable to the code for your terminal.

►**NOTE** The **tset** command uses the values of the **SHELL** and **TERM** variables. Make sure that they are set and exported before the **tset** command is executed.

Command	Action
:	Null command
.	Execute a program or script as part of the current process
`` `command` ``	Replace with the output of *command*
break	Exit from loop
cd	Change current directory
continue	Start with next repetition of loop
echo	Echo arguments (System V only)
eval	Scan and evaluate the command line
exec	Execute a command in place of the current process
exit	Exit from the current shell or script
export	Make a variable available to subshells and scripts
getopts	Parse arguments to a shell script (System V only)
hash	Remember the search path of a command (System V only)
newgrp	Change the user's group
pwd	Print the current (working) directory (System V only)
read	Read a line from the standard output to a variable
readonly	Make it impossible to change a variable or display read-only variables
return	Exit from a function with a return value (System V only)
set	Set variables or command-line parameters or display all variables
shift	Shift each command-line parameter to the next lower parameter
test	Evaluate conditional expressions (System V only)
times	Display times
trap	Trap a signal
type	Display how each argument should be interpreted as a command (System V only)
ulimit	Limit the size of files written by the shell (System V only)
umask	File-creation mask
unset	Remove a variable or function (System V only)
wait	Wait for a background process to terminate

Table 9-1.   *The Bourne Shell Built-in Commands*

If you regularly log in from several different terminal types, put the following line in your **.profile** instead:

```
eval `tset -s -m :?wy50`
```

When you log in, the shell will display the following:

```
term=(wy50)
```

You may press RETURN to accept the default terminal type or type the code for your terminal and press RETURN.

To learn more about **tset**, see the *UNIX User's Reference Manual*.

The commands in Table 9-1 are built into the Bourne shell.

The Bourne shell is both a user interface and a programming language. As a user interface, the shell executes your commands as you type them at the prompt. As a programming language, the shell executes commands from a file called a shell script. Besides the usual command-line commands, shell scripts allow you to alter the flow of control with conditional and looping constructions. Various types of variables are available to the shell script programmer: user variables, environment variables, and read-only shell variables. By setting the environment variables and modifying the **.profile** file, you can tailor your environment to your needs.

10 *The C Shell*

In many respects, the C shell is like the Bourne shell. It is both a command interpreter and a programming language. It has user-created variables and shell variables. It can run shell scripts and has a complete shell programming language with conditional and looping commands. In addition, it has files with which you can automatically control your environment when you log in.

However, the C shell offers you more features than the Bourne shell. The *history* feature allows you to reexecute and manipulate previous commands. The *alias* feature lets you define new commands. The C shell on Berkeley systems also brings you *job control*, which allows you to suspend processes, place them in the background, or bring them back to the foreground. These features make the C shell the first choice of many UNIX users, although, unfortunately, the C shell is not supplied with all versions of UNIX.

On the command line, the C shell ordinarily uses the percent sign (%) as a prompt (although it is often changed), while the Bourne shell uses the dollar sign prompt.

To enter the C shell from the Bourne shell, type the command **csh** at the command line, as in the following example:

```
$ csh
%
```

If, for instance, your login shell is the Bourne shell and you want this login session to use the C shell, use the **exec** command to run the specified command in place of the current shell, as follows:

```
$ ps
   PID TTY  TIME COMMAND
   295 i1a  0:03 sh
   344 i1a  0:05 vi
$ exec csh
% ps
   PID TTY  TIME COMMAND
   295 i1a  0:03 csh
   344 i1a  0:05 vi
```

To leave the C shell, use either the **logout** command in your login shell or **exit** in other shells. To prevent you from logging out by mistake, if you type **logout** from a shell other than your login shell, you will get an error.

Unique Features to the Shell

The C shell is the first choice of many users because it offers features that are unavailable in the Bourne shell. These features are covered in the following sections.

The History Feature

Starting when you log in, the C shell automatically keeps a list of previous commands. The history feature allows you to reexecute and manipulate the commands in this list. You can use the history list to make minor changes to similar commands, to correct command-line mistakes, or to keep a record of what you have done.

The shell assigns a number to each command you issue. The first command issued is number one and subsequent commands are numbered sequentially. A command in the history list is also called an *event* and the number associated with each event is called the *event number*.

If you type **history** on the command line, the shell displays all commands in the history list. For example,

```
% history
    24   time
    25   cat /u/bin/dates
    26   deadline
    27   vi .login
    28   c 11
    29   pwd
    30   ls -l
    31   c 10
    32   ch 10
    33   prep -x c10 &
    34   kill 28617
    35   ps
    36   ls
    37   rm c10*
    38   prep -x ch10 &
    39   c 11
    40   vi outline
    41   cd
    42   vi .exrc
    43   history
```

The history list has a default length of about 20. It only holds the number of commands specified by the **history** environment variable. As more commands are executed and added to the list, the earliest commands will be removed from the history list and lost. You can change the number of commands saved in the history list with the **history** variable. However, if the history list is too long, your shell may run out of memory. The following shell command sets the history list to a length of 100:

```
% set history = 100
```

The **set** command associates a value with a variable and will be covered in the "Variables" section in this chapter.

▶**TIP** You can set the **history** variable in your **.cshrc** file to automatically set the size of the history list every time you enter a shell (see the section "Modifying Your Environment").

On some systems, you can automatically save your history list between login sessions by assigning a value to the **savehist** environment variable. This way, you may log out and log in and the commands in your history list from the first login session will be available to you in the second. The value that you give the **savehist** variable is the number of commands from the history list that are saved. For example, the following command tells the C shell to save the previous 25 commands when you log out:

```
% set savehist = 25
```

The commands are saved in your home directory in a hidden dot file called **.history**.

▶**TIP** You can also set the **savehist** variable in the **.cshrc** file to set automatically the number of history list entries saved when you log out.

Reexecuting Commands The history feature lets you reexecute any command in the history list. You can also reference the previous command (even if there is no history list) by its event number, by its position relative to the current event, or by text within the command.

The exclamation point (!) usually tells the C shell to activate the history feature and reexecute a command.

▶**NOTE** You may want to use the exclamation point in another context (network addressing, for example, which is covered in Chapter 8). To tell the shell not to perform history substitution, you must precede each exclamation point that is not history-related with a backslash (\).

The Previous Command   You can reexecute the previous command with the following command:

```
% !!
```

The shell substitutes every occurrence of !! on the command line with the text of the previous command. After substitution, the shell will usually echo the resulting command, as shown here:

```
% cat test.1
This is the contents of test.1
% !!
cat test.1
This is the contents of test.1
```

Although you will often use !! alone to repeat the previous command, other text may appear on the command line with !!. If text precedes or follows !!, the shell will substitute the previous command in the proper place. In the following example, the previous command is substituted for !!:

```
% cat test.1 test.2
This is the contents of test.1
This is the contents of test.2
% !! > test.both
cat test.1 test.2 > test.both
```

Event Numbers   Each command you type on the command line is assigned a sequential number, called an event number, in the history list. You can use an event number to reference a command deep in the history list. An exclamation point followed by a number specifies a particular event and is called an *event specification*. If the event is in the history list, the shell substitutes the command on the command line. The

following example specifies a command several events into the history
list:

```
% history
    44  vi remind
    45  remind &
    46  w -q
    47  ps
    48  history
% !46
w -q
  7:28pm  up 15 days,  1:53,  3 users
User      Tty    Idle  What
schumann ila            w
randy3    ilc      21  vi
```

A negative number following an exclamation point specifies an event
preceding the current event number. The next example specifies a
command three events back in the history list:

```
% history
    74  /u/bin/randcall
    75  randcall
    76  ps
    77  csh -v remind
    78  history
% !-3
ps
   PID TTY  TIME COMMAND
 29858 ila  0:11 csh
  2850 ila  0:00 ps
```

Event Text   You can also reference previous commands by mentioning
text within the command. The shell searches for the most recent event
that matches the pattern you specify. Text following an exclamation
point references the most recent command that begins with the given
pattern text, as shown here:

```
% history
    71  rm xx*
    72  csplit fingers 5 10
```

```
    73  ls
    74  more xx*
    75  history
% !r
rm xx*
```

You can use the question mark (?) as a wildcard character in history substitution. The ? matches any number of characters in the command text. If you surround the pattern text with question marks, the shell will match the most recent command containing the text. The following example reexecutes the most recent command matching the pattern **reports**:

```
% history
    58  mail peche
    59  vi tables
    60  ls reports/
    61  prep tables
    62  history
% !?reports?
ls reports/
final       final.asc  final.fig
```

Words Within Events   You can reference the individual words of a command line stored in the history list. The words are numbered sequentially, with the first command on the line numbered 0. To specify a particular word in the command, follow the event specification with a colon and the number of the word in the command. For example, to specify the second word (excluding the initial command, which is numbered 0) of event number 43 in the history list, enter

```
% !43:2
```

You can specify a range of words by separating two numbers by a hyphen. You can specify the first word of a previous command with a carat (^) and the last word by a dollar sign ($). The following examples use the **echo** command to print the first through third words, the first word, and the last word of previous commands:

```
% history
     97  vi table.1 table.2
     98  vi table.3
     99  cat table.1 table.2 table.3 > tables
    100  more tab*
    101  history
% echo "!99:1-3"
echo "table.1 table.2 table.3"
table.1 table.2 table.3
% echo "!97:^"
echo "table.1"
table.1
% echo "!100:$"
echo "tab*"
tab*
```

You can reference individual words in previous commands with any method of event specification, as well as by event number. You can specify particular words in the previous command with !! followed by a colon and the word specification, as in

```
% !!:2
```

You can reference words matching a particular pattern with text after the exclamation point, as in

```
% !cat:^-3
```

Modifying Previous Events   You can modify a previous command using the history mechanism. If you make a mistake in a complex command, it is easier to correct the mistake than to retype the entire command. If you execute a series of commands, each with only minor differences, it is easier to modify a few parameters than to type a similar command over and over again.

You can fix a typo in the previous command by typing a caret (^), the mistyped text, another caret, and the replacement text. The following example corrects a mistake in the previous command:

```
% nroof -mm -rL60 -rW60 -r05 report.asc
nroof: Command not found.
% ^nroof^nroff
nroff -mm -rL60 -rW60 -r05 report.asc
```

The caret notation is actually a convenient shorthand. Here is a more general way to write the preceding event modification:

```
% !!:s/nroof/nroff/
```

The **s** modifier stands for substitute. You can modify a previous command by following an event specification with a colon and any one of the following modifiers:

r (root)	Removes the file name extension of a file name
h (head)	Removes the last element of a pathname
t (tail)	Removes all but the last element of a pathname
p (print)	Prints but does not execute the modified event
q (quote)	Quotes the modified event and prevents its further modification
s/*old/new/* (substitute)	Substitutes *new* for *old*
gs/*old/new/* (global substitution)	Substitutes *new* for *old* wherever it occurs within the command

As with the **vi** substitution command, an ampersand (**&**) in the *new* string of a history substitution is replaced with the *old* string. If the *old* string of a history substitution is null (as in **s//new/**), a previous *old* string is used.

You can use these event modifications in combination, separated by colons. Each new modifier acts on the results returned by the previous modifier. Furthermore, you can use these event modifications in combination with any event specification, including the specification of particular words. This flexibility makes history tremendously powerful.

Alias

With the C shell, you can create a whole set of simple commands. These new commands are called aliases because they allow you to rename and group existing commands. For each new alias you must define a command or a set of commands that the alias will perform. When you type on the command line one of the words to which you have assigned an alias, the shell substitutes and executes the full alias. The alias function simplifies complex new commands and redefines existing ones.

Making an Alias You assign an alias with the **alias** command. You must supply the **alias** command with the word to which you want to assign the alias and the commands the alias is to execute. The following example creates an alias **lsl** that displays a long directory listing:

```
% alias lsl "ls -lFs"
% lsl
total 26
    2 drwx------    2 modes    group      48 Aug 16 15:51 bin/
    4 -rwx------    1 modes    group    1354 Sep  1 16:21 julian*
    6 -rw-------    1 modes    root     2187 Jul 26 07:55 kingcity
    8 -rw-------    1 modes    group    3474 Sep 10 16:27 mbox
    2 -rwx------    1 modes    group     408 Sep  1 13:58 phone*
    2 -rwx------    1 modes    group     239 Sep  8 17:32 remind*
    2 drwx------    7 modes    group     224 Sep  7 11:13 text/
```

You could name the alias **ls** instead of **lsl** in the previous example to make the long directory listing replace the standard **ls** command. In fact, you can use **alias** to change the behavior of any command. This is useful with potentially damaging commands. In the following example, the **-i** option is made the new default of the **rm** command and causes **rm** to ask for verification before removing each file:

```
% alias rm "rm -i"
% rm kingcity
kingcity: ?
```

It can be helpful to make simple modifications of UNIX commands. However, you shouldn't make extensive changes to the way UNIX commands function. Shell scripts that expect commands to perform a certain way may malfunction if the commands they use are unexpectedly changed.

If you do change a command with an alias, you can prevent the alias substitution by either preceding the command with a backslash (\) or enclosing the UNIX command within single quotes ('), as in the following example:

```
% alias ls "ls -lFs"
% ls bank
   2 -rw-r--r--   1 modes    group         365 Sep  2 14:10 bank
% \ls bank
bank
% 'ls' bank
bank
```

▶**NOTE** Often aliases are set in your **.cshrc** file (discussed later in this chapter). These aliases will apply to any subshell or script you enter. If you instead set certain aliases in your **.login**, they will only apply to your login shell.

In fact, you may need to use the backslash or single quotes within an alias assignment. Consider this example:

```
% alias pwd "echo 'The current directory is \c' ; pwd"
% pwd
Alias loop.
```

The example creates an alias named **pwd** that contains the command **pwd**. When you type **pwd**, the shell substitutes and attempts to execute the alias commands. But when it gets to the command **pwd** in the alias, it attempts another alias substitution, getting trapped in an endless "alias loop." Surrounding the **pwd** command with single quotes solves this problem by preventing alias substitution.

```
% alias pwd "echo 'The current directory is \c' ; 'pwd'"
% pwd
The current directory is /u/bin/schumann
```

▶**NOTE**   The odd mixture of single and double quotes in the previous example is essential. Without the double quotes, the shell executes the **alias** command and assigns the **echo** and its text to the **pwd** alias. Then it executes the final **pwd** command, incorrectly interpreting the semicolon as a separator between the **alias** and **pwd** commands. Without the first set of single quotes, the **\c** does not prevent **echo** from echoing a newline character. Without the second set of single quotes, the **pwd** command causes an alias loop.

Displaying an Alias   Without any arguments, the **alias** command displays a list of the current aliases assigned with the **alias command**:

```
% alias
ls      (ls -FCs)
lsl     (ls -lFs)
note    echo "Enter note (end w/CTRL-D):";cat >> $home/.note
notes   more -10 $home/.note
nroff   'nroff' -mm -rL60 -r03 -rW70
pwd     echo 'The current directory is \c' ; 'pwd'
rm      (rm -i)
```

With one argument, the **alias** command displays the alias for that argument:

```
% alias note
note    echo "Enter note (end w/CTRL-D):";cat >> $home/.note
```

The **unalias** command removes an alias from the list of aliases. For example,

```
% alias lsl
lsl     (ls -lFs)
% unalias lsl
% lsl
lsl: Command not found.
```

Argument Substitution   You can use command-line arguments within your aliases. In the same way that the history mechanism handles command-line arguments, the **alias** command uses the exclamation point followed by a colon and a modifier. The modifiers are the same as those used by the history function. With the **alias** command, you must precede exclamation points with a backslash so that the shell passes them to the **alias** command.

```
% alias print 'echo "print: \!:*:t" ; pr \!:* | lpr'
% alias print
echo "print: !:*:t" ; pr !:* | lpr
% print /u/schumann/text.draft
print: text.draft
lpr: request id is 1034
```

Job Control

Available only on Berkeley UNIX, *job control* allows you to suspend processes temporarily, place them in the background, or bring them back to the foreground. You can temporarily suspend a command while it is executing by pressing CTRL-Z. A suspended command, also called a *stopped job,* is placed on hold in exactly the condition in which it was suspended. You can continue the execution of a suspended command by placing it either in the background or in the foreground.

The **bg** command places a previously suspended command in the background. Placing a command in the background is like executing the command on the command line followed by an ampersand. If you execute a command that may take a while to finish, you may want to suspend it and place it in the background.

The **fg** command places a previously suspended command in the foreground. This resumes execution of the stopped command at the point at which it was suspended. Being able to suspend commands and return them to the foreground makes it easy to switch between applications. For example, if you are editing a file with **vi** and you wish to put the editor on hold and check your mail, you can press CTRL-Z, suspend **vi**, execute **mail**, and resume **vi** with the **fg** command.

Job control is covered in detail in the Chapter 12, "The UNIX Multiuser Environment."

Directory Stack Manipulation

The C shell can store a list of the directories that you are using and allow you to move between them easily. The list is referred to as the *directory stack.* You can put directories on the stack, take them off the stack, or switch them around. The stack is organized like a stack of plates: The first ones on are the last ones off. The last directory you placed on the stack is always at the top of the stack and is readily available.

The two principal commands that handle directory stack manipulation are **pushd** and **popd**. The **pushd** command pushes directories on to the stack. The **popd** command pops them off of the stack. It is easiest to use **pushd** and **popd** is without arguments.

Use the **pushd** command to place the current working directory on the stack. The stack will remember this directory until you want to return to it. After placing a directory on the stack, you may change directories as many times as you like. You can even push another directory onto the stack. Use the **popd** command to return to the last directory you placed on the stack, as shown here:

```
% pwd
/usr/hatch/bin
% pushd
% cd ../text
% popd
/usr/hatch/bin:
```

▶**NOTE** On some systems, you can use the **pushd** command to switch the top two elements of the directory stack, making the second element in the stack the new current directory. This allows you to move back and forth between directories with ease.

Shell Scripts

Like the Bourne shell, the C shell can be used as a programming language. As a programming language, the shell reads and executes commands from a file called a shell script. In a shell script, you can use any command that you can enter at the command line, including UNIX utilities, compiled programs, or other shell scripts. You can also use ambiguous file references, input and output redirection, and piping within a shell script. C shell scripts also offer flow control commands that allow you to change the order of execution of commands in the shell scripts.

Creating a Shell Script

Shell scripts are simply executable text files that contain shell commands. Creating a shell script involves two simple steps: making the text file and setting the permissions to make it executable. You can create the text file with an editor such as **vi**, covered in Chapter 6, or by redirecting to a file the output of the **cat** command.

The first line of a C shell script should contain a single pound sign (#) on a line by itself. This tells the shell that the script is a C shell script. Even if you are running the script from the C shell, the pound sign is essential since the C shell assumes that any script without the pound sign is a Bourne shell script. You cannot run a C shell script directly from the Bourne shell, which assumes that all scripts are Bourne shell scripts (even with the pound sign). A colon at the top of a shell script explicitly identifies the script as a Bourne shell script. Another more explicit method of identifying a script as a C shell script is to place **#/bin/csh** on the first line of the script.

A newly created text file will not usually have execute permission set. Use the **chmod** command, discussed in Chapter 4, to change the permissions of your shell script.

The following example creates a shell script called **search** that uses **grep** and **find** to search the current directory (and deeper) for files containing text that matches a specified pattern. Use an editor to create the text file or just redirect the standard output of **cat** to the file **search**, as shown here:

```
% cat > search
#
# search
#    search current directory (and below) for files containing pattern
#
grep -l "$*" 'find . -print'
```

▶ **NOTE**   Lines beginning with the pound sign (#) are comments and are ignored by the shell (see the section "Shell Programming"). The symbol

$*** represents the arguments from the command line and is short for the variable **$argv or **$argv[*]**. Command-line arguments are discussed under "Variables."

You cannot execute the script yet, because the shell would not recognize **search** as an executable file. Since the proper execute permissions are not set, the shell would give you an error message such as

```
% search
search: Permission denied.
```

You need to set the proper permissions to make the shell script **search** executable. Use the **chmod** command to give the owner (you) execute permission. The **ls** command and the **-l** option show the access privileges for the **search** file.

```
% ls -l search
-rw-r--r--   1 modes     group        112 Sep 19 16:18 search
% chmod u+x search
% !ls
ls -l search
-rwxr--r--   1 modes     group        112 Sep 19 16:18 search
```

At this point, the file **search** is executable.

Executing a Shell Script

As with Bourne shell scripts, you execute C shell scripts by typing their file name on the command line. The shell executes each command in the script, one by one. You can run the script created in the previous section by typing the command **search** at the command line and supplying a pattern to search for.

```
% search pattern
```

Variables

Variables in the C shell are much the same as variables in the Bourne shell. Remember, variables are symbols to which you may assign values. The value may be a number, a word, or a string of words. The shell has variables that you create and assign values to, as well as variables that are set by the shell itself. Unlike the Bourne shell, however, the C shell has numeric variables that you can treat as numbers and variable arrays to which you can assign multiple values.

Variables that you create and assign are called user variables. User variables that contain single words or strings of words are *string variables*. User variables that contain only numbers are called *numeric variables* and can be manipulated mathematically. These mathematical manipulations are called *expressions*. The C shell allows you to create *arrays* of both string variables and numeric variables. Arrays allow you to assign multiple values to a single variable name. The values of an array are numbered sequentially.

Variables that are set by the shell are called shell variables. These variables include variables to read command-line arguments, process identification numbers, and exit status. A group of these variables, called environment variables, play an important part in determining the shell environment.

User Variables

You can create user variables from any sequence of letters and digits as long as the first character is a letter. Three commands declare and manipulate user variables: **set**, **@**, and **setenv**. Use the set command to declare nonnumeric string variables. The @ command works only with numeric variables. The **setenv** command typically sets environment variables, although you can also use it to declare user variables. The **set** and @ commands declare local variables — that is, variables that are only available within the shell in which they were created. The **setenv** command declares global variables, variables available to all child processes (this is similar to using the **export** command in the Bourne shell).

String Variables   In the C shell, you declare string variables with the **set** command. Use the equal sign (=) to assign a value to your variable. In the following example, the variable **district** is assigned the value **southern**:

```
% set district = southern
```

The spacing around the equal sign is unimportant. To print the contents of a variable, use the **echo** command. As in the Bourne shell, whenever you reference a variable in the C shell you must precede the variable name with a dollar sign ($). Without the dollar sign, the shell does not recognize a variable reference.

```
% set district = southern
% echo district
district
% echo $district
southern
```

Because of the leading dollar sign, the shell recognizes **$district** as a variable. It immediately substitutes the variable reference with the value of the variable and passes this value to the command line.

▶**NOTE**   You can display a dollar sign by preceding it with a backslash (\) or by placing single quotes around the text. This prevents variable substitution.

When assigning a variable, put double quotes around values that contain spaces or tabs. Without double quotes, the shell assumes that only the first word is the variable's value, as shown here:

```
% set district = zone five
% echo $district
zone
% set district = "zone five"
% echo $district
zone five
```

You should also put double quotes around references to variables whose values might contain multiple spaces or tabs. If you do not enclose the variable within quotes, multiple spaces are treated as single spaces.

```
% set district = "zone      seven"
% echo $district
zone seven
$ echo "$district"
zone      seven
```

In addition, you must put double quotes around references to variables that contain the characters * and ?. If you do not use quotes, the shell interprets these special characters as wildcard characters or ambiguous file name references.

String Arrays   A *string array* is a list of nonnumeric values referenced by a single variable name. An *index number* specifies which element of the array is to be referenced. You declare string array a bit differently than you declare a regular string variable: You use the **set** command and the equal sign, but you surround the values of the variable by parentheses. The following example declares an array of the variable **region**. The parentheses tell the shell that **region** is an array.

```
% set region = (northwest southwest northern)
% echo $region
northwest southwest northern
```

▶**NOTE**   To specify an element containing spaces, enclose the text of the element in quotes.

You reference elements of the array by following the string array name with an index number in square brackets. Two numbers separated by a hyphen within the square brackets specify a range of elements in the array. An asterisk within square brackets specifies all the elements of the array.

```
% set region = (northwest southwest northern "rocky mountain")
% echo $region[*]
northwest southwest northern rocky mountain
```

```
% echo $region[1]
northwest
% echo $region[4]
rocky mountain
% echo $region[2-3]
southwest northern
```

To assign a value to an individual element in an array, use the variable name and the index number surrounded by square brackets, as with an ordinary string variable.

```
% set region[4] = midwest
% echo $region[*]
northwest southwest northern midwest
```

The number of elements in an array is determined by the number of elements you specify when you first declare the array. However, suppose you don't know what values the array will hold when it is declared but still wish to declare an array of a certain size. You can specify the necessary number of null elements, as in

```
% set state = (California "" "" "" "")
% echo $state
California
% set state[2] = Oregon
% echo $state
California Oregon
```

You can determine the number of elements in an array after it has been declared with a special form of the user variable. If you precede the array name with a dollar sign and a pound sign, the shell will give the number of elements in the specified array. For example,

```
% set region = (northwest southwest northern "rocky mountain")
% echo $#region
4
```

Numeric Variables   You declare numeric variables with the @ command. Unlike the **set** command, which only assigns a constant value to a variable, the @ command can assign the results of a complex mathematical expression to a variable. The expressions that the @ command can evaluate and the operations that it performs are derived from the C programming language (covered in the next chapter). The @ command has the following format:

@ variable operator expression

The *variable* is the variable to which you are assigning a value or expression. The name of a variable assigned with the @ command may not contain numeric characters. The *operator* is one of the following C assignment operators:

=	Assigns the value of the expression to the variable
+ +	Increments the variable
− −	Decrements the variable
+ =	Adds the expression to the variable and assigns the result to the variable
− =	Subtracts the expression from the variable and assigns the result to the variable
* =	Multiplies the expression by the variable and assigns the result to the variable
/ =	Divides the variable by the expression and assigns the result to the variable
% =	Takes the remainder, after dividing the variable by the expression, and assigns the result to the variable

The *expression* is a mathematical expression that may contain constants, other variables, or C operators. Arithmetic and logical operators are commonly used in expressions with the @ command. Expressions are also used by the **if** and **while** commands and will be covered in detail in the section "Shell Programming." The following examples illustrate the @ command and some of its operators and expressions:

```
@ members = 4
@ members ++
@ members -= 3
@ hourpm = ($miltime - 12)
@ minute = ($hour * 60)
```

```
@ regtime = ($miltime - (12 * ($miltime >= 12)))
```

The C shell's ability to handle numbers and perform arithmetic allows you to accomplish complex tasks without having to learn a full programming language such as C.

Numeric Arrays   A *numeric array* is a list of numeric values referenced by a single variable name. It is just like a string array but contains only numeric values. An *index number* specifies which element of the array is to be referenced. Before you can use @ to assign values to the elements of a numeric array, you must declare the array with the **set** command. With the **set** command, you can assign any values to the elements of a numeric array, including zeros, other numbers, and null strings. You use the **set** command much as you did to declare string arrays. For example,

```
% set quarterly = (0 0 0 0)
```

You may assign values to the individual elements of the array with the @ command by following the variable name with the index number of the array element in square brackets. The index number can be a constant or another variable. For example,

```
% set store = (0 0 0 0 0 0)
% @ store[1] = 75000
% @ store[3] = 125000
% @ store[4] = 1200
% echo $store[1]
75000
% echo $store
75000 0 125000 1200 0 0
```

Reading User Input   The script can prompt the user for information and store the input in a user variable. On many systems, you can do this with the **set** command and a special symbol; on others, you need to use command substitution.

Some versions of the C shell use the symbol $< to read user input. The following example reads a line of input into the variable **newline**:

```
% set newline = $<
dubious undertaking
% echo $newline
dubious undertaking
```

On other systems, you can use the **head** command and command substitution with backquotes (´) (both described in Chapter 5, "UNIX Command-Line Fundamentals"), as in the following example:

```
% set newline = ´head -1´
forensic jurisprudence
% echo $newline
forensic jurisprudence
```

▶**NOTE**   The command **head -1** displays a single line from the standard input. The command enclosed in backquotes is substituted for the output of the command. Thus, a single line from the standard input is assigned to the variable **newline**.

Shell Variables

The shell variables are automatically set by the shell. They include command-line arguments, process numbers, exit status, and environment variables. Although many environment variables are set by the shell when you first enter the C shell, some are not placed in the environment until you set them.

Command-Line Arguments   The shell stores each word of the command line in a string array variable **argv**. The variable **argv[0]** typically holds the name of the calling program, since it is usually the first word on the command line. Succeeding words on the command line are stored in **argv[1]**, **argv[2]**, and so on. A reference to an element of the **argv** array with a higher index number than the actual number of command-line arguments produces an error. The variable **argv[*]** or **argv** alone gives all the command-line arguments. The following shell script demonstrates the **argv** variable:

```
% cat getargs
#
echo Arguments: $argv[*]
echo Calling program: $argv[0]
echo Argument 1: $argv[1]
echo Argument 2: $argv[2]

% getargs one two
Arguments: one two
Calling program: getargs
Argument 1: one
Argument 2: two
% getargs one
Arguments: getargs one
Calling program: getargs
Argument 1: one
Subscript out of range.
```

You can use the **set** command to change any element of the **argv** array except **argv[0]**, as shown here:

```
% cat chgarg
#
echo Old argument 2: $argv[2]
set argv[2] = new
echo New argument 2: $argv[2]
echo Arguments: $argv[*]

% chgarg one two three
Old argument 2: two
New argument 2: new
Arguments: one new three
```

▶**NOTE** You can abbreviate the variable **argv[0]** to **$0**, **argv[1]** to **$1**, **argv[2]** to **$2**, and so on. You can abbreviate the variable **argv[*]** to **$***.

The special variable **$#argv** (abbreviated **$#**) gives the number of arguments on the command line excluding the element **argv[0]**, as shown here:

```
% cat argnum
#
echo There are $#argv arguments

$ argnum one two three four
There are 4 arguments
```

Process Identification Numbers   The **$$** variable holds the process identification number of the current shell. It is often used by shell scripts to create unique temporary file names. The following example illustrates the **$$** variable:

```
% echo $$
12647
% ps
  PID TTY  TIME COMMAND
 12647 i1a  0:01 csh
 12651 i1a  0:00 ps
```

The **child** variable holds the process identification number of the last process you ran in the background. The following example runs **nroff** as a background process, prints the process number, and kills the process using the **child** variable:

```
% nroff bigreport &
% echo $child
12153
% kill -9 $child
12153: nroff: Killed
```

Exit Status   The **status** variable holds the exit status of the last command executed. It is identical to the Bourne shell's **$?** variable. When a process stops, for any reason, it returns an exit status (sometimes called a *condition code* or return code) to the parent process. A nonzero exit code indicates that the command failed. A zero indicates that the command was successful. You can return your own exit status from your shell scripts with the **exit** command.

Environment Variables Most of the environment variables are either inherited with the environment or assigned by the shell when it is started. You can change these values from the command line or in your **.login** and **.cshrc** files, described in the section "Modifying Your Environment."

■ **home** Stores the location of your home directory. It works the same as the **HOME** variable in the Bourne shell. Your default home directory is the directory you are in when you first log in. It is originally set by the system administrator. The **cd** command without arguments puts you in the directory named by the **home** variable.

▶**NOTE** On some systems, the **HOME** variable is used instead of **home**.

■ **path** Determines the search path the shell uses to find a file or command you have specified on the command line. The C shell **path** variable works similarly to the **PATH** variable in the Bourne shell. The search path is a list of directories that the shell searches in an attempt to find your command.

When you log in, the shell assigns a default value to the **path** variable. On most systems, **/bin** and **/usr/bin** are the standard directories for holding utilities and must, therefore, be included in the search path.

Reset the search path by changing the value of the **path** variable. The following example tells the shell to look for files first in **/bin**, then in **/usr/bin**, next in **/usr/schumann/bin**, and finally in the current directory.

```
% set path = (/bin /usr/bin /usr/schumann/bin .)
```

▶**NOTE** It is best to set the path in your **.cshrc** file so that the path will be set automatically each time you enter the C shell.

■ **prompt** Specifies the C shell prompt. It is similar to the **PS1** variable in the Bourne shell. When you change the value of this variable, the appearance of the prompt changes. The prompt is initially set to a percent sign followed by a space.

If you are working on more than one machine from the same terminal, it is sometimes hard to keep track of which machine you are currently logged on to. You can change the prompt to help keep track of which machine you are currently connected to. For example, to change the prompt to the machine name **sparta**, enter

```
% setenv prompt = "sparta% "
sparta%
```

If you regularly use the C shell history function, the prompt can display the current event number. This allows you to see the event numbers of the most recent commands. An exclamation point in a prompt string is replaced by the current event number. The following example places the current event number in the prompt:

```
% set prompt = '! % '
23 %
```

▶**NOTE**   You should set your prompt in your **.cshrc** file so that it will be set automatically every time you enter a shell.

■ **mail**   Like the Bourne shell's **MAIL**, **MAILCHECK**, and **MAILPATH** variables combined. When you specify a single file with **mail**, the shell will notify you whenever mail arrives in that file with the message "You have new mail." If the first word of the **mail** value is a number, the number specifies the interval in seconds at which the shell checks to see if mail has arrived. The default interval is 600 seconds or 10 minutes.

If multiple files are specified, the shell will notify you with the message "New mail in *filename*" when mail arrives in the file *filename*.

The following example specifies a mail check interval of one minute and a mail file located at **/usr/spool/mail/williams**:

```
% set mail = (60 /usr/spool/mail/williams)
```

▶**NOTE**   You should set the **mail** variable in your **.cshrc** file so that it will be set automatically every time you enter the C shell.

■ **cdpath**   specifies the search path of the **cd** command and provides the **cd** command with a list of directories in which to look for the specified subdirectory.

■ **histchars** specifies the characters used to trigger history substitution. It can be assigned a two-character string. The first character is used in place of the ! history character, the second in place of the ^ history character. For example, **set histchars = "#@"** changes the history characters to the pound sign and the at sign.

■ **history** specifies the size of the history list.

■ **savehist** specifies the number of commands that will be saved from the history list when you log out. These commands are saved in a file called **.history** in your home directory.

■ **shell** specifies the default shell in your environment.

■ **SHELL** is similar to the **shell** variable, but is used by the **tset** command to help set your terminal type.

■ **TERM** identifies your terminal type. You should set this variable before you configure your terminal with the **tset** command. This variable is usually set in your **.login** file (see the section, "Modifying Your Environment").

■ **TERMCAP** contains information about your terminal. It is usually set by **tset** in your **.login**.

The following environment variables act as switches; they do not take on values, but are either set or not set.

■ **echo**   When set, causes each command and its argument to be echoed just before it is executed. This is the same as calling the C shell with the **-x** option.

■ **ignoreeof**   When set, prevents a shell from accidentally being terminated with a CTRL-D. If this variable is set, you must use **exit** or **logout** to leave the shell.

■ **noclobber**   When set, ensures that files are not accidentally destroyed with output redirection and that ≫ redirections refer to existing files. Use the redirection symbols >! and ≫! to override **noclobber**.

■ **noglob**   When set, inhibits file name expansion. The symbols *, ?, ~, and [ ] are not interpreted as ambiguous file names. This is sometimes useful within shell scripts that do not deal with file names but make use of these symbols in other contexts.

■ **nonomatch**   When set, passes ambiguous file names without matching files to their commands without file name expansion. Ordinarily, when **nonomatch** is not set an ambiguous file reference with no matching files causes an error.

■ **verbose**   When set, causes the shell to display each command after a history substitution. This is the same as calling the C shell with the **-v** option.

Shell Programming

The shell programming language offers the following features:

■ Comments allow you to document your shell scripts.

■ The here document allows you to include within the shell script lines to be redirected to the input of a command in the script.

■ The **exit** command allows you to terminate a script and return an exit status to the calling program.

■ The conditional commands **if** and **switch** execute a set of commands only if particular conditions are met.

■ The looping commands **foreach** and **while** repeatedly execute a set of commands in a loop.

■ The **break** command allows a script to exit unconditionally from a loop, while the **continue** command allows the script to skip to the top of a loop. The **goto** command unconditionally moves to a location in your shell script.

Comments

You enter comments in your C shell scripts as you enter them in Bourne shell scripts. You can enter a comment in your shell script with the pound sign (#). Put the pound sign at the beginning of a line to have the line ignored by the shell. Put the pound sign after a command to have the remainder of the line ignored. The following example demonstrates good commenting:

```
% cat search
#
# search
#    search current directory (and below) for files containing pattern
#    created:    Karri Mendivil  23 Dec 85
#    modified:   Ravi Swami      10 Apr 86
#
grep -l "$*" 'find . -print'    # find supplies grep with filenames
```

You should document even the simple scripts this thoroughly. As a script grows in size and complexity, it becomes increasingly important to know who created it, who modified it, what the script does, and how it does it. Comments are essential to good programming.

▶**NOTE**   Most of the useful shell scripts in this chapter are commented, although the commenting is sparse for the sake of simplicity. Some scripts that illustrate only a single concept are uncommented.

The Here Document

A here document allows you to redirect the input of a command in a shell script to lines that you place within the shell script. You can thus provide input to a command without having to use a separate file. Remember, it is called the here document because the input is *here,* within the shell script, not *there,* in another file.

The C shell's here document works exactly like the Bourne shell's here document. The beginning of a here document consists of the redirection symbol ≪ followed by a delimiter. The delimiter can be one or more characters and tells the shell where the here document begins and ends. The text of the here document is followed by the delimiter on a line by itself. The following shell script uses the here document and the **cat** command to catenate a standard header to the top of a memo. This example uses **fini** as the delimiter.

```
% cat memo
#
# memo
#   prepare and attach the following header to a specified memo
#
cat - $argv[1] <<fini
MEMORANDUM

Date: `date +"%d %h %y"`
From: Gerard McDowell
      Director, Internal Affairs
fini

% memo koladov.3
MEMORANDUM

Date: 4 Jun 90
From: Gerard McDowell
      Director, Internal Affairs
To:   Vladimir Koladovich

Check your audit trail at the second juncture.  Call me later.
```

Notice the substitution for the date command in backquotes. Within a here document, the shell continues to perform variable substitution and substitution for commands in backquotes.

The exit Command

You can use the **exit** command in two ways: to terminate a shell script before it is finished, and to make your shell scripts return exit codes. When the shell encounters an **exit** command in a shell script, the script is terminated immediately.

Normally, a shell script returns the exit status of the last command executed in the shell script. When the **exit** command followed by a number is encountered in a shell script, the shell script is terminated and the number is returned as the exit status. The following example demonstrates the **exit** command:

```
% cat mkerr
echo "mkerr: This is an error."
exit 1
echo "This command is never executed."

% mkerr
mkerr: This is an error.
% echo $status
1
```

The exit status of a shell script is available to the parent process through the **status** variable, described in the section "Variables."

▶**NOTE**   The **exit** command and the **status** variable are especially useful with the **if** constructions discussed in the section "Conditional Commands." You can use **if** in a script to check that certain vital conditions are met before the rest of the script is executed. If the conditions are not met, the **exit** command can terminate the script and return an unsuccessful exit code.

Expressions

Expressions were mentioned under numeric variables and the @ command. Expressions are also used with the **if** and **while** commands (covered in the next two sections). An expression is an arithmetic expression that can contain constants, other variables, and the following C operators:

Parentheses

( )   Change the order of evaluation

Unary Operators

-                              Unary minus
~   One's complement
!   Logical negation

Arithmetic Operators

+   Add
-                              Subtract
*   Multiply
/   Divide
%   Remainder

Shift Operators

>>   Right shift
<<   Left shift

Relational Operators

>   Greater than
<   Less than
>=   Greater than or equal to
<=   Less than or equal to
!=   Not equal to (used for strings)
==   Equal to (used for strings)

Bitwise Operators

&   AND
^   Exclusive OR
| Inclusive OR

Logical Operators

&&   AND
|| OR

The = = and != operators compare their arguments as strings; all others operate on numbers. Numbers that begin with 0 are considered octal numbers. Null or missing arguments have a value of 0. All results are decimal numbers. Each element of an expression must be surrounded by spaces.

The following operations that deal with files and directories may also appear in expressions. Each must be followed by a file name or directory name.

-r *file*	True if *file* exists and is readable
-w *file*	True if *file* exists and is writeable
-x *file*	True if *file* exists and is executable
-e *file*	True if *file* exists
-o *file*	True if *file* exists and is owned by the user
-z *file*	True if *file* exists and has a size of zero
-f *file*	True if *file* exists and is an ordinary file
-d *file*	True if *file* exists and is a directory

Conditional Commands

Conditional commands only execute if a certain condition is met. The **if** construction is the simplest of these commands. The **if . . then,** **if . . then . . else,** and **switch** constructions are more complex variations.

The if Construction   The **if** construction executes a single command only *if* some condition is met. It has the following format:

if (*expression*) *command*

The **if**, the expression, and the command must all appear on the same line. If the expression is successful (zero), the command is executed. If the expression fails (nonzero), the command will not execute and the shell will execute the line following the **if**. This construction is useful if you have a simple expression and a single command to execute conditionally.

```
% cat day
#
# day
```

```
#     print the day and date
#
date +"%a %h %d, 19%y"
set day = 'date +%a'
if ($day == Sat || $day == Sun) echo "Happy Weekend"
```

The if .. then Construction   The **if .. then** construction is similar to the **if** construction. This construction works like this: *if* some condition is met, *then* execute the following commands. It has the following format:

if (*expression*) **then**
   commands
endif

The **if**, the expression, and the **then** must be on the same line, and the **endif** must be on a line by itself. The **endif** statement marks the end of the **if .. then** construction. If the expression evaluates to true (zero), the commands following **then** are executed. If the expression evaluates to false (nonzero), the commands following **then** will not be executed and the shell will continue execution with the commands following **endif**. The following shell script illustrates the use of **if .. then**.

```
% cat view
#
# view
#   view a file paginating it for the terminal screen
#
if ("$1" == "") then
    echo "view: No arguments"
    exit 1
endif
pr -122 $* | more
```

▶**NOTE**   The **$1** variable is an abbreviation for **$argv[1]** and **$*** is an abbreviation for **$argv[*]**. Both refer to arguments on the command line. The **argv** variable is covered in the section "Variables."

The if .. then .. else Construction   The idea behind the **if .. then .. else** construction is this: *if* some condition is met, *then* execute one set of commands, or *else* (if the condition is not met) execute another set of commands. It has the format:

if (*expression*) **then**
   commands
else
   commands
endif

Again, the **if**, the expression, and the **then** must be on the same line; the **else** and **endif** must be on lines by themselves. If the expression evaluates to true (zero), the commands between the **then** and **else** are executed, after which control is passed to the commands after **endif**. If the expression evaluates to false (nonzero), the commands following the **else** are executed. The following shell script shows the **if . . then . . else** construction.

```
% cat remind
#
# remind
#    print a reminder file (if it exists)
#
if (-e ~/.reminder) then
    echo "remind: Reminder file does not exist.
else
    more ~/.reminder
endif
```

▶**NOTE** The **-e** option in an expression tests whether a file exists. It returns true (zero) if the file exists and false (nonzero) if the file does not exist. The options and operations used in expressions were discussed in the section "Expressions."

The switch Construction The **switch** construction is similar to the Bourne shell's **case . . esac** construction. It has a multiple-choice format that matches one of several patterns and executes a corresponding set of commands. It has the format

```
switch (input)
   case pattern1:
      commands
      breaksw
   case pattern2:
      commands
      breaksw
   default:
      commands
      breaksw
endsw
```

The input is typically a variable that matches one of the several patterns in the **switch** construction. The patterns following the **case** statements are tested one by one for a match with the input. If the input matches a pattern, the commands following the matching **case** statement are executed. The **breaksw** marks the end of a set of commands for a particular branch of the **switch** structure. When the shell reaches a **breaksw**, control is shifted to the commands following the **endsw**.

A **default** statement in place of a **case** is used to match input that does not match any other pattern. This provides a useful way to detect erroneous or unexpected input. The **default** statement is optional.

Patterns can contain variables as well as the metacharacters *, ?, and [ ]. The asterisk matches any sequence of characters. The question mark matches any single character. The square brackets match any single character contained within the brackets.

The following shell script illustrates the **switch** construction:

```
% cat report
#
# report
#    Manage administrative reports
#
echo "[r]ead report, [w]rite report, [f]ile report"
echo "command: \c"
set command = $<
switch ($command)
   case [Rr]:
      more $1
      breaksw
```

```
    case [Ww]:
       vi $1
       breaksw
    case [Ff]:
       mail admin < $1
       breaksw
    default:
       echo "Command not found."
endsw
```

Looping Commands

Commands normally execute one after the other from the top of a shell script to the bottom. Conditional commands are one way of altering the shell's path through the script; looping commands are another. Unlike conditional commands, which specify a single path through the script, looping commands repeatedly execute a command or set of commands. The **foreach** and **while** loops execute their commands several times.

The foreach Loop   The **foreach** loop is similar to the **for . . in** loop in the Bourne shell. The **foreach** loop executes a set of commands once for each member of a list. It has the format

foreach *variable (argument-list)*
   commands
end

For each repetition of the loop, the next member of the list is assigned to the variable given after the **foreach** statement. You can use this variable within the commands of the loop, as in the following example:

```
$ cat backup
#
# backup
#    backup files with given extension
#
foreach file ('ls *.$1')
```

```
    cp $file backup/$file
end
```

▶ **NOTE**   Using the variable **argv** for the *argument-list* in the **foreach** loop does the same thing as the **for** loop in the Bourne shell. The loop executes once for each element on the command line, each element being assigned, one at a time, to the variable after the **foreach** statement.

The while Loop   The **while** loop repeatedly executes a set of commands *while* some particular condition is met. It has the following format:

while (*expression*)
 commands
end

The shell will execute the commands between the **while** and **end** as long as the expression evaluates true (zero). When the expression evaluates false (nonzero), control is passed to the commands following the **end** statement. The following shell script illustrates the **while** loop:

```
% cat getinput
#
# getinput
#    gets input from the terminal, ends with a single dot
#
set input = ""
while ($input != ".")
   set input = $<
   echo $input
end
```

Unconditional Commands

The **break** and **continue** commands are designed to interrupt a **foreach** or **while** loop. The former exits the loop, while the latter jumps to the top of the loop. The **break** and **continue** commands always occur within a loop.

The **goto** command is an unconditional jump to a specified place in the shell script. It may occur inside or outside a loop.

The break Command   The **break** command exits a loop completely, transferring control to the command after the **end** statement. It is useful to exit a loop when some event happens that is not in the loop condition.

The following example executes a loop once for each file in an argument list. If one of the files is not found, the loop is exited prematurely with **break**.

```
% cat ccmany
#
# ccmany
#
foreach file (lexer animate parse)
   if (! -e $file.c)
      echo "File not found."
      break
   endif
   cc -o $file $file.c
end
```

The continue Command   The **continue** command immediately begins the next execution of the loop, transferring control to the **end** statement, which continues the loop. It is useful to skip to the top of a loop when you do not want the remainder of the loop executed.

The following example executes once for each file in an argument loop. If one of the files is not found, it is not necessary to execute the rest of the loop. Skip to the top of the loop with the **continue** command.

```
% cat exmany
#
# exmany
#
foreach file (section.1 section.2 section.3)
   if (! -e $file)
      continue
```

```
    endif
    echo "Editing $file"
    ex $file
end
```

The goto Command   The **goto** statement immediately transfers control to the commands following a specified label. The *label* names a specific line in the shell script. The **goto** command is most often used in combination with the **if** and **if . . the** statements. The following shell script illustrates the use of **goto**:

```
% cat toc
#
# toc
#
#
if ("$1" == "-q") then
    shift
    goto quiet
endif
echo "Making a table of contents for $1"
quiet:
grep '^([1-9])' $1 | sed -f toc.sed >! $1.toc
```

The label must be a single word on a line by itself and must be followed by a colon.

Redirecting Standard Error

Chapter 5, "UNIX Command-Line Fundamentals," discussed redirecting the standard input and output. To redirect the standard output of a command such as **sort**, use the output redirection symbol >, as in

```
% sort list > sorted
```

In addition to the standard output, many commands produce output to the standard error (by default, your terminal screen). A command can send error messages to the standard error to prevent them from becoming mixed up with the text it sends to the standard output. As with the standard output, the shell sends the standard error to your terminal unless you redirect it. If you redirect the standard output with >, commands will still send their error messages to your terminal.

Although the Bourne shell allows you to redirect the standard output and standard error separately, the C shell does not. In the C shell, you must combine standard error with the standard output before you may redirect the standard error. You can combine and redirect standard output and standard error with the > & symbol.

▶ **TIP**   To write to a file that already exists, use > &! to redirect standard output and standard error.

It is useful to combine and redirect output when you want to run a slow command in the background and don't want its output cluttering up your terminal. The following example redirects of the output and standard error of the **cat** command:

```
% !cat /usr/bin/* &> cat.out
```

Modifying Your Environment

If the C shell is your login shell, a shell script in your home directory called **.login** is run when you first log in. The **.login** file is similar to the Bourne shell's **.profile** file. Furthermore, every time you enter a C shell (both your login shell and subshells) another file in your home directory called **.cshrc** is run. The **.login** and **.cshrc** files set much of your environment. You can modify both of these files to customize your environment or alter the actions taken when you log in.

Because **.login** and **.cshrc** are regular shell scripts, you can usually edit them with an editor such as **vi** (covered in Chapter 6). On some systems, you can edit these files yourself. On others, the system administrator must do it for you. Since both files are hidden dot files, they do not ordinarily appear when you type **ls**. Use **ls -a** to list all the files in your home directory, including dot files.

Modifying Your .login

The **.login** shell script is run only once when you log in. It is typically used to set environment variables that are passed to other shells through the environment or to perform actions that need execution only once per login session. You can use **.login** to configure your terminal, check your mail, or print a welcome message. For example, to automatically check your mail when you log in, you may want to put the following lines at the end of your **.login** file:

```
if (! -z /usr/spool/mail/williams) then
   echo "You have mail, wanna read it now? \c"
   set query = $<
   if ("$query" == "y") mail
else
   echo "So sorry, no mail now.  Try later."
endif
```

▶**TIP**   Before you change your **.login** file, you should make a copy of the file for safekeeping.

Modifying Your .cshrc

The **.cshrc** file is run each time you enter a new shell. Thus, it is run each time you log in, each time you enter a subshell, and each time you run a shell script. It is most often used to set C shell aliases and to set user variables and shell variables that must be available to other shells. You can use **.cshrc** to set your **prompt, path,** and **mail** variables, as well as other environment variables, and to create new commands and abbreviations with the **alias** command. For example, the following lines from the .cshrc file set several important variables and define several useful commands:

```
# set prompt string
set prompt = ") % "
# set path
set path=(. .. $home/bin /usr/bin /u/bin /etc $home/bin)
# set mail and mail interval
set mail=(10 /usr/spool/mail/modes)
# set history
set history=25

# aliases
alias lsl ls -lFs
alias time date +%T
alias rm rm -i
alias ls ls -FCs
alias note  'echo "Enter note (end w/CTRL-D):";cat >> $home/.note'
alias notes 'more -10 $home/.note'
```

▶**NOTE**   The shell environment variables were discussed in the section "Variables." The **alias** command was discussed in the section "Unique Features to the Shell."

Setting Terminal Options

If you want to use a full-screen program, such as the **vi** editor, the system must know what type of terminal you are using. Since the system needs this information every time you log in, you should set your terminal type in your **.login**. For example, the following lines in your **.login** automatically set your terminal type when you log in:

```
set SHELL = /bin/csh
set TERM = tvi920
eval 'tset -s'
```

Of course, you should substitute your terminal code in place of **tvi920**.

▶**NOTE** The **tset** command uses the values of the **SHELL** and **TERM** variables. Make sure that they are set before you issue the **tset** command.

If you regularly log in from several different terminals, put the following lines in your **.login** instead:

```
set termstat = 1
while ($termstat)
    set term = ('tset -S -m:?tvi920')
    set termstat = $status
end
setenv TERM    $term[1]
setenv TERMCAP $term[2]
unset termstat term
```

When you log in, the shell will display the following:

```
term=(tvi920)
```

You can press ENTER to accept the default terminal type or type in the code for your terminal and press ENTER. The **while** loop causes your **.login** to request your terminal type again if you supply a terminal code it does not recognize.

▶**NOTE** To find out more about **tset**, refer to the *UNIX User's Reference Manual.*

_____

The commands listed in Table 10-1 are built in to the C shell.

The C shell is like the Bourne shell in many ways: It is both a user interface and a programming language. But the C shell has additional features such as history substitution, aliases, and job control that make it tremendously powerful. Besides user variables and shell variables, the C shell offers arrays of both string and numeric variables. The C shell programming language is designed to resemble the C programming language, and is therefore much like an advanced high-level programming language. Furthermore, in the C shell you can modify your **.login** and **.cshrc** files to customize your environment.

Command	Action
@	Sets a numeric variable to the value of an expression
`command`	Backquotes are replaced with the output of *command*
alias	Creates and displays aliases
alloc	Reports used and free memory
bg	Places a previously stopped job in the background (Berkeley UNIX only)
break	Exits from loop
cd	Changes the working directory
continue	Starts with next repetition of loop
dirs	Displays the directory stack
echo	Displays its arguments. The symbol **\c** or the option **-n** suppresses a newline character.
eval	Scans and evaluates the command line
exit	Exits from the current shell or script
fg	Restores a previously stopped job to the foreground (Berkeley UNIX only)
glob	Like **echo** but with no spaces between arguments
history	Displays the history list
jobs	Lists stopped and background jobs (Berkeley UNIX only)
kill	Terminates jobs or processes
logout	Terminates a login shell
nice	Lowers the processing priority of a job
nohup	Allows you to log off while processes are running in the background without terminating the processes
notify	Causes the shell to notify you immediately when the status of a job changes (Berkeley UNIX only)
rehash	Causes internal hash tables to be recomputed. Often necessary after adding a file to a directory in your path
repeat	Repeats a command a specified number of times
set	Declares, initializes, and displays the value of variables
setenv	Declares and initializes the value of environment variables

Table 10-1. *C Shell Built-in Commands*

Command	Action
shift	Shifts each command-line argument to the next lowest argument
source	Executes a shell script as part of the current process
stop	Stops a job that is running in the background (Berkeley UNIX only)
suspend	Temporarily suspends the current shell (Berkeley UNIX only)
time	Executes a given command and displays elapsed time when the command finishes
umask	Identifies or changes the access permissions of your files
unalias	Removes an alias
unhash	Turns off the hash mechanism
unset	Removes a variable declaration
unsetenv	Removes an environment variable declaration
wait	Waits for all child processes to terminate

Table 10-1. *C Shell Built-in Commands* (continued)

11 *Program Development with C*

It is natural for a book on UNIX to talk about the C programming language. UNIX was conceived as a development system—a workshop full of tools for the software engineer—with C as its primary development tool. C, in turn, was designed to be the systems language for UNIX, but it is also used for numerical, text-processing, and database applications. Virtually all UNIX applications programs and all software tools written for UNIX are in C—including the operating system and the C compiler itself. Because C enables you to build complex programs out of simple elements, it is well suited to UNIX.

This chapter discusses two of UNIX's primary development tools: the C programming language and the **make** utility. This chapter presents an overview of C; it will not teach you how to program. The **make** utility keeps track of which modules of a program have been updated, helping to ensure that you use the latest version of all program modules when you compile a program.

The C Programming Language

This section examines the features of the C programming language and the C library. It also covers the basics of creating, compiling, debugging, and executing a C program.

Language Features

C is a general-purpose programming language. Like UNIX, C was created as a development tool, but it is not specific to any application. Although C is useful for writing operating systems and utilities, it is also used for business, educational, and scientific programming.

C is a small language. It includes relatively few control structures and data types, yet allows you to use them with very few restrictions. It has fewer keywords than Pascal, yet it is the more powerful language. Because of its economy, a C compiler can be simple and compact.

C is portable. Since C is not tied to any particular machine or hardware, you can easily write programs that will run without change on any machine that supports C. The C library handles input, output, and file operations. The system utilities and preprocessor allow you to isolate possible machine dependencies outside of the main code. This makes C programs easy to move from one machine to another.

C is modular. C supports one style of routine, the function. A C program is a collection of functions in which each function usually performs only one task. To write a C program, you first create functions and then combine them.

C is simple. It has no operations to deal directly with complex data types such as character strings, sets, lists, or arrays considered as a whole. C deals mainly with characters, numbers, and addresses; you must build more complex data types from these. C has a small set of well-chosen control structures: tests, loops, grouping, and functions. It has no built-in input-output facilities: there are no statements to read input and print output, and no built-in file access methods. These higher level mechanisms must be provided by explicitly called functions.

C is a powerful language. Its absence of restrictions and its generality make it convenient and effective. C has no run-time checking of array subscripts and argument types. It is relatively permissive about the data types supplied to functions and operations. Even if you supply a function with an argument of an unexpected type, in most cases the function will treat the argument as if it were the expected type. C is a succinct language, but it has a powerful set of operators allowing a great deal of flexibility. You can combine many operations within expressions to accomplish in one statement or expression what would require many statements in another language. Although it is a relatively high-level language with modern control structures and data types, C places no limits on your access to the machine at a low level.

The C Libraries

In C, function libraries provide operating system services, such as input and output, and a variety of essential operations not explicitly provided by C. The *libraries* are collections of related functions that are included in your program at your request. You can use library functions exactly as you use your own functions. The *standard library* contains a set of library files for a wide variety of applications, including system calls and the standard I/O library. System calls are the routines that make operating system services available to programmers. The standard I/O library has functions that use the system calls to create files, read from and write to files, and collect information about files. There are also libraries of mathematical operations, string functions, screen handling, graphics, and many other specialized operations. Most C systems include at least the standard and mathematical libraries.

Because you can place machine-dependent and specialized functions in libraries outside of the C language, C can remain small and general. You can also build a specialized set of tools you will use in your program. For example, if you need complex mathematical operations, just include the mathematical library in your program.

To include a particular C library in your program, you must use the **#include** compiler directive. For example, to take advantage of input and output functions contained in the standard I/O library, the following statement near the top of your C source code tells the compiler to make the library functions in **stdio.h** available to your program.

```
#include <stdio.h>
```

▶**NOTE**   The pound sign (#) tells the compiler that the statement is a preprocessor directive—in this case, an order to include the file **stdio.h**.

The C Program

Writing and running a C program involves the following steps:

1. Create a C source file with an editor such as **vi**. The name of the file must have a **.c** extension. For example, to create or edit a file called **agency.c**, type

```
% vi agency.c
```

The **vi** editor is covered in Chapter 6.

2. Compile the program using the **cc** compiler. If there are no errors in the code, **cc** will automatically create an executable file named **a.out** and you may skip to the final step. For example, to compile the file you created in the previous example, type

```
% cc agency.c
```

3. If there are errors in the program, you must debug (fix) the code. You can use another version of the compiler called **lint** that carefully checks your code before it is run. Generally, code that checks out fine with **lint** will have no problems at compile time with **cc**. For example, to check your program with **lint**, type

```
% lint agency.c
```

4. When the program has compiled properly, the executable program is, by default, left in the file **a.out**. Execute the program by typing its name on the command line, as in

```
% a.out
```

A sample C source file appears in Figure 11-1.

```
% cat show.c
/*show.c -- show control characters                          */
/*    created:   B. Jarvis          14 Mar 84                 */
/*    modified:  Carl Ansite        1 Jan 85                  */
/*        created the putcontrol function                     */
/*    modified:  B. Jarvis          12 Feb 85                 */
/*        improved the putcontrol function                    */

#include        <studio.h>
#define         MARK        '^'

main( )
{
     int c;      /* raw input character*/

     while ((c = getchar()) != EOF)
          if (c >= 0 && c <= 31)
               putcontrol(c) ;
          else
               putchar(c) ;
}

/*putcontrol -- output printable translation                 */
putcontrol(cc)
int cc;          /* raw control character */
{
     putchar(MARK);
     putchar(cc + 'A' - 1) ;
}
```

Figure 11-1.   *A simple C program*

Writing a C Program

You must use an editor, such as **vi** (discussed in Chapter 6), to write a
C program. The C program file is called the *source file,* because the
compiler generates the executable program from this file. The source
file must have a **.c** extension. Figure 11-1 illustrates the structure of a
simple C program.

Comments   Comments at the top of the file supply important information to anyone reading the code. In C, comments begin with **/*** and end with ***/**. Although comments are ignored by the compiler, they are an essential part of all computer programs. As with shell scripts, C programs should be commented thoroughly. As a simple program grows in size and complexity, it becomes more and more important to know who created it, who modified it, what the program does, and how it does it.

Compiler Directives   Compiler directives appear after the comments. A compiler *directive*, also called a *preprocessor directive*, is a statement that directs the compiler to perform some action before it compiles your program. Each directive is preceded by a pound sign (**#**). The compiler expands the directives in the initial phases of compilation.

The **#include** directive tells the compiler to include in the code at that point a copy of the specified file. Typically, the **#include** statement appears at the beginning of a program. The included file is generally called a *header file*. In Figure 11-1, the header file **stdio.h** (the standard I/O library) is included in the program, since the functions **getchar** and **putchar** (defined in **stdio.h**) are used. The angle brackets (< >) in the **#include** directive tell the compiler to look for the header file in a standard directory (**/usr/include**, in most cases). If you want to include a header file from one of your own directories, put the file name and its full pathname in double quotes, as in

```
#include "/usr/keith/include/stat.h"
```

You can use the **#define** directive to define symbolic constants. A *symbolic constant* is a name to which you have assigned a constant value. In the example, the name **MARK** is associated with the character value ^. By convention, the names of symbolic constants are uppercase. Using symbolic names can make your program easier to read and modify. If you have defined a constant symbolically with the **#define** directive and used it throughout a program, you can easily change it later if necessary. You update all the code by simply changing the constant in the **#define** line.

The Function main( )   In every C program there is exactly one function, **main( )**, where execution begins. The parentheses following

main( ) are indicative of a function. Typically, **main( )** will call other functions, which may call other functions, and so on.

Other Functions A *function* is a set of C statements that act as a unit and define one task to be done. By placing different operations into separate functions, you can make a program easier to read and maintain. You can also put frequently used code segments in a function to facilitate program development and maintenance. This way, if you want to alter the code, you only need to change it once.

If your program is long and involves many functions, you may want to split it into two or more files, grouping related functions together. You can divide a C program into any number of source files; however, each function must be wholly contained within a file. You should put all **#define** directives into a single header file and use the **#include** directive to include the header file in any source file that uses the definitions. Each source file must have a **.c** extension. You can compile these into a single program with **cc**. If your program involves many different source files, you will want to use the **make** utility discussed in the next section.

Compiling a Program

Use the **cc** compiler to compile your C source file. To compile the example in Figure 11-1, type

```
% cc show.c
```

The **cc** utility actually calls up to four programs: the C preprocessor, the C compiler, the assembler, and the link editor. The C preprocessor expands symbolic constants and includes header files. The *compiler* creates assembly language code from the instructions in the source file. The *assembler* creates machine-readable object code, one object file for each source file. Each object file has the same name as its source file but has an **.o** extension. (You can use these object files when recompiling your program.) The *link editor,* also called the *loader,* searches the C libraries for the library functions called by your program, combining these object modules with your program's object code.

To compile a program divided into several files, follow the **cc** command with the names of each of the files that make up the whole program. For instance, if your program consists of the files **ap.c**, **ar.c**, and **gl.c**, the following command will compile your program into a single executable file:

```
% cc ap.c ar.c gl.c
```

When recompiling your program, you can save time by recompiling only the source files you have changed. For the files that have not changed, you can use the already compiled object code files. For instance, if you initially compiled several source code files with the command

```
% cc menus.c options.c programs.c
```

and you later changed the source file **options.c**, you only need to recompile the one file. You can do this with the command

```
% cc menus.o options.c programs.o
```

Because the compiler recognizes the file name extension **.o**, it recognizes that the files only need to be linked.

▶**NOTE** If the object files with the **.o** extension are not left in your directory, use the **-c** option when you compile. For instance, in the preceding example, you would use **cc -c menus.c options.c programs.c** to preserve object code files.

Normally, the executable version of your program is left in a file called **a.out**. You can tell the **cc** utility to give your executable program a different name with the **-o** option.

```
% cc -o mkreport print.c graph.c
```

This will compile the two source code files **print.c** and **graph.c** into a single executable file called **mkreport**.

By default, the C compiler searches the standard C library, **libc.a**, for the library functions called by your program. If you use another library, such as the mathematical library **libm.a**, use the **-l** option with **cc**. In the following example, the C compiler searches the math library (specified by **m**):

```
% cc inven.c -lm
```

This then requires that the line

```
#include <math.h>
```

be included in the source file.

Executing a Program

A C program without errors compiled with the **cc** utility produces an executable program—called **a.out** by default. To run your compiled program, type its name at the command line like any other executable UNIX utility, as in

```
% a.out
```

Debugging C Programs

If your program has compilation errors or does not run properly, you must correct or debug it. The UNIX system provides several tools to make debugging easier. The C program checker, **lint**, is one of the most useful. It checks programs for errors and portability problems. Unlike the C compiler, which is virtually unrestrictive, **lint** is very strict. It detects and reports a wide variety of problems and potential problems, including variables that are used before they are set, arguments to functions that are not used, functions that use nonexistent return values, and mismatched data types. A warning from **lint** usually means that the

program has an obvious error, a nonportable construct, or that you have
violated a standard of good programming. Always using **lint** on your
programs will improve your programming. Programs that pass through
lint unscathed seldom have any problems when they are compiled. The
next command uses **lint** to run a full check of a group of source files
making up a single program; **lint** produces the following warnings,
including the file and line number of the problem:

```
% lint -p gl.c ap.c ar.c
gl.c(28): warning: loop not entered at top
gl.c(60): warning: statement not reached
ap.c(9): warning: balance unused in function main
```

▶**NOTE**   The **-p** option checks portability between various versions of C.
Portability checking is the only test that is not done by default.

UNIX also provides debuggers for tracking problems that cannot be
uncovered with **cc** and **lint**. System V's debugger is called **sbd** (for
symbolic debugger). Berkeley UNIX's debugger is called **dbx**. Both
programs let you look at the execution of the program step by step in
terms of its C language statements and let you examine values as the
program is executed. For more information on the UNIX C debuggers,
look at the *UNIX Programmer's Guide,* which accompanies the UNIX
development software.

The definitive C language reference book is *The C Programming
Language,* by Brian Kernighan and Dennis Ritchie (Englewood Cliffs,
N.J.: Prentice-Hall, 1978); both authors were instrumental in the cre-
ation of the C language. A good starting point for learning C is *The C
Puzzle Book,* by Alan Feuer (Englewood Cliffs, N.J.: Prentice-Hall, 1982).

The make Utility

When you have a large program with many source files and header files,
the files are often interdependent, with changes in one file affecting
several other dependent files. When recompiling a program, you must
recompile all modified files as well as all files that are dependent upon
the modified files. With a large program, it can be difficult to determine

which files need to be recompiled. The **make** utility automates this process.

The **make** utility requires that file dependencies be described in a file named **makefile**. Once you create the **makefile**, the single command

```
% make
```

will recompile modified and dependent files, if necessary. A **makefile** consists of a series of target files, followed by a colon, and then a series of prerequisite files. The target files are dependent in some way on the named prerequisite files and must be updated when the prerequisite files are modified. You specify the updating action, such as compilation, after a semicolon or after a tab character at the start of a new line. For example, the following example shows the **makefile** needed to maintain the program **account**, which is made by compiling the C source programs **gl.c**, **ap.c**, and **ar.c**. The three source files use the header file **account.h**.

```
% cat makefile
account: gl.o ap.o ar.o
        cc gl.o ap.o ar.o -o account

gl.o ap.o ar.o: account.h
```

The program **account** is dependent upon **gl.o**, **ap.o**, and **ar.o** (**make** knows that these files are dependent upon their **.c** source files), which, in turn, are dependent upon **account.** If any one of the three source files are changed, the **make** command recompiles the appropriate source code, combines the unchanged object code files, and creates the program **account**. If the header file **account.h** is modified, the **make** command recompiles all three source code files before combining them to form **account**.

For more information on **make**, consult the *UNIX Programmer's Guide*.

The C language and a variety of software tools make the UNIX system well suited to program development. The C language offers simplicity

and elegance, generality and power. The C libraries encourage portability and modularity and provide ready access to a wide variety of useful
functions.

Writing and running a C program is typically a four-step process:
writing, compiling, debugging, and executing. Write your C program
with an editor such as **vi**. Compile it with the C compiler **cc**. Check it
with **lint** or debug it with **sbd** or **dbx**. And, finally execute your program
(by default **a.out**) at the command line.

You can use the **make** utility to keep current the various files of your
program. It keeps track of interdependencies between modules in a file
named **makefile**. Once you create **makefile**, a large number of programs
can be maintained automatically.

12 *The UNIX Multiuser Environment*

You have now learned how to use a great number of UNIX utilities. For the most part, these utilities help you do your work more efficiently. With the exception of **mail**, however, you use most of these utilities in isolation. Of course, you are always connected to the UNIX system when you are logged in, but it is sometimes easy to forget this.

This chapter explains more about what goes on behind the scenes. Just what happens when you type a command? How can you tell if other people are logged into the system? How does your account get created? You will learn something about the multiuser properties unique to a UNIX system and about how a system is administered and maintained. You may never administer a UNIX system yourself, but knowing something about what system administration involves will help you understand UNIX better.

Processes

Each time anyone executes a UNIX command, a process is initiated. "Process" is the official name for a program that is running. Each process is assigned a unique number so that the computer can allocate processing time among all processes running at a given time. Since a UNIX system usually has just one central processing unit (CPU), it works on each process for a very short time and then switches to another process, thus appearing to run many processes simultaneously. In this way, each process is executed relatively quickly, and users don't have to wait for another process to be completed before theirs is executed.

The process associated with each command *lives,* or remains active, only as long as the command is being executed. When the command has been completely executed, the process associated with it *dies,* which means that it no longer exists. When you execute a command, you *own* the process associated with that command. As long as that process lives, you have some control over it. You can list the processes you and other users are running and terminate any processes that you own.

User Processes

Whenever you are logged in to your UNIX account, you are necessarily running at least one process: the one associated with your shell (**sh** or **csh**). If you execute any commands, these become processes and are assigned process numbers as well. The process associated with the command you are executing at any given time is called the *current process.* Some commands are executed so quickly that the processes associated with them live only for a few milliseconds. Others, such as the text formatters **nroff** and **troff**, take a considerable amount of time to run, depending on the number of users on the system and the length of the file being formatted.

You can list all the processes you are currently running by typing the command **ps** (process status). This will display the *process identification number* (PID) assigned to each process, the name of the command being executed, and the amount of time the CPU has worked on the process. Remember, your process is only one of many running at any given time and is allotted only a portion of CPU time. For example, suppose it takes five minutes from the time you type a command to the time it is finished running. The CPU may spend only a few seconds of that five minutes working on your process. The rest of the time will be spent switching between the other currently running processes.

The following example shows a typical output of the **ps** command:

```
% ps
  PID TTY  TIME COMMAND
 3157 ilc  0:00 ps
 2880 ilc  0:04 csh
 3045 ilc  0:23 nroff
```

The number in the PID column is the process identification number. The code in the second column is the terminal associated with the process. In this case, only one user's processes are displayed so all of the processes are associated with the same terminal. The third column shows the CPU time spent working on the process, and the last column shows the name of the command the process is associated with.

In Chapter 5, "UNIX Command-Line Fundamentals," you learned how to execute a command in the background by following it with **&**. When you do this, the process associated with that command runs in the background. Since the process takes place off screen, this command seems to have disappeared, but any processes you have put in the background are assigned PID numbers and can be displayed with the **ps** command. In the preceding example, **ps** is the current process. The C shell **csh** is always running while you are logged in. Process number 3045 is running the **nroff** command. Since the current process must be **ps**, **nroff** must be running in the background, since only one process can run in the foreground at a given time.

System Processes

When a UNIX system is running, some processes will always be running, even when no users are logged in. Some of these processes may be commands that users have put in the background before logging out or commands executed with the **at** utility (see Chapter 13, "Command Reference"). Others are *system processes*, processes that the UNIX system executes automatically to keep everything running smoothly. For example, a utility called **getty** runs on every login port that is not in use, displaying the **login:** prompt on the terminal connected to that port and waiting for someone to log in.

By typing

ps -e

you can see all of the processes that are running on the whole system, including those you own, those that other users are running, and the system processes. When you type **ps -e**, some additional information is added to the information displayed with **ps** alone. Along with the PID number, name of the command, and time the process has been worked on, a second column displays the number of the terminal associated with the process.

▶**BERKELEY VERSION** The **ps** options on Berkeley UNIX work differently from those on AT&T UNIX. To see a list of all the processes on a Berkeley UNIX system, you could use the **-x** and **-a** options rather than the **-e** option. An example of the **ps -xa** command follows:

```
PID TT STAT   TIME COMMAND
  0 ? D      0:12 swapper
  1 ? I      1:15 init
  2 ? D      0:02 pagedaemon
 41 ? I      0:40 /etc/syslogd -m10
 48 ? S     11:40 /etc/routed
 57 ? I      1:07 /etc/timed -M
 62 ? I      1:45 -accepting connections (sendmail)
 78 ? S     17:35 /etc/update
 81 ? I     11:01 /etc/cron
```

This is not a complete list of processes on a system, but it gives you a good idea of what you will see with the command **ps -xa**.

Interrupting a Process

You can terminate the current process in mid-execution with the *interrupt key*. Usually, CTRL-C is the interrupt key. If CTRL-C doesn't work for you,

you can use the **stty** command (see Chapter 13, "Command Reference") to find out what key is your interrupt key or to choose a new interrupt key.

When you press the interrupt key, the current process (with the exception of the shell) will be terminated at whatever point has reached in its execution. Whatever work is already done will not be undone. For example, if the command created a new file with a redirection symbol (see Chapter 5, "UNIX Command-Line Fundamentals"), that file will have been created before any output was directed to it. Pressing the interrupt key will not uncreate the file, and if any output has already been directed to the file, the file will contain that output. You cannot use the interrupt key to reverse the effects of a command. Furthermore, the interrupt key only works while the process is still being executed. Once the process has died, you cannot interrupt it. In other words, it is usually futile to press the interrupt key after giving a command that is executed almost instantaneously, such as **date** or **rm**. The interrupt key is mainly used to terminate a process that is taking too long to run or that you decide you don't want to execute, such as formatting a file with **nroff** or viewing a very long file with **cat**.

Killing a Process

Once you have placed a process in the background, you cannot terminate it with the interrupt key. To terminate, or *kill*, a background process, you must use the **kill** command. In order to kill a process, you must know its PID number, which you can determine with the **ps** command. (The number assigned to a process is also printed after you type a command followed by **&**, but you will probably not remember what that number was.) Once you know the PID number of the process you want to kill, you just type

kill *PID number*

where *PID number* is the PID number of the targeted process. For example, to kill the process associated with the **nroff** command in the previous example, you would type

% **kill 3045**

Now if you type **ps** again, that process should no longer be listed.

You can terminate most processes with the **kill** command, but processes associated with certain commands cannot be killed in this way. The process associated with your current shell is one example. If, when you type **ps** after trying to kill a process, that process is still listed, you can use **kill -9** to kill it. The **9** option makes **kill** send a different signal to the process than it sends when used without an option. You can even kill your current shell with **kill -9**. Of course, if you kill your shell you will be automatically logged out, since the shell is the only way you can communicate with the computer.

You can only use the **kill** command to terminate processes that you own. However, if you are logged in on two different terminals, you can kill processes on the terminal you are not currently using from the one you are using. This can be very useful if your terminal *freezes* (refuses to accept input or print output) for some reason. You can log in on another terminal and log yourself out on the frozen terminal by typing **ps -e**, finding the PID number of the shell running on that terminal, and killing it with the **kill -9** command. Of course, to do this, you must know the number of your terminal, which is *not* the same as the code for your terminal type.

▶**BERKELEY VERSION**   To find the PID number of your shell on another terminal, you can type **ps -ax**, which displays all the processes currently running on the system, or **ps -g**, which shows all the processes you own on any terminal.

Job Control (Berkeley UNIX Only)

In the C shell on a Berkeley UNIX system, there is a set of commands that allows you to suspend processes, bring to the foreground background processes, and restart suspended processes. First, you can press CTRL-Z during execution of a command (even **vi**) to suspend the process. This means that the process will be placed on hold (also called *stopping a job*). The CTRL-Z function is handy if you start running a command that takes too long to execute. Whereas the interrupt key and the **kill** command (both available on Berkeley UNIX as well) kill a process forever, CTRL-Z just suspends the process temporarily, keeping it in the background, ready to be restarted.

A *job* is a process that is either running in the background or stopped. To see a list of your current jobs, use the **jobs** command. The following example shows what the output of the **jobs** command looks like:

```
[1]  + Stopped        cat *
[2]    Done           cat t001.* t002* t003* | nroff -ms > tables
[3]  - Stopped        ls / | more
[4]    Running        cat * | nroff -ms > newfile
```

Notice that neither the shell nor the current process (**jobs**) shows up as a job. Column 1 shows the number of the job in square brackets. Each time a new job is created, it is given a job number according to how many other other jobs you are currently running. For example, if no other jobs are running, a new job is numbered 1. The next job will be numbered 2, and so on. This is different from how processes are numbered, since PID numbers are assigned relative to all other processes running on the system. Column 2 shows the status of the job. The status indicators are fairly self-explanatory: **Running** indicates a job running in the background, **Stopped** means that the job has been stopped with CTRL-Z, and **Done** means that the job has just finished running. Column 3 shows the commands that the job consists of.

Suppose that you are running a lengthy process in the foreground and you want to put it in the background without killing it and restarting it. You can do this by first stopping the current job with CTRL-Z, and then starting it up again in the background with the **bg** (background) command. For example, suppose you were formatting a very long file with **nroff** and got tired of waiting. You would first press CTRL-Z to stop the job. If you now typed **jobs**, the **nroff** job should show up as the last numbered job. At the next prompt, you can type

bg *%job number*

where *job number* is the number of the job. The % character tells the shell that the following number is a job number. The **nroff** job will now resume execution in the background. Typing **jobs** again should show that that job is running. You can now execute other commands in the foreground while the **nroff** job is running in the background.

In addition, you can use the **fg** command to put in the foreground either a stopped job or a job that is running in the background. The syntax of the **fg** command is the same as that of the **bg** command. First, type **jobs** to find the number of the job, which may be either stopped or running in the background. Then type

fg *%job number*

where *job number* is the number of the job you want to put in the foreground. If the job takes a long time to execute, you will have to wait until it is done before you can execute a new command.

▶**TIP**   You can use the CTRL-Z key and **fg** command to switch back and forth between two different jobs. Suppose you are editing a file with **vi** and want to leave the file just temporarily to do something else. Simply press CTRL-Z while editing the file, and you will be returned to the shell. Now execute the other command (perhaps edit another file) and when you are done, type **fg** and you will be returned to where you were before in **vi**.

Finally, if you decide you want to suspend a job running in the background, you can do so with the **stop** command, whose syntax is the same as that of **bg** and **fg**. Find the number of the job you want to stop and type

stop *%job number*

where *job number* is the number of the job you want to stop. You can also kill a job as you kill a process, with the **kill** command. Killing a job has exactly the same effect as killing a process. The only difference is how you refer to the process to be killed. If you refer to it as a process, you must specify its PID number. If you refer to it as a job, type

kill *%job number*

where *job number* is the job number displayed with the **jobs** command.

Multiuser Operation

One of the best features of UNIX is its ability to support many users at one time. A UNIX system with several terminals is much more valuable than the same number of personal computers, because UNIX allows users to communicate with each other and share data without using networking software. Also, because a UNIX system (except one adapted for a PC) is usually overseen by a system administrator, there is always someone for you to turn to when you have a problem.

Much of the time you will be unaware of other users on your UNIX system. However, if you want you can find out quite a bit about who else is using your system. The next few sections explain how to find out about the other system users.

Getting Information About Other Users

The files and directories in your account may be read and changed only by authors that you authorize to do so. However, information about your activity on the system is accessible to every system user. Other users can find out what processes you have running, when you last logged in and out, and how long it has been since you last entered anything. You can also access information about other users. Chapter 3, "Getting Started," explained the **who** command, which displays a list of users currently logged on to the system and the time each one logged in. There are other commands that you can use to find out more about other system users, who are either logged in or not.

The w Command The **w** command displays a list of current users. It also gives some information about the system, where users are logged in, and what they are doing. The following example shows the output of the **w** command on a small UNIX system:

```
% w
 10:07am  up 6 days, 16:05,  3 users,  load average: 0.08, 0.02, 0.01
User      Tty        Login@  Idle   JCPU   PCPU  What
sheila3   ttyi1c     9:59am          7            w
modes     ttyi1a     8:22am    2     5      12    vi chapt10
root      tty01      9:03am    2     19      1    bc
```

The first line includes the current time, the amount of time the system has been *up* (running), the time it was last started up, the number of users currently logged in, and the current processing load on the system.

▶**NOTE**   The load average information does not appear on some UNIX System V systems.

The columns below the first line contain information about each user currently logged in. The first column is the user's login name. The next three columns show the code for the terminal the user is logged in on, the time the user logged in, and how many seconds the terminal has been idle (not receiving any input from the user). The next two columns show the CPU time used by all processes on the user's terminal and the CPU time used by the current process. The last column shows what command the user is currently executing. As you can see, you can find out quite a bit about other users by using the **w** command.

The finger Command   On some UNIX System V systems, you can also learn a few things about users who are not currently logged into the system. You can use the **finger** command to display some information about a user if you know his or her login name. The utility can come from different sources, so its format varies widely. This section will give you a general idea how the **finger** command works. To see information, type **finger** *user*, where *user* is the login name of the user you want information about. For example, to find out about a user whose login name is **cleveland**, you would type

```
% finger cleveland
```

UNIX systems will differ but the output of the **finger** command will be of the general format shown here:

```
Login name: cleveland   In real life: Cleveland Wall
Writeable.
Directory: /b/l/cleveland     Shell: /bin/csh
On since Aug 23 11:02:55 on ttyp1
Uses and interests:
Product research.
```

```
Writer, technical and otherwise.
Current project: The effects of coffee on normal sleep cycles.

  Dept.: Research and Development
  Ext.: 3362
```

The amount of information displayed with the **finger** command depends on how much the user wants you to know. The minimum information displayed is the user's home directory, the date of her or his last
login, and the login shell assigned to her or his account. The **finger**
command will compile and display this data automatically. On some
systems, **finger** also tells you whether the user is writeable (see the next
section). If the user wants you to know, **finger** will also display her or his
real name (**In real life:**) and any additional information she or he wants
to make public. In the preceding example, this information includes
everything below the line **Uses and interests:**. Different systems have
different titles for this information.

The information below the Uses and interests line must be entered
in a dot file in the user's home directory. The name of this file differs
from system to system. Ask your system administrator what the file must
be called on your system. If you use **finger** without a user name, **finger**
displays pertinent information about each of the users currently logged
in.

Communicating with Other Users

In Chapter 8, you learned how to send electronic mail to other UNIX
users. Other users need not be logged on for you to send mail to them.
Two UNIX utilities let you communicate more interactively with other
logged-on users. You can use the **write** command to send text directly
to another user's terminal. The other user may or may not reply. For
you to be able to write to another user's terminal with **write**, her or his
account must be *writeable*. This means that she or he must have set **mesg**
y in her or his **.login** or **.profile** file. If you want others to be able to
write to you (even to reply to your messages), you must do this too.
You can set **mesg y** either by typing the command at the shell

prompt or by entering it as a line of your **.login** or **.profile** file. See Chapter 13, "Command Reference," for more information about the **mesg** command.

Once you have selected a user to send a message to (use **who** to find out which other users are logged in), you must check that she or he is only logged in on one terminal. If not, you will have to specify which terminal you want to write to. To send a message to a user, you type

write *login name* [*terminal*]

where *login name* is the login name of the user you want to write to and *terminal* is the number of the terminal you want to write to (necessary only if the user is logged in on more than one terminal). This terminal number is the number displayed by the **who** command, *not* the code you enter when you log in. Note that the terminal number must be separated from the login name by a space. The brackets indicate that the terminal code is not always necessary. To use **write** to send a message to a user named **dale**, you would type

```
% write dale
```

The cursor would then be on a blank line, and you would type lines of text, pressing RETURN at the end of each line. To end transmission of the message, press CTRL-D as the first character on a line. If **dale** were logged in on more than one terminal, you would have to specify which terminal you wanted to write to after the login name.

System Administration

Many of the tasks involved in administering a UNIX system are taken care of automatically by the system itself. Since UNIX is a multiuser system, each user's activity on the system must be authorized and, to some extent, controlled. The unique components of a UNIX system, such as the user accounts and any special software, must be set up by a person. Also, a human being must perform certain tasks that help keep the UNIX system running more smoothly and efficiently. In the next few sections, you will learn what some of these tasks are and how they are carried out.

The System Administrator

The system administrator is the person (or people) who takes care of the tasks on a UNIX system that must be done by a person. Being a system administrator does not require any special training, it just means being in charge of your UNIX system. If you don't know who your system administrator is, ask the person who assigned you your account name and password. He or she probably either *is* the system administrator or knows who is. Most system administrators have a UNIX account to which you can send electronic mail if you have any questions or problems.

The system administrator usually logs in to the UNIX system as **root**, a user whose home directory is **/**. A person logged in as **root** is called the superuser because he or she has read and write permission on all files in the system. Only the superuser can execute most of the system administration commands.

Installing the System Software

The first task of any system administrator is to install the UNIX system software on the computer. During installation, the system administrator supplies information about the type of hardware the system has and sets up any special file systems that need to be reserved for user accounts or other purposes. The system administrator also decides at this point which parts of the UNIX software to install. Because this decision is up to the system administrator of each UNIX system, and because different UNIX systems have slightly different sets of utilities, no two UNIX systems are likely to have exactly the same set of utilities.

If a utility whose name you have typed has not been installed or is not available on your UNIX system, you may get the message "Command not found." If a utility that you want is not available on your UNIX system, consult your system administrator.

Starting Up and Shutting Down the System

Many UNIX systems remain on and running 24 hours a day, while others are turned on and off each day. Even a system that is always on may at times need to be shut down and restarted for maintenance, installation of new software, or updating of the old software. The next three sections explain briefly what happens when a UNIX system is started up or shut down, and what the system administrator does to turn the system on or off.

Starting Up the System   You start up a UNIX system from the system console. Since UNIX software usually resides on a hard disk, the first step in starting up the system is often simply to turn on the computer. As a system starts up, or *boots,* it checks the hard disk to make sure that everything is okay. The system administrator supplies a new time and date if necessary and decides whether to put the system into multiuser mode or single-user mode. (In single-user mode, only the superuser can be logged in for system maintenance or backups.) If you can log in normally, the system is in multiuser mode.

Shutting Down the System   Anyone who has access to the CPU could shut down the system by simply unplugging it or turning it off. However, this would be a dangerous way to shut down a system. Even if no users are logged on to a system, any background or system processes that may be running when the system is improperly shut down will be instantly terminated, resulting in possible losses or scrambling of data. The situation is even worse if users *are* logged on and running their own processes. To ensure that no data are lost or scrambled when a system goes down, it must be shut down with special commands that ensure that everything is in order and all processes are properly terminated. The superuser is the only person authorized to use these commands.

A system administrator usually uses the **shutdown** command to shut down a UNIX system. When the system administrator gives this command, she or he specifies with it a number that determines how many minutes the system will wait before terminating all processes and shutting down. After this, a message is sent to any users currently logged on to the system, warning them of the impending shutdown. If you are editing a file or executing another command and you receive a message such as "System going down in x minutes," quickly finish up what you are doing and log out. Any background processes that you have running will be terminated when the system goes down, and the work they are doing will not be completed. You can either kill them yourself before logging out or let the system terminate them—the result will be the same.

Accidental Shutdowns   Occasionally, a UNIX system will accidentally be shut down by a power outage, hardware malfunction, or human error (such as someone tripping over the power cord). In such a situation, known as a *system crash,* a UNIX system does its best to see that as little data as possible is lost. For example, if you are editing a file, a copy of the buffer is usually saved so that you can retrieve any changes you might have made since writing the file to disk. When this happens, mail from **root** will usually tell you how to recover this buffer. Unfortunately, the system cannot always save editing buffers in a crash. This is one important reason why you should write files to disk often while using **vi**.

Another type of crash, which is often more devastating than a system crash, is a *disk crash,* which occurs when the hard disk (where all files and directories on a UNIX system are stored) is damaged. Depending on the extent of the damage to the disk, some or all of the data stored on it may be lost. A disk crash is very rare and with any luck you will never experience one. If there is a disk crash on your system, however, it is not the end of the world. You may lose some work, but most UNIX systems are *backed up,* or copied on other media, at regular intervals, so most of your files will be safe, especially those that have not been recently modified.

Creating and Administering User Accounts

Before anyone can use a UNIX system, she or he must be authorized to do so. The system administrator must create either a special login account for each person or a public account accessible by many users. Only the superuser can create or remove new user accounts, but doing so is a simple matter. Since a user account initially consists of just one directory, to create a new account the system administrator simply creates that directory and changes its ownership from himself or herself to the user of that directory. If the account is to be used by only one person, the system administrator also assigns it a password.

To assign a password to a user, the system administrator puts an entry in a file called **/etc/passwd**. This entry also contains information about which is the user's login shell, her or his user ID number, group number, and any comments the system administrator wants to include, such as the user's telephone number or department. Users usually have read permission on the **/etc/passwd** file. User passwords are listed in this file, but they are *encrypted* (translated into a special code) so no one can read them. Some systems have a utility called **mkuser**, which creates new user accounts in one fell swoop. To remove a user from the system, the system administrator simply removes all of the files from that user's home directory and removes the entry from the **/etc/passwd** file.

Backing Up the System

A UNIX system should be backed up regularly (copied on tapes or floppy disks) so that, in case of a system or disk crash or accidental file removal, as little data as possible will be lost. It is rare for a system crash to cause a substantial loss of data on a UNIX system, because UNIX has ways of checking and repairing data after the system is shut down improperly. A disk crash, however, will usually result in some lost data. Thus, system backups are very important to all UNIX users. The system administrator usually arranges a regular backup schedule, so that the most recently modified files get backed up very often. Using the **backup** or **tar** command, the system administrator can back up entire file systems or just the most recently modified files.

Maintaining System Security

The system administrator must also maintain the security of a UNIX system. As you know, each individual user account has a password that a user must type to access her or his account.

▶**NOTE** If you ever forget your password, don't panic. Although even the superuser cannot determine your password, she or he can change it so that you can log in again.

Additional security for user accounts is provided by the system of permissions, which allows users to deny others access to their files and directories. The security of your account is not only for your protection, but for the protection of the whole UNIX system. Only by gaining access to the system could an unauthorized user break in and read confidential material, change programs or other files, or otherwise wreak havoc. Unprotected user accounts are an easy way for people to access the system illicitly. Even if you have nothing of value in your account, don't take its security lightly.

The system administrator also protects the **root** account from corruption by unauthorized users with an all-important password. The password must be kept secret, since anyone who logged in to the **root** account without authorization could potentially do irreparable damage to the system. It is equally important that the system administrator not lose or forget the **root** password, since without a password there is no way to access the account and perform system administration tasks.

Many files not in user accounts (those in **/bin, /lib**, and other subdirectories of **/**) are protected against reading and writing by all users except the superuser. Thus, while you can execute most of the commands stored in the subdirectories of **/**, you cannot read or make changes to the source code that runs the programs.

Accounting

On UNIX systems with many users, it may be necessary to allocate resources such as printing, CPU time, and disk space among the users to ensure that all users get their share. To this end, a collection of UNIX accounting programs keeps track of the system resources used by all users and stores this information in files accessible by the system administrator. Accounting programs are usually used only to keep track of the use of system resources; on some systems, however, users or their departments may actually be charged for CPU time or printing.

An important accounting task for the system administrator is to make sure that the available space on the hard disk is not used up and that no user or group of users monopolizes too much disk space. The number of files you can have in your account may be limited by the amount of space on the disk and the number of users on your system. If you ever accumulate an exceptionally large number of files in your account, you may be asked to remove some of them.

To a new user, a UNIX system sometimes appears to be a mysterious black box. You issue a command and it gives you some output. Although you can use UNIX for a long time without ever looking beneath the surface of this black box, you will probably feel more comfortable with UNIX if you know something about the workings of the operating system. This chapter aimed to explain some of the features of UNIX and to make it seem less bewildering.

You now know how to use the **ps** and **kill** commands to exercise greater control over your processes. On a Berkeley UNIX system, the job control commands add a degree of convenience to the execution of commands in the C shell. You may not really need to know about the other users of your system. However, you now have the tools to find out about them if you ever want to. Finally, this chapter's overview of system administration should help you understand some of what makes a UNIX system run smoothly.

13 Command Reference

This chapter consists of an alphabetical list of commands. The arguments and options of each command are fully explained. In addition, many of these commands are discussed in detail in one of the other chapters (in which case you will be referred to that chapter). What follows is a list of all commands in this command reference, ordered by subject for easy reference. A short description of each command follows its name.

Communication

mail	Allows you to communicate with other users
mesg	Allows or denies messages sent to a terminal
who	Lists the users currently logged on to the system
write	Writes to another user's terminal

Text Processing

nroff	Formats text for printing on a line printer or letter-quality printer
pr	Paginates files
sed	Edits files noninteractively
spell	Finds spelling errors in a file or the standard input
troff	Formats text for printing on a typesetter or laser printer
vi	Invokes the visual text editor

File and Directory Management

cat	Creates, joins, and displays files or standard input
cd	Changes the user's current, or working, directory
chgrp	Changes the group ID of a file
chmod	Changes the read, write, and execute permissions on files and directories
chown	Changes the ownership of a file or directory
compress	Compresses a file to a smaller size for storage
cp	Copies files
cpio	Copies files into and out of archives for storage, moving, and backups
csplit	Splits files into sections determined according to context
file	Examines a file or directory and reports what type of file it is
find	Recursively searches directories for files that meet certain criteria
grep, egrep, fgrep	Search standard input for specified regular expressions
ln	Makes a link to a file

ls	Lists the contents of directories
mkdir	Creates a directory
mv	Moves and renames files and directories
pwd	Prints the full pathname of the working, or current, directory
rm	Removes files or directories
rmdir	Removes directories
split	Splits a file into pieces of equal length
tar	Saves and restores files to and from archive media
touch	Updates a file's access and modification times
umask	Sets the file create mode mask
wc	Counts the number of lines, words, and characters in a file or the standard input

System Information

cal	Prints a calendar
date	Prints and sets the current time and date
df	Reports the amount of free disk space on file systems, devices, or directories
du	Reports the number of blocks used by a directory or a file
id	Prints your user and group ID names and numbers
news	Displays system news items
ps	Reports process status
tty	Prints the pathname of a terminal's device file

Date Manipulation

awk	Scans for patterns and performs actions on lines of input
banner	Prints strings in large letters

bdiff	Compares files too large to be compared with diff
comm	Compares two sorted files and reports on differences and similarities
csplit	Splits files into sections determined according to context
diff	Compares two files and reports on the differences
echo	Reads arguments and displays them on the standard output
head	Gives the first few lines of input as output
more	Displays files one screenful at a time
paste	Merges lines of files
pg	Displays files for reading one screenful at a time
pr	Paginates files
sed	Edits files noninteractively
sort	Sorts files according to the ASCII collating sequence and merges files
split	Splits a file into pieces of equal length
tail	Gives the last few lines of input as output
tee	Pipes the standard input to both the standard output and specified files
uniq	Prints one occurrence of each input line, even if that line is duplicated

Process Control

at	Executes commands at the time you specify
batch	Executes commands at a later time as soon as the processing load on the system allows
kill	Terminates a process
nice	Executes commands with a different scheduling priority level than usual
nohup	Makes a command keep running after the user logs out
ps	Reports process status

sleep	Suspends execution of a process for a specified interval
time	Times a command

Terminal Control

clear	Clears the user's terminal screen
lock	Locks a user terminal
mesg	Allows or denies messages sent to a terminal
stty	Displays and sets terminal parameters
tty	Prints the pathname of a terminal's device file

Printing

lp	Sends and cancels requests to a line printer
lpstat	Reports the status of the **lp** printing service
pr	Paginates files

Shell Management

csh	Invokes the C shell
newgrp	Temporarily changes a user's group membership
sh	Invokes the Bourne shell command interpreter
shl	Manages shell layers
su	Temporarily switches your effective user ID to that of another user

Program Development

cc   Compiles, assembles, and loads programs writ-
                      ten in the C programming language

make   Keeps a set of programs current

The at and batch commands

The **at** and **batch** commands execute commands at a later time. The **at**
command executes commands at the time you specify, and the **batch**
command executes them as soon as the processing load on the system
allows. After you type the **at** or **batch** command, type one command per
line and press CTRL-D alone on the last line.

Syntax for at

at *time* [*date*] [+ *increment*]
at **-r** *job* . . .
at **-l** [*job* . . .]
at **-q** [*letter*] [*date*] [+*increment*]

Syntax for batch

batch

Options

-l [*job*]   Shows the jobs currently scheduled with **at** and the
                      queue number assigned to them. Shows only those that
                      you have scheduled

-r [*job*] Removes a job that you have scheduled from the **at** or **batch** queue. First you must know the queue number of the job as displayed with the **-l** option

-q*letter* Places the job in the queue specified by *letter*. Each queue has its own scheduling priorities. You can use any lowercase letter, but three letters have special significance, as follows:

  a This places the job in the **at** queue, the default queue

  b This places the job in the **batch** queue. When you use the batch queue, you may or may not specify a time. If you do not specify a time, commands will be executed as soon as the processing load permits, just as with the **batch** command

  c This places the job in the **chron** queue

Arguments

time You can specify the time for an **at** command to be executed with one, two, or four digits. One- and two-digit numbers are interpreted as hours, while four-digit numbers are interpreted as hours and minutes. If a colon separates the hours and minutes (*hour:minute*), you can use three-digit numbers such as 3:35 in addition to two- and four-digit numbers. A 24-hour clock is assumed unless you specify **am** or **pm** as a suffix to the time. If you don't specify a date, the commands are executed at the next occurrence of the specified time. The **at** command also recognizes the times **noon**, **midnight**, and **now**

  You can increment the time by using the special symbol **+**, followed by a number and a unit of time. The acceptable units are **minutes, hours, days, months,** and **years**. The singular of any of these units can be used with the number 1. See the following "Examples" section

date　　　　You can specify a date as well as a time for commands to be executed. You can specify the date as either a month, day, and optional year, or as a day of the week. If you specify a month, day, and year, the format is

month day(, year)

where *month* is the name of month spelled fully or abbreviated to three characters, *day* is a one- or two-digit number, and *year* is an optional two- or four-digit number. If you specify a day of the week, you can use either the full name or the first three letters. You can precede either type of date by the special word **next**. (See the following "Examples" section.) If you specify no date, the date **today** is assumed. The special date **tomorrow** is also recognized

Notes

■ The Berkeley UNIX **at** command behaves much like the System V **at** command, but has a different set of options.

■ You must have permission to use **at** or **batch**. If you are unable to use **at**, look at the file **/usr/lib/cron/at.deny**. If your login name is in this file, or if the file does not exist, you probably don't have permission to use **at**.

■ If you use the **at** or **batch** command with the redirect symbol <, all the commands in a command or script file are executed without your having to press CTRL-D (see the first example that follows).

Examples

The following example shows how you would use **at** to run a script file called **prepare** at noon on October 23rd:

```
% at noon oct 23 < prepare
```

The following example shows how you would use **batch** to join three files into another file, remove the three original files, and then format the resulting file with **nroff**. After you pressed CTRL-D, these commands would be executed as soon as the processing load on the system allowed.

```
% batch
cat proj1 proj2 proj3 > projn
rm proj1 proj2 proj3
nroff -mm projn > proj.fin.n
^D
```

The following example shows how you would mail a file called **report** to users **murray** and **baldwin** at 2:00 P.M. next Wednesday:

```
% at 2pm next wed
mail murray baldwin < report
^D
```

The following example shows how you would do the same thing as in the preceding example but at 2:00 p.m. in two days:

```
% at 2pm + 2 days
mail murray baldwin < report
^D
```

The awk Command

The **awk** command looks for and processes patterns in the input. The **awk** utility can perform mathematical calculations on numerical input and make changes to textual input.

Syntax

awk *'program'* [*file* . . .]

awk [**-F***c*] **-f** *program-file* [*file* . . .]

The **awk** utility can scan input for particular patterns or fields and perform actions on lines or fields of the input. The patterns to search for, and the actions to be performed on them, are specified in the form of a *program*.

Arguments

You may type an **awk** command in one of two formats. In the first format, you specify on the command line the program **awk** is to execute on the input. In the second format, the program is contained in a file that you give as an argument to the **-f** option.

Options

-F*c*	Specifies a different character *c* as the input field separator instead of the default whitespace separators (spaces and tabs). The field separator can be only one character
-f *program-file*	Causes **awk** to read the program of patterns and actions to be performed from the file *program-file* instead of from the command line

Programs

An **awk** program consists of a pattern and an action to be performed on lines or portions of lines matching that pattern. The format of an awk program is *pattern { action }*

where the action is enclosed in braces following the pattern. If an **awk** program does not contain a pattern, the action is carried out on every line of the input. If no action is given, lines matching the pattern are printed.

Patterns

A pattern in an **awk** command can be a regular expression enclosed in slashes or a numerical value that matches a line or a particular field on a line. To test whether a pattern matches a specific field on the line or a variable, you can use the operator ~ (tilde) as follows:

variable ~ /regular expression/

where *variable* is the field or other variable you want the pattern to match. The section "Variables" explains how to refer to fields and other variables. The operator !~ tests for a field that does *not* match a pattern. If the pattern is a regular expression alone, a line will match this pattern if the regular expression occurs anywhere on the line.

A numeral not enclosed in slashes is treated as a number and can be used to compare numerical values. The format for comparing numerical values of variables is

variable operator number

where *variable* is the name of a field or other variable (as explained in "Variables") and *operator* is one of the following operators:

<	Less than
< =	Less than or equal to
= =	Equal to
!=	Not equal to
>	Greater than
> =	Greater than or equal to

Two patterns separated by a comma indicate a range of lines beginning with a line matching the first pattern and ending with the next line matching the second pattern. An action following two patterns separated by a comma will apply to all lines in the range.

Two patterns may also be separated by one of the two Boolean operators ||, which stands for "or," or &&, which stands for "and." That is, the pattern

/pattern1/ || */pattern2/*

will match all lines that contain either *pattern1* or *pattern2*. In contrast, the pattern

/pattern1/ && */pattern2/*

will match only those lines that contain both *pattern1* and *pattern2*.

The special pattern **BEGIN** allows you to specify actions to be performed before **awk** begins processing the input lines. The pattern **END** allows you to specify actions to be performed after **awk** has finished processing the input lines.

Actions

The action portion of an **awk** program tells **awk** what action to take on the lines matched by patterns. If you do not specify an action following a pattern, lines matching the pattern are printed as output.

You can use the **print** command to print one or more fields of a line, text, or the value of a variable. The format of the print command is

{print *x*}

where *x* is the name of any field or other variable, or ordinary text enclosed in double quotes. For example, to print the words "Number 1 is" and then the first field of a line, you would use the following action:

```
{print "Number 1 is " $1}
```

The section "Variables" explains how to refer to fields and other variables. See the following "Examples" section for more examples of the **print** command.

Variables

You can create your own variables to stand for anything you want. In addition, **awk** maintains a set of built-in variables that you can use in both the pattern and the action portion of an **awk** program. The built-in variables include the following:

NR	The current record number. By default, a record is one line, but you may change this by assigning a different value to the RS variable
$0	The current record (all fields on the line)
NF	The number of fields on the current record
$1-$n	The fields in the current record, where *n* is the last field in the record
FS	Input field separator. By changing this variable, you could use different field separators in different lines of the input. By default, spaces and tabs are the input field separators
OFS	Output field separator. By default, spaces are the output field separators
RS	Input record separator. By default, this is a newline character, which means that a record is one line
ORS	Output record separator. By default, this is a newline character
FILENAME	The name of the current input file

When you use the name of a variable in either the pattern or the action portion of an **awk** program, the name refers to the current value of that variable. You can change the values of these variables with any of the operators discussed in the next section.

Operators

You can use the following operators to perform mathematical operations on the values of variables:

e1 + *e2*	Adds the expressions *e1* and *e2*
e1 - *e2*	Subtracts the expression *e2* from the expression *e1*
e1 * *e2*	Multiplies the expression *e1* by the expression *e2*
e1 / *e2*	Divides the expression *e1* by the expression *e2*
e1 % *e2*	Divides *e1* by *e2* and gives the remainder
v = *e*	Assigns the value of the expression *e* to the variable v, where *v* is any built-in variable or any of the variables that you have initialized. This works for assigning strings, as well as numerical values, to variables
v ++	Increments the variable *v*
v --	Decrements the variable *v*
v += *e*	Increases the value of the variable *v* by the value of the expression *e*
v -= *e*	Decreases the value of the variable *v* by the value of the expression *e*
v *= *e*	Multiplies the value of the variable *v* by the value of the expression *e* and assigns the result to the variable *v*
v /= *e*	Divides the value of the variable *v* by the value of the expression *e* and assigns the result to the variable *v*
v %= *e*	Divides the value of the variable *v* by the value of the expression *e* and assigns the result to the variable *v*

Functions

Here are some of the functions you can use to manipulate numbers and strings:

length(*s*)	Returns the number of characters in the string *s*
int(*n*)	Returns the integer portion of the number *n*
sub(*old*,*new*,*in*)	Replaces the first occurrence of the regular expression *old* with the regular expression *new* in the string *in*. The regular expressions *old* and *new* must be enclosed in double quotes

gsub(*old*,*new*,*in*)   Replaces all occurrences of the regular expression *old* with the regular expression *new* in the string *in*. The regular expressions *old* and *new* must be enclosed in double quotes

index (*s1*,*s2*)   Reports the position in the string *s1* where the string *s2* first occurs. If the strings are regular expressions, they must be enclosed in double quotes

Notes

■ Only the rudiments of the **awk** utility are explained here. For more information on **awk**, refer to the Bell Labs publication, *Awk — A Pattern Scanning and Processing Language*. This text is written by the creators of **awk**: Alfred V. Aho, Peter J. Weinberger, and Brian W. Kernighan.

Examples

The **awk** examples in this section all take as input the file **radio**, which is displayed here with **cat**:

```
% cat radio
Sun    10am    Breakfast-in-Bed         KZSC  88.1  $35
Mon    7pm     Closet-Free_Radio        KZSC  89.1  $35
Tues   12n     Latin-American_Music     KRMR  93.1  $10
Tues   9pm     The_Living_Spirit        KKUP  91.5  $60
Tues   9pm     Ragtime/Dixie_Show       KAZU  90.3  $40
Wed    9am     Spirit_of_Africa         KRMR  93.1  $10
Wed    9am     Brazilian/Cuban_Music    KZSC  88.1  $35
Thu    7pm     Just_Jean-Bluegrass      KKUP  91.5  $60
Fri    3pm     Roses_of_Portugal        KZSC  89.1  $35
Sat    5pm     African_Music,Etc.       KAZU  90.3  $40
Sat    7pm     Latin-American_Music     KAZU  90.3  $40
```

Each line in this file contains six fields separated by tabs. The fields show the day of the week, the time, the name of a radio show, a radio station, its number, and a subscription amount.

The following example shows how a simple **awk** program specified on the command line operates on the file **radio**. The program selects all lines on which the first field contains the pattern "Tues" and prints the first four fields of those lines. The commas between the names of the field variables cause the output fields to be separated by spaces.

```
% awk '$1~/Tues/ {print $1,$2,$3,$4}' radio
```

The next example uses a program in a file called **sort.by.day** to print some of the information in **radio** in a different format. The file **sort.by.day** is first displayed with **cat**.

```
% cat sort.by.day
NR == 1 {ST = $1
print ""
print "The shows on " $1 " are: "
print $3 " at " $2 " on " $4"."
}
$1 == ST {print $3 " at " $2 " on " $4"."}
$1 != ST {ST = $1
print ""
print "The shows on " $1 " are: "
print $3 " at " $2 " on " $4"."
}
```

This program first initializes a variable **ST** to be equal to the first field of the first input line and prints some text and some of the fields from that line. For each other line, **awk** checks to see if the first field matches the value of the variable **ST**. If it does, fields 3, 2, and 4 of the line are printed, along with some text. If it does not, the value of **ST** is reset to this value and the process repeats. The following example shows the output of **awk** with this program on the file **radio**:

```
% awk -f sort.by.day radio

The shows on Sun are:
Breakfast-in-Bed at 10am on KZSC.

The shows on Mon are:
Closet-Free_Radio at 7pm on KZSC.

The shows on Tues are:
Latin-American_Music at 12n on KRMR.
The_Living_Spirit at 9pm on KKUP.
Ragtime/Dixie_Show at 10pm on KAZU.

The shows on Wed are:
Spirit_of_Africa at 9am on KRMR.
Brazilian/Cuban_Music at 9am on KZSC.
```

```
The shows on Thu are:
Just_Jean-Bluegrass at 7pm on KKUP.

The shows on Fri are:
Roses_of_Portugal at 3pm on KZSC.

The shows on Sat are:
African_Music,Etc. at 5pm on KAZU.
Latin-American_Music at 7pm on KAZU.
```

The next example uses the program file **late** to print out only information about shows that begin at 7 P.M. or later. The file **late** is first displayed with **cat**.

```
% cat late
BEGIN {print "The late evening shows are:"
$2~/pm/ && int($2) >= 7 {print $3,"at",$2,"on",$4}
```

Before **awk** begins processing the input file, the "BEGIN" pattern causes text to be printed. Then two patterns select the lines from which fields are to be printed. The first pattern selects only lines where the second field contains the regular expression "pm". The second pattern selects only lines where the integer portion of the second field is greater than or equal to 7. Because these two patterns are separated by the Boolean operator **&&**, both of them must be matched for a line to be selected. The following example shows the output of **awk** with this program on the file **radio**:

```
% awk -f late radio
The late evening shows are:
Closet-Free_Radio at 7pm on KZSC
The_Living_Spirit at 9pm on KKUP
Ragtime/Dixie_Show at 10pm on KAZU
Just_Jean-Bluegrass at 7pm on KKUP
Latin-American_Music at 7pm on KAZU
```

The banner Command

The **banner** command prints any string of up to ten characters in large letters composed of pound signs. This command is useful for printing names at the beginning of printouts.

Syntax

banner *string*

Notes

■ The **banner** utility on some systems prints only uppercase letters. However, it is case sensitive and prints lowercase input letters as small capitals and uppercase input letters as large capitals.

Examples

The following example shows how to print the word "Jack" in large letters. Notice that the "J" is slightly larger than the other letters.

```
% banner Jack
        #
        #    ##        ####    #    #
        #   #  #     #     #   #    #
        #   #   #   #          ####
 #      #   ######  #          #    #
 #      # #     #   #     #     #    #
 ####   #      #     ####    #    #
```

The bdiff Command

The **bdiff** command compares files too large to be compared with **diff** by first splitting them into smaller segments. It finds lines that are different in the two files, and prints them as output that is the same as the output of **diff**.

Syntax

bdiff *file1* *file2* [*n*] [-**s**]

Options

n   Specifies the number of lines the files are to be split into before being compared

-**s**   Keeps **bdiff** diagnostics from being printed

If either *file1* or *file2* is replaced with a hyphen (-), the standard input is
read in place of a file.

Notes

■ Because files are segmented, and only lines within segments are
compared, more than the actual number of differences may be reported
with **bdiff**.

■ If the first difference is not found in the first segment, an error will
be received. If this happens, specify segments large enough so that at
least the first difference is in the first segment.

Example

The following example shows how you would compare two files,
personnel1 and **personnel2**, in 300-line segments:

```
% bdiff personnel1 personnel2 300
```

The cal Command

The **cal** command prints a calendar for the current month and adjacent months or for a specified month and/or year.

Syntax

cal [*month*] [*year*]

You can type months either as numbers (1-12) or as enough lowercase letters of the name to uniquely identify it (**d** for December, **mar** for March, and so on). The whole name of the month is also acceptable.

Notes

■ If you specify no month or year, the current month and the two adjacent months are displayed.

■ If you specify only a month, that month for the current year is displayed.

■ If you type only one number, **cal** interprets it as a year.

■ If you specify only a year, all months for that year are displayed.

■ You must specify all digits in a year number. That is,

```
cal 90
```

displays the calendar for the year 90, not 1990.

Examples

The following command displays a calendar for April of the current year:

% **cal ap**

```
      April 1990
 S  M Tu  W Th  F  S
 1  2  3  4  5  6  7
 8  9 10 11 12 13 14
15 16 17 18 19 20 21
22 23 24 25 26 27 28
29 30
```

The following example displays a calendar for June of the year 2000:

% **cal 6 2000**

```
      June 2000
 S  M Tu  W Th  F  S
 1  2  3
 4  5  6  7  8  9 10
11 12 13 14 15 16 17
18 19 20 21 22 23 24
25 26 27 28 29 30
```

The calendar Command

The **calendar** command consults the file **calendar** in your home directory and sends you mail if there are any entries containing today's or tomorrow's date. This program is usually run automatically under the care of **cron**.

Syntax

calendar [-]

If you give the - option, **calendar** checks the **calendar** files in every user's home directory, mailing to everyone any lines with relevant dates.

To have **calendar** send you messages, simply create the **calendar** file in your home directory and put one event per line with its date. Most ways of specifying dates are recognized. For example Nov. 28, november 28, and 11/28 are all valid ways of specifying that date.

Notes

■ For **calendar** to work, the **calendar** file in your home directory must be readable by everyone.

■ See also **mail**.

The cat Command

The **cat** command reads lines from the input and gives them as standard output. You can use **cat** to create, display, and join files.

Syntax

cat [**-svte**] *file* . . .

Options

-s	Suppresses error messages that are usually printed when you attempt to use **cat** on a nonexistent file
-v	Prints nonprinting characters such as control characters as the printable character ^X, where X is a letter, rather than as the actual control character
-t	Prints tabs in a file as ^I. Works only if used in conjunction with the **-v** option

-e   Prints an $ at the end of each line. Works only if used in conjunction with the **-v** option

Notes

■ The **cat** utility is usually used with redirection symbols. Only with redirection symbols can you join two or more files into another file.

■ See Chapter 4, "Files and Directories," and Chapter 5, "UNIX Command-Line Fundamentals," for more information about **cat**.

Examples

The following example shows how you would display a file called **assets**:

```
% cat assets
```

The following example shows how you would create a file called **assets**:

```
% cat > assets
```

The following example shows how you would combine the **stocks** and **bonds** files into a file called **assets**:

```
% cat stocks bonds > assets
```

The cc Command

The **cc** command compiles, assembles, and loads programs written in the C programming language. It also assembles and loads assembly language programs, and loads object programs. See Chapter 11, "Program Development with C," for more discussion of **cc**.

Syntax

cc [**-cgOS**] [**-o** *file*] *file* . . . [**-l***arg*]

The cd Command

The **cd** command changes the current, or working, directory to the user's home directory or to a specified directory.

Syntax

cd [*directory*]

If you do not specify a directory, **cd** makes your home directory the current directory. If the directory is a subdirectory of the current directory, you can use its short name. Otherwise, you must use either the full or relative pathname of the directory.

Notes

■ The **cd** program is not actually a UNIX utility, but a built-in part of the Bourne shell, the C shell, and the Korn shell.

■ See Chapter 4, "Files and Directories," for a discussion of **cd**.

Examples

The following example changes the current directory to a directory called **receipts**, which is a subdirectory of the current directory:

```
% cd receipts
```

The following command changes the current directory to the directory **/usr/bin** (the current directory is not **/**, so the whole pathname of the directory must be specified).

```
% cd /usr/bin
```

The chgrp Command

The **chgrp** command changes the group ID of a file. This is useful if you want to make a file readable or writeable for a group other than your own, but not for everyone on the whole system. Since the only permission categories are owner, group, and others, you can make a file readable by one group and not another only by having the file associated with that group.

Syntax

chgrp *group file* . . .

Notes

■ Unless you are the superuser, you can only change the group ID of files that you own.

■ See also **chmod** and **chown**.

Example

The following example shows how you would change the group ID of a file called **suggestions** to the group **accounting**:

```
% chgrp accounting suggestions
```

The chmod Command

The **chmod** command changes the read, write, and execute permissions on files and directories.

Syntax

chmod *mode file* . . .
chmod *who* **+-=** *permission* . . . *file* . . .

There are two ways of changing the permissions on a file. You can use a *mode* number that represents all the permissions on the file. This number is known as the *absolute mode*. Alternately, you can specify which users or (*who*) the permission is to be given to or taken away from, followed by the specific permissions to be given or taken away. This way of setting the permissions is called the *symbolic mode*.

Symbolic Mode Arguments

The format for setting permissions in symbolic mode is

chmod *who* **+-=** *permission* . . . *file* . . .

The symbols used for each of the symbolic mode arguments are listed next.

who (the classes of users for whom permissions are granted or denied):

u (user)	The owner of the file
g (group)	The group to which the file belongs (a file may belong to a group other than that of its owner)
o (others)	All other users besides the owner and his or her group
a (all)	All users – the owner, the group, and others

Operations (granting and denying permissions):

+	Grants the following permissions to the specified classes of users
-	Takes away the following permissions from the specified classes of users
=	Assigns the following permissions to the specified classes of users and takes away all other permissions for those users. If no permission is assigned, all existing permissions are taken away

Permissions:

r	Permission to read, or view, the file or directory
w	Permission to write, or make changes to, the file
x	Permission to execute the file as a program
s	Sets the user or group ID to that of the owner upon execution of the file. If the specified user is **u**, the user ID is set. If the specified user is **g**, the group ID is set
t	Sets the *sticky bit*, which saves a program in memory when it is executed. Only the superuser can set this permission

Absolute Mode   Absolute mode numbers are a bit more complex than the symbolic codes. You can use them to set *all* the permissions for a file with one number. Each permission is represented by an octal number. To set all the permissions, simply add the individual permissions you want the file to have. The numbers assigned to the permissions are listed here, and examples of absolute modes are shown in the "Examples" section.

4000	Sets the user ID when the program is executed
2000	Sets the group ID when the program is executed
1000	Sets the sticky bit
0400	Read permission for the owner
0200	Write permission for the owner
0100	Execute permission for the owner
0040	Read permission for the group
0020	Write permission for the group
0010	Execute permission for the group
0004	Read permission for others
0002	Write permission for others
0001	Execute permission for others

Note that the first digit is 0 unless a special permission is set. The second digit indicates the owner permissions, the third digit indicates the group permissions, and the fourth digit indicates the permissions for others.

Notes

■ No matter what permissions you have set on your files, the superuser has read and write permission on all files on the system and execute permission on all files with execute permission for anyone.

■ When the first digit in a mode number is 0, you do not have to include it in the mode number.

■ See Chapter 4, "Files and Directories," for a discussion of **chmod**. See also **chgrp** and **chown**.

Examples

Following are examples for both symbolic mode and absolute mode.

Symbolic Mode To give read permission on a file called **forum** to all users, you would type

```
% chmod a+r forum
```

To take away execute permission on a directory called **private** for users in your group, you would type

```
% chmod g-x private
```

To take away all existing permissions on a file called **data.base** for users not in your group, you would type

```
% chmod o= data.base
```

Absolute Mode To set read permission only on a file called **california** for the owner of the file, you could type

```
% chmod 0400 california
```

Since the first digit in this number is 0, you can leave it out. The following example sets the same permission:

```
% chmod 400 california
```

For the remainder of these examples, first digits of 0 will be omitted.
    To set only write permission for the owner on the same file, you would type

```
% chmod 200 california
```

The number that represents both read and write permission for the owner is 600, the sum of the numbers for the individual permissions. To set these permissions, you would type

```
% chmod 600 california
```

To set read, write, and execute permission for the owner, you would type

```
% chmod 700 california
```

To set all permissions for the owner and read permission only for the group and other users, you would type

```
% chmod 744 california
```

The chown Command

The **chown** command changes the ownership of a file.

Syntax

chown *user file* . . .

The *user* argument may be either a user's ID number or his or her login name.

Notes

■ Unless you are the superuser, you can only change the ownership of a file that you own.

■ Once you change the ownership of one of your files, you will no longer be able to access that file unless it has access permissions for other users besides the owner. (Of course, this does not apply if you are the superuser.)

■ See also **chgrp** and **chmod**.

Example

The following example shows how you would change the ownership of a file called **smith.acct** to the user **mcdowell**:

```
% chown mcdowell smith.acct
```

The clear Command

The **clear** command clears the user's terminal screen.

Syntax

clear [*termtype*]

The **clear** command gets the terminal type from the TERM environment variable in the **.login** or **.profile** file. If this variable is not set, you can supply the terminal type on the command line.

Notes

If a user's terminal cannot clear the screen, **clear** outputs enough new lines to scroll all text off the screen. If the terminal is a printing terminal, **clear** advances the paper to the top of the next page.

The comm Command

The **comm** command compares two sorted files and displays lines unique to each file and lines common to the two files.

Syntax

comm [- [**123**]] *file1 file2*

Ordinarily, the output is displayed in three columns:

- Lines unique to the first file are not indented.
- Lines unique to the second file are indented by one tab.
- Lines common to the two files are indented by two tabs.

The flags **1**, **2**, and **3** suppress the output of the corresponding columns. If you substitute a - for *file1*, *file2* will be compared with the standard input.

Notes

- Since the input files must be sorted in order for **comm** to work, this utility is not very useful for comparing text files.

Examples

The following command would print only the lines common to the two files **stat1** and **stat2**:

```
% comm -12 stat1 stat2
```

The following command would print only those lines unique to either of the two files:

```
% comm -3 stat1 stat2
```

The compress Command

The **compress** command compresses a file to a smaller size for storage. You can later uncompress files with the **uncompress** command. This command is useful when disk space is at a premium.

Syntax

compress [-cdfF]

Options

-d	Decompresses a compressed file (same as **uncompress**)
-c	Writes output to the standard output without removing the original file. Since the output is not readable, you must use a redirection symbol if you use this option
-f	Overwrites a previous output file with the same name
-F	Compresses the file even if compression saves no space

Notes

■ Compressed files are not readable except with the command **zcat**. If you attempt to read one, your terminal will probably lock.

The cp Command

The **cp** command copies files.

Syntax

cp *file1 file2*

cp *file . . . directory*

The first syntax will copy one file to another file with a different name in the same directory. The second copies a file or group of files into a different directory.

Notes

■ See Chapter 4, "Files and Directories," for a discussion of **cp**.

Examples

The following example shows how you would make a copy of a file called **results** in the same directory. The copy will be called **res.backup**.

```
% cp results res.backup
```

The following example shows how you copy the file **results** into another directory, whose pathname is **$HOME/backups**. The copy will have the same name as the original file: **results**.

```
% cp results $HOME/backups
```

The cpio Command

The **cpio** command copies files into and out of archives for storage, moving, and backups. Archives can be ordinary files, directories, or backup media such as floppy disks.

Syntax

cpio -o [acBv]
cpio -i [*options*] [*patterns*]
cpio -p [*options*] *directory*

The **cpio** command has three different formats, each of which uses a different required option. These required options may not be used in combination. There are additional options that you can combine with the required options and with each other. The **cpio** command takes its input from the standard input, not from files typed as arguments. If you do not use a redirection symbol or a pipe to redirect input to **cpio**, it will wait for input. Type file names, one per line, and then press CTRL-D on a line by itself. With the **cpio -o** form of the command, you must also direct the *output* to a file.

Required Options

-o[*options*]	(Copy out) Causes **cpio** to read a list of file names from its standard input and combine them into an archive file, which it prints as the standard output
-i[*options*] [*patterns*]	(Copy in) Causes **cpio** to retrieve files from its standard input, which must be an archive created with **cpio -o**. These files are then copied to the current directory. The *patterns* select the files that are to be copied. You can use the wildcard characters ? and * in these patterns, but each pattern must be enclosed in double quotes. If you specify no pattern, all files are copied
-p[*options*] *directory*	Causes **cpio** to read a list of ordinary files from its standard input and copy them to the named *directory*. This is useful for copying directories and their contents

Other Options

-a	Resets access times of input files after they are copied
-c	Writes the header information in ASCII characters for portability. You must use this option if you plan to transfer files to a machine of a different type from the original

-d   Creates directories as needed. Use this option when some of the files you are copying are directories. Do not use **-d** with the **-o** option

-f   Copies only files *not* matched by patterns specified with the **-i** option

-l   If you use this option, **cpio** will create links to files in the new directories instead of copies of them whenever possible. You can use **-l** only with the **-p** option

-m   Does not change the modification time of files when they are copied. This does not work for directories

-r   Lets you rename files as they are copied. As **cpio** copies each file, it pauses and waits for you to type a new name. If you press RETURN, the file will not be copied. If you type . (period), the original name will be used

-t   Lists the names of the input files without copying them. You can use this option with the **-i** option to determine the names of the files in an archive

-u   Ordinarily, **cpio** will not overwrite a newer file with an older one. This option causes a file to be copied even if it overwrites a newer file with the same name

-v   Prints a list of the files being copied

Notes

■ See also **find,** particularly the **-cpio** and **-depth** expressions.

Examples

The following example shows how you would copy all the files in the current directory to floppy disk on the device **/dev/dsfd048ds9**. Directories will not be copied. The input to the **cpio** is the list of file names generated by the **ls** command. This list is piped to the **cpio** command, and the output is redirected to the device **/dev/dsfd048ds9**.

```
% ls | cpio -o > /dev/dsfd048ds9
```

The following example shows how you would retrieve all the files from the archive created in the previous example. Since a file's pathname is preserved when it is copied into an archive, when it is retrieved, it will be copied to its original directory. The **-v** option causes the names of all the files retrieved to be printed on the standard output.

```
% cpio -iv < /dev/dsfd048ds9
burble
keats
kirkwood
steele
velasquez
walker
```

The next example shows how you would retrieve all files beginning with the letter "c" from an archive called **products.arc**. Since a file's pathname is preserved when it is copied into an archive, each file will be copied to its directory of origin.

```
% cpio -iv "c*" < products.arc
cat.convert
cushions
custard
```

The following example copies all files and subdirectories in the current directory into another directory whose relative pathname is **$HOME /backups**. Only with the **-d** option can the subdirectories be copied.

```
% cpio -pd $HOME/backups
```

The csh Command

The **csh** command invokes the C shell command interpreter. See Chapter 10, "The C Shell", for a detailed discussion of **csh**.

Syntax

csh [*-options*]

The csplit Command

The **csplit** command splits files into sections determined according to context. By default, sections are placed in files called **x00, x01**, and so on, up to **x99**.

Syntax

csplit [-s] [-f *prefix*] *file arg1* [. . .*argn*]

The first file gets that part of the original file from the beginning up to, but not including, the first line referenced by *arg1* (see "Context Arguments"). The second file gets the lines from the first one referenced by *arg1* up to but not including the line referenced by *arg2,* and so on. The last file gets from the line referenced by *argn* to the end of the file.

Options

-s	Suppresses printing of character counts for each file created
-k	Causes **csplit** to leave intact files created previous to the error if an error occurs. (Ordinarily, these files are removed if an error occurs.)
-f *prefix*	Changes the default prefix for created files from **xx** to *prefix,* where *prefix* is any string of characters that are legal in file names (see Chapter 4, "Files and Directories")

Context Arguments

The context arguments *arg1* through *argn* can be any combination of the following:

/rexp/	A regular expression enclosed in slashes. If the regular expression includes spaces or characters that are magic characters to the shell, they must be enclosed in single quotes. This creates a section beginning with the current line and up to, but not including, the first line containing the regular expression. This argument may be followed by an optional **+** or **-** and a number of lines, as is illustrated in the following "Examples" section
%rexp%	The same as */rexp/* except that no file is created for the section ending with this expression
line	Any line number. A section is created starting with the current line and up to, but not including, the line specified with number *line,* which then becomes the current line
{num}	Repeats the previous argument *n* times. If it follows a regular expression argument, it will apply that argument *n* times. If it follows a line number argument, it will split the files every *line* lines

Notes

■ If you want to split a file into sections of equal length, it is simpler to use the **split** command than to use **csplit** with line number context arguments.

■ If you are using the C shell, the braces **{** and **}** used with the *num* argument must be preceded by backslashes to be correctly interpreted (that is \{*num*\}).

■ See Chapter 5, "UNIX Command-Line Fundamentals," for a discussion of regular expressions.

■ Because **csplit** is a filter, the original file is not removed when it is split. You must remove the file if you want it removed.

Examples

The following example shows how you would split a file called **lecture** into three sections, the first from the beginning of the file to the first line containing the pattern "Section 2", the second beginning at that line and continuing to the first line containing the pattern "Section 3", and the third starting with that line and continuing to the end of the file. Note that because the regular expressions "Section 2" and "Section 3" contain spaces, they must be enclosed in single quotes.

```
% csplit lecture /'Section 2'/ /'Section 3'/
```

The following example illustrates how you would split a file into several sections, the first ending with the line before the first occurrence of the word "Section." Since the {*num*} argument specifies that the context argument be repeated nine times, up to ten sections will be created. Since the −k option is given, if there are not ten occurrences of "Section" in the file, **csplit** will create as many as possible.

```
% csplit -k lecture /Section/ {9}
```

The date Command

The **date** command prints and sets the current time and date.

Syntax

date [*mmddhhmm*[*yy*]]

date [+*format*]

The **date** command has two formats, one to set a new date, and one to display the date. To set a new date, you would type

date *mmddhhmm*(*yy*)

where the first *mm* is two digits that represent the month, *dd* is two digits that represent the day of the month, *hh* is two digits that represent the hour, and the second *mm* is two digits that represent the minute. *yy* is optional and represents the last two digits of the year. You can only set a new date if you are the superuser.

If you type **date** without arguments, the current date is displayed in the format *day month date hour:minute:second zone year*. However, you can change this format by selecting which fields you want to be displayed with which format. Format arguments follow a **+** and each one is preceded by a %. If you specify any format argument, the regular output of **date** will be suppressed, and the item specified by that argument will be the only output. If you use more than one format argument, you must enclose the whole list in single quotes to protect the spaces between the arguments from the shell.

Anything after a **+** not preceded by a % is treated as ordinary text. By typing words or punctuation between format arguments, you could label and punctuate the date, as shown in the "Examples" section. The following list explains each of the format arguments.

Format Arguments

a	Weekday abbreviated to three letters
d	Day of the month
D	Date in *month/day/year* format
h	Month abbreviated to three letters
H	Hour on a 24-hour clock
j	Day of the year (001-366)
m	Month in two digits (01, 09, and so on)
M	Minutes in two digits
n	Inserts a newline character
r	Time in A.M./P.M. notation
S	Seconds in two digits
t	Inserts a tab character (used to separate fields)
T	Time in *hour:minute:second* format
w	Day of the week as a number from 0 through 7 (Sunday is 0)
y	Last two digits of the year

Notes

■ The format arguments of **date** are most useful in an alias or shell script, so you don't have to type them out every time you want to see the date.

Examples

The following example sets the new date to 3:03 P.M., September 1, 1990. Only the superuser can execute this command.

```
% date 1001150390
```

The following example shows the date displayed in its ordinary format:

```
% date
Mon Aug 20 14:06:45 PDT 1990
```

The next example shows a different way of displaying the date, using some formatting arguments and textual labels. Notice that the text and format arguments can all be integrated within the single quotes.

```
% date +'Today is: %a %h %d, and it is now %r.'
Today is: Mon Aug 20, and it is now 02:06:45 PM.
```

The final example shows yet another way of displaying the date using different formatting arguments. Notice that the **%n** format command inserts a newline character between the two parts of the date.

```
% date +'Today's date: %D %n Current time: %r'
Today's date: 08/20/90
 Current time: 02:06:45 PM
```

The df Command

The **df** command reports the amount of available disk space for the root file system and any other mounted device or directory. The free disk space is reported in terms of blocks.

Syntax

df [**-ftv**] [*file systems*]

If no *file systems* are specified, **df** reports on all mounted file systems. If a list of *file systems* is given, **df** reports only on those.

Options

f   Reports only the number of free blocks, not the number of free inodes

t   Reports the total blocks allocated to the file system, along with the number of free blocks

v   Reports the number of blocks used, as well as the number available

The diff Command

The **diff** command compares two files and tells what lines you would have to change to make the two files identical. That is, all differing lines are displayed as output along with the **ed** editing commands that you would perform to convert *file1* into *file2*.

Syntax

diff *file1 file2*

If you replace either *file1* or *file2* with the name of a directory, the remaining file will be compared with a file of the same name in the named directory.

Options

-b   Ignores trailing strings of whitespace characters, and treats as equal all other strings of whitespace characters

-e   Creates a script for the **ed** editor that will edit *file1* to make it the same as *file2*

-f   Creates a script that shows how *file2* would be converted into *file1*. Scripts produced with this option cannot be used with **ed**

Notes

■ You can use the **-e** option of **diff** to make *file1* identical to *file2*. However, a simpler way to get two identical files is to make a copy of a file with **cp**. Users often use **diff** just to see the differences between two files.

■ If you are using **diff** only to view the lines that make two files different, it is helpful to pipe the output of **diff** to **more,** since a long list of differing lines would scroll off the screen too quickly for you to read.

■ The **diff** utility does not work well on very long files. To compare very large files, you should use **bdiff**.

Example

The following example shows how you would compare a file called **synopsis** with a file called **synopsis2**. It also shows a sample output of the **diff** command. The lines containing numbers are editing commands that indicate the changes needed in **synopsis** to make it identical to **synopsis2**. For example, the first line shows that you would have to change lines 2 and 3 of **synopsis** to lines 2 and 3 of **synopsis2**. Lines preceded by < are lines in the first file (in this case **synopsis**), while lines preceded by > are lines in the second file (in this case **synopsis2**).

```
% diff synopsis /u/bin
2,3c2,3
< national conference, held this year at our headquarters in
< Barstow. We expect a turnout of over 50,000,000 members from
> conference, held this year at our national headquarters in
> Barstow. We expect a turnout of over 50 million members from
8c8,10
< seminar/exhibit portion of the conference.
> seminar/exhibit portion of the conference.
>     We advise all members from this branch who plan on
> attending the conference in any capacity to familiarize
```

The du Command

The **du** command reports the number of blocks used by a directory (including all of its subdirectories and files) or a file.

Syntax

du [**-ars**] [*directories*] [*files*]

Information for files will only be displayed if you give either the **-a** or **-s** option (see the "Options" section). If you don't specify any files or directories, **du** displays information for the current directory.

Options

-a   Displays information for files as well as directories
-r   Prints error messages for each file or directory in the named list that cannot be opened or is not readable
-s   Displays total disk usage for the directories and files you specify, but not for any subdirectories or unnamed files

Examples

The following example shows how you would display information for all files and subdirectories in your home directory. Remember, if you are using the C shell, you can substitute ~ for **$HOME**.

```
% du -a $HOME
```

The following example shows how you would display information only for the files **mcgill.a, kraz.a, and fuller.a**:

```
% du -s mcgill.a kraz.a fuller.a
```

The echo Command

The **echo** command reads one or more arguments and displays them on the standard output, separated by spaces and ending with a newline character. You can use the **echo** command to send messages to a terminal or to a file from a shell script.

Syntax

echo *arguments*

Arguments

The *arguments* may consist of ordinary text, in which case the text will simply be printed. An argument may also contain wildcard characters, in which case it is interpreted as the names of a set of files and/or subdirectories in the current directory (illustrated in the "Examples" section). Finally, an argument may contain special escape sequences, which must be enclosed in single quotes to be properly interpreted by the shell. The escape sequences meaningful to **echo** are as follows:

\n	Inserts a newline character
\b	Inserts a backspace
\c	Suppresses the newline character normally printed at the end of the line
****	Prints a backslash

Notes

■ It is a good idea to enclose an entire message in single quotes in case you use any wildcard characters or escape sequences.

■ Escape sequences will not work if there are arguments containing wildcard characters on the same line.

■ Only the arguments given on the same line as the **echo** command will be printed as output. If your arguments take up more than one line, you must precede each newline character with a backslash. Also, the entire output will be printed as one line unless you insert newline characters with the escape sequence **\n**.

Examples

The following example prints the message "Hello! How are you?" to the standard output. Note that **?** is interpreted by the shell as a wildcard character; it must be either preceded by a backslash or enclosed in single quotes. Here, the entire message is enclosed in single quotes.

```
% echo 'Hello! How are you?'
Hello! How are you?
```

The following example prints the phrase "The files ending with .a are:" followed by a list of the files in the current directory ending with **.a**. Since a redirection symbol follows the arguments, the output is sent to the file **log** instead of to the terminal screen.

```
% echo The files ending with .a are: *.a > log
```

The file Command

The **file** command examines a file or directory and reports what type of file it is (text file, C program file, directory, and so on).

Syntax

file [-m] *file* . . .

file [-m] **-f** *namesfile*

The **file** command takes as arguments a list of file or directory names (or pathnames) specified on the command line.

Options

-m	Sets the access time for the named file to the current time. If you don't give this option, **file** does not affect the access time of a file it looks at
-f *namesfile*	Causes **file** to take its list of files from the file of file-names (or *namesfile*) you specify, rather than from names specified on the command line. The file you specify should consist only of a list of file names

Notes

■ The **file** program sometimes mistakes shell scripts for C programs, perhaps because of the structural similarity of C commands and shell scripts.

Examples

The following command shows how you would use **file** to determine the file types of several files. It also illustrates typical output of the **file** command:

```
% file accounts search c.morgan s.r.let report
accounts:       directory
search: commands text
c.morgan: ascii text
s.r.let:        roff, nroff, tbl, or eqn input text
report: English text
```

The find Command

The **find** command recursively searches directories for files.

Syntax

find *directory-list expression*

The *directory-list* is a list of directories to be searched recursively. That is, **find** will search not only each named directory, but also each subdirectory of that directory, and so on until the lowest level is reached.

Expressions

The *expression* consists of one or more arguments, which may be either criteria the file must meet, actions for **find** to take, or both. If an expression consists of multiple arguments, they must be separated by spaces. The valid arguments are explained here:

-name *filename*	A file meets this criterion if its name matches *filename*. *Filename* may contain wildcard characters (such as ∗), but they must be preceded by a backslash to be protected from the shell
-type *x*	A file meets this criterion if it is of type *x*, where *x* is one of the following types:
	b Block special file
	c Character special file
	d Directory
	f Ordinary file
	p Fifo (named pipe)
-links *n*	A file meets this criterion if it has *n* links, where *n* is an integer
-inum *num*	A file matches this criterion if its inode is *num*
-user *uname*	A file matches this criterion if its owner is the user *uname*
-group *gname*	A file matches this criterion if it belongs to the group *gname*
-size *n*	A file matches this criterion if it is *n* blocks long. If the number *n* is followed by the letter "c," the size will be measured in characters instead of blocks
-atime *n*	A file matches this criterion if it was last accessed *n* days ago
-mtime *n*	A file matches this criterion if it was last modified *n* days ago
-exec *cmnd*	Executes the shell command *cmnd*, which must be followed by an escaped semicolon (\;). If the command returns a 0 exit status (a true value), the file meets this criterion. The command argument { } is replaced by the file name of the file being evaluated. See the "Examples" section
-ok *cmnd*	Like **-exec** except that the generated command line is printed with a question mark. The command is only executed if you type **y**

-cpio *device*	Writes any found files on *device* in **cpio** format. You can use the **find** command with the **-cpio** expression in place of the **cpio** command
-depth	Causes the entries in a directory to be searched or acted upon before the directory itself. If used with the **-cpio** expression, this allows you to transfer files in which you do not have write permission
-print	Causes the pathnames of any found files to be printed. If this argument is not included in an expression, the files the expression selects will not be printed. If this argument is printed after other criteria, only files that meet the other criteria will be printed. If **-print** is the first argument in the expression, the pathnames of all files in the *directory-list* will be printed
-newer *filename*	A file meets this criterion if it has been modified more recently than the file *filename*

The arguments can be combined with following operators:

(*expression*)	Used for grouping expressions for evaluation, usually with the **-o** operator. Since parentheses are special to the shell, they must be preceded by backslashes (**\(\)**). The expression must also be separated from the parentheses by spaces
!	Negates the next argument. For example, the sequence
	!-name *filename*
	selects a file whose name is *not* matched by *filename*
-o	If two criterion arguments are separated by spaces, a file must meet both criteria in order to be selected by the expression. Placing the **-o** operator between two arguments creates an expression that selects a file that meets *either* of the two criteria. For example, the expression

-name *filename* -**user** *uname*

selects only files whose name matches *filename* and whose owner's name is *uname*. On the other hand, the expression

-**name** *filename* -**o** -**user** *uname*

would select a file that either has an appropriate name or belongs to the specified user, but not necessarily both

Notes

■ When you use **find** to search large directories such as the root directory, it must check whether every file in every subdirectory meets the specified criteria. This can take a while, so you might want to redirect the output of **find** to a file and run this process in the background. Remember that you must still use the -**print** argument to **find** even when you redirect the output to a file.

Examples

The following example shows how you would find and print the pathnames of all files in your home directory and its subdirectories whose names begin with the sequence **char**. Because the -**print** argument is included, the pathnames of all the found files matching the specified file name are printed as output.

```
% find $HOME -name char\* -print
/u/sheila3/U.U/chart.master
/u/sheila3/character.refs
/u/sheila3/s.carolina/charleston
```

```
/u/sheila3/shannon.inc/chart
/u/sheila3/U.U/C7/sect1/charge
```

The next example finds all files in a directory called **accounts** and its subdirectories that were either last accessed three or more days ago or whose names end with the sequence **temp**. Again, the **-print** argument causes the output to be printed. To print files matched by either criterion instead of just the one after the **-o** operator, group the two expressions with escaped parentheses.

```
% find accounts \( -atime 3 -o -name \*temp \) -print
/u/sheila3/accounts/1temp
/u/sheila3/accounts/abc/better
/u/sheila3/accounts/abc/crane
/u/sheila3/accounts/conventions
/u/sheila3/accounts/def/r.temp
/u/sheila3/accounts/m.temp
```

The grep, egrep, and fgrep Commands

The **grep**, **egrep**, and **fgrep** commands search standard input for specified patterns. By default, **grep** prints matching lines as output.

Syntax

grep [-**chlnvy**] [-**f** *expfile*] [-**e**] *expression* [*file* . . .]
egrep [-**chlnvy**] [-**f** *expfile*] [-**e**] *expression* [*file* . . .]
fgrep [-**clnv**] [-**f** *expfile*] [*string*] [*file* . . .]

The **grep**, **egrep**, and **fgrep** utilities all search for patterns in files and report matching lines. The difference between the three utilities is in the type of patterns they can search for. You can use a number of magic characters with **grep** to search for patterns that match regular expressions, and **egrep** recognizes even more special characters. The **fgrep** utility, on the other hand, does not recognize any magic characters and can only find fixed strings.

Options

-c	Causes **grep** to display only the line numbers of lines matching the regular expression
-e *expression*	Keeps *expression* from being interpreted as an option if it begins with a **-** (hyphen). You could enclose the expression in single quotes to achieve the same effect
-f *expfile*	Instructs **grep** to take regular expressions to search for from the file *expfile* instead of from the command line
-h	Prevents the name of a file from preceding the output lines, as **grep** ordinarily does when searching more than one file. Does not work with **fgrep**
-y	Causes **grep** to ignore the case of letters in matching regular expressions. Useful when searching for a word either in the middle or at the beginning of a sentence
-l	Prints only the names of files containing matching lines. Each name is printed only once, even if the file contains more than one match
-n	Causes **grep** to precede each printed line with its line number, which indicates where that line occurs in the input file
-v	Causes **grep** to display all lines *except* those matching the expression

Notes

■ See Chapter 5, "UNIX Command-Line Fundamentals," for more on the **grep** family of utilities. Chapter 5 also explains the magic characters that work with **grep** and **egrep**.

The head Command

The **head** command takes a file or the standard input and gives the first few lines as output.

Syntax

head [*-count*] [*file* . . .]

By default, **head** prints the first ten lines of the input as output. If you specify a count, **head** prints *count* lines.

Notes

■ See Chapter 5, "UNIX Command-Line Fundamentals," for more on **head**.

The id Command

The **id** command prints your user and group ID names and numbers.

Syntax

id

The kill Command

The **kill** command sends signal 15 to a specified process and terminates that process.

Syntax

kill [-*signal*] *process* . . .]

The **kill** utility ordinarily sends signal 15 to a process. Some processes cannot be killed with this command, however, and must be killed with signal 9.

Notes

■ See Chapter 12, "The UNIX Multiuser Environment," for more on kill.

■ See also **ps**.

The In Command

The **ln** command makes a link to a file so that the file can be referred to by different names or in different directories. The **ls -l** command displays the number of links a file has (along with other information).

Syntax

ln [-**f**] *file1 file2*
ln [-**f**] *file . . . directory*

Arguments

You can link a file either to another file with a different name in the same directory or to a file of the same name in a different directory. You can link one or more files to a different directory with the command

ln *file . . . filen directory*

where *file1 . . . filen* are the files you want to link and *directory* is the file you want to link them to. When you list the contents of *directory,* you will now see the files that you have linked.

You can link one file to another in the same directory by typing

ln *file1 file2*

where *file1* is the name of an already existing file and *file2* is the name you want the other link to have.

Option

-**f**   Ordinarily, you cannot make a link in a directory for which you do not have access permissions. The −**f** option forces a link even if you don't have access permissions

Notes

■ When you link a file to another file name, you are not creating another file but simply giving the old file another address. Changes made to one link of the file will affect all other links as well.

■ The permissions are the same for every link to a particular file. If you change the permissions on one link, they are automatically changed on the other links. Thus you cannot create a link to a file for which you do not have read and write permission.

■ Links created with **ln** can be removed with **rm**. This will not remove the file as long as there is still at least one link left.

■ See also **ls**.

Examples

To add a link to a file called **standards** in a directory whose pathname (relative to the current directory) is **int.af/bulletin**, you would type

```
% ln standards int.af/bulletin
```

To link all files in the current directory to a directory with the pathname **/u/bin**, you would type

```
% ln * /u/bin
```

The lock Command

The **lock** command locks a terminal so that you can leave it without anyone accessing your account or taking over your terminal. The **lock** utility requests that you type and verify a password , which can be any word or sequence of characters you want . The terminal will only be unlocked when you retype that password and press RETURN.

Syntax

lock [**-v**] [*-number*]

Options

-number   If you do not return and unlock your terminal within a certain amount of time, you will automatically be logged out and the terminal will be unlocked. If you don't specify a *number,* this amount is determined by the environment variable **DEFLOGOUT**, which is set in the file **/etc/default/lock**. If you specify a *number,* the terminal will be logged out after the specified number of minutes as long as the number is not greater than the limit. The maximum time a terminal can be locked is determined by the environment variable **MAXLOG-OUT**

-v   Sets the visual mode of **lock**, which displays a large message on the screen stating that the terminal is locked

The lp Command

The **lp** command sends and cancels requests to a line printer.

Syntax

lp [*-options*] *file* . . .
lp -i *request-ids printing-options*
cancel [*request-ids*] [*printers*]

The first form of the **lp** command sends a request to a printer. If no file name is specified on the command line, the standard input is presumed (this is most useful when piping the output of another filter to **lp**). You can also send the standard output together with a file or files by including a **-** as one of the file names. The **lp** command assigns a unique *request-id* with each printing request and prints that ID on the standard output after you press RETURN. This is a number that you can use when later changing the printing options or canceling a request.

The second form the **lp** command, using the **-i** option, is for changing the printing options for a request already sent to the printer. The printing options available with this option are the same as those for making the original request. The **-i** option may not be available on all systems.

You can use the **cancel** command to cancel a request made with the **lp** command. The arguments to the **cancel** command may be either *request-ids* (as printed with the **lp** command) or printer names. Specifying a *request-id* will cancel the printing of that request if it has not yet printed or even if it is currently printing. Specifying a printer name will cancel the request currently printing on that printer.

Printing Options

-c	The **-c** option causes copies to be made immediately; **lp** gets the data from the copies instead of from the actual file (without this option, **lp** gets its data from the files themselves). If you do not use this option, removing or making changes to the file before it has finished printing will affect the printed output
-d *destination*	Prints the request on the printer or class of printers specified by *destination*. By default, **lp** gets the destination from the environment variable **LPDEST** (if this option is set). Otherwise, the system default printer is used as the destination. This varies from system to system (you can find out your system's default with the **lpstat** command)

-H   Prints the request according to the special handling command you specify. The special handling commands are as follows:

        hold   The request will not be printed until you resume it. If it has already started printing, it will stop until you resume it

        resume   Resumes a request held with the **hold** command

        immediate   Prints the specified request next, regardless of other requests waiting to be printed. If another request is currently printing, you will have to put it on hold or wait until it is finished (available only to LP administrators)

-m   Sends mail after the files have been printed

-n *number*   Prints *number* copies of the output. By default, **lp** prints one copy

-o *options*   Specifies printer- or class-dependent *options*. To specify more than one of these options, use the **-o** option as many times as needed, each followed by one *option*. Printing options are defined by the system administrator, so they vary from system to system. The following are sample options:

        nobanner   Does not print a banner page (usually the user's name in large letters and the date) along with the request. The system administrator can disallow this option

        nofilebreak Supresses insertion of a form feed between files if a request includes more than one file. Ordinarily, a form feed is inserted

length = *decimal number(units)*

> Prints the output with pages that are *number* lines long. The *decimal number* indicates the number of lines, centimeters, or inches. If you want to specify the length of the page in inches or centimeters, replace *units* with **i** or **c**, respectively. A length or width setting with no following units indicates the number of lines or columns (lines for length, columns for width)

width = *decimal number(units)*

> Specifies the width of the output pages in columns, inches, or centimeters. Follow the instructions for setting the length to set page width in inches or centimeters

lpi = *decimal number*

> Sets the line pitch to *decimal number* lines per inch

cpi = *decimal number*

> Sets the character pitch to *decimal number* characters per inch. You can also set the character pitch to **pica** (ten characters per inch), **elite** (twelve characters per inch), or **compressed** (as many characters per inch as the printer can handle)

stty = *stty options*

> Sets the printer with any options valid for the **stty** command. If the list of **stty** options contains spaces, you must enclose the entire list in quotes

-P

> Prints only the specified *pages*. This option will be rejected if your system is not equipped to print only certain pages. The *pages* may be either a range of numbers, single page numbers, or a combination of both. The pages will be printed in order

-s	Supresses **lp** messages (for example, the message that tells you the ID of your request)
-t *title*	Prints *title* on the banner page. By default, no title is printed
-w	Writes a message after the printing request is completed. If you are logged out when it is completed, the printing service will send you mail instead

Notes

■ The number and kind of printers available on UNIX systems varies widely. Your system might not even have any printers. To find out if your system is set up for printing and what printers are available, ask the system administrator or another user.

■ See also **lpstat**.

■ Berkeley UNIX systems have the command **lpr** instead of **lp**. Although **lpr** serves the same purpose as **lp**, the options for the two commands differ substantially.

Examples

The following example shows how you would print a file called **abstract** using the default printer and without any printing options. The line following the command line shows a sample message from **lp**, indicating the request ID. What this message says depends on the system and the type of printer.

```
% lp abstract
request id is nec-765 (1 file)
```

The next example shows how you would cancel the printing request established in the preceding example. A sample message given with **cancel** follows the command line.

```
% cancel nec-765
request "nec-765" canceled
```

The following example shows how you would print the same file, setting the page length to 11 inches. A message similar to the one in the first example would be printed with this and the following examples.

```
% lp -o length=11i abstract
```

This example shows how you would print only pages 1 through 5 of this file:

```
% lp -P 1-5 abstract
```

The following example shows how you would pipe the output of **nroff** to the **lp** command, thus printing the formatted version of a file without having to create a new file.

```
% nroff -mm abstract | lp
request id is nec-778 (standard input)
```

The lpstat Command

The **lpstat** command reports the status of the **lp** printing service. You can use this command to find out the request ID of a printing job you want to cancel.

Syntax

lpstat [*options*] [*request-ids*] [*printers*]

Without options or arguments, **lpstat** prints the status of all requests made to **lp** by all users. Any arguments that are not options are interpreted as *request-ids,* names of printers, or classes of printers. Options can be repeated and mixed with arguments.

For options that can be followed with a *list,* the list may consist either of items separated by commas and no spaces (*item1,item2,item3*. . .), or of items enclosed in double quotes and separated by a comma and/or spaces ("*item1*" "*item2*" "*item3*". . .). For options that take optional *lists,* **lpstat** gives information for all relevant items if you do not specify a *list.*

Options

-a[*list*]	Prints acceptance status of request destinations in *list.* The list can consist of both printer names and class names
-c[*list*]	Prints a list of all printer classes and the members of each class
-d	Prints the system default destination
-o[*list*] [**-l**]	Prints the status of output requests. If you specify the **-l** option, a more detailed list is printed
-p[*list*] [**-D**] [**-l**]	Prints the status of printers and printer classes in the list. If you specify the **-D** option, a brief description of each printer in the *list* is printed. With the **-l** option, a full description of each printer's configuration is printed
-r	Prints the status of the **lp** request scheduler
-t	Prints all status information
-u[*list*]	Prints status of requests for users in *list*
-v[*list*]	Prints the names of printers in *list* and the paths of the devices associated with them

Notes

■ See also **lp**.

Examples

The following example shows a sample output of **lpstat** with the **-o** option. Since no *list* is given, all output requests are shown.

```
% lpstat -o
nec-24      sheila3  62491    Sep17    13:50
texas-25    modes    46781    Sep17    13:59
nec-26      sheila3  62491    Sep17    14:00
daisy-27    leblond1 98667    Sep17    14:19
```

The following example shows a sample of **lstat** with the **-t** option.

```
% lpstat-t
Scheduler is running
System default destination: nec
device for nec: /dev/lp1
device for texas: /dev/lp0
device for daisy: /dev/lp2
nec accepting requests since Jun 13 18:13
texas accepting requests since Aug 6 13:17
daisy accepting requests since Mar 22 08:02
printer texas now printing texas-25. enabled since Aug 6 13:17

nec-24      sheila3  62491    Sep17    13:50
texas-25    modes    46781    Sep17    13:59 on texas
nec-26      sheila3  62491    Sep17    14:00
daisy-27    leblond1 98667    Sep17    14:19
```

The ls Command

The **ls** command lists the contents of directories.

Syntax

ls [*-options*] [*names*]

By default, directory contents are listed in alphabetical order, one item per line. However, you can use one or several options to change both the order and the format in which contents are listed.

Options

-A   Lists all entries, including those whose names begin with a period. Only the files . and .. are not listed with this option

-a   Lists all entries, including ., .., and others whose names begin with a period

-C   Lists the items in a multiple-column output. Entries are sorted alphabetically down the columns

-F   Places a slash after each entry that is a directory and an asterisk after each entry that is an executable file

-p   Places a slash after each entry that is a directory

-d   If an argument is a directory, lists only its name and not its contents. Often used with the **-l** option to determine the status of a directory

-l   Lists the contents in long format. See Chapter 4, "Files and Directories," for an explanation of long format

-m   Formats output as one stream, entries separated by commas

-R   Recursively lists all directories encountered

-r   Reverses the order of sorting to get reverse alphabetical ordering or the oldest file first, depending on which other options are used

-s   Gives the size in blocks of each entry

-t   Sorts the entries by time of last modification (most recent first) instead of alphabetically

-u   Used with the **-t** option, the **-u** option causes sorting by time of last access rather than last modification

-c   Used with the **-t** option, the **-c** option causes sorting by last modification of the inode the file is associated with. The inode is modified whenever a file is created or its mode changed

-x   Lists the items in a multiple-column output, with entries sorted across the page rather than down the columns

Notes

■ See Chapter 4, "Files and Directories," for more on the **ls** utility.

The mail Command

The **mail** command allows you to communicate with other users.

Syntax

mail [-*options*] [*user* . . .]

Notes

■ See Chapter 8 for a detailed discussion of **mail** and its options.

The make Command

The **make** command keeps a set of programs current. See Chapter 11, "Program Development With C," for a discussion of **make**.

Syntax

make [-*options*] [files]

The mesg Command

The **mesg** command allows or denies messages sent to a terminal. This determines whether other users can write messages to your terminal with the **write** command.

Syntax

mesg [**n**] [**y**]

With no argument specified, the **mesg** command reports the current status (**y** or **n**). If you specify the argument **n**, **mesg** will revoke the write permission on your terminal. If you specify the argument **y**, other users will be permitted to write to your terminal.

Notes

■ If it is not already there, you may want to place this command in your .**login** or .**profile** file so that it will be executed every time you log in.

■ If someone writes to your terminal while you are editing a file with **vi**, your screen will be temporarily scrambled. The **nomesg** environment option of **vi** will revoke the write permission on your terminal whenever you are using **vi**. See Chapter 6, "The vi Editor."

The mkdir Command

The **mkdir** command creates a directory.

Syntax

mkdir [-**p**] [-**m** *mode*] *dirname*

Options

-**m** *mode*   Ordinarily, directories are created with the mode 777 (readable, writable, and executable by everyone). The -**m** option allows you to set a different permissions mode for the directory when you create it, thus saving you the trouble of having to modify it later

-**p**   If you specify this option, **mkdir** creates a directory by first creating all nonexistent parent directories. Use this option if you want to create a subdirectory several levels down from the current directory (see "Example")

Notes

■ The options **-p** and **-m** may not be available on all System V UNIX systems or on Berkeley UNIX systems.

■ The initial permissions on a directory you create may be altered if you execute **umask** as part of your login procedure. See **umask** for more information.

■ See Chapter 4, "Files and Directories," for more on **mkdir**.

■ See also **chmod** and **rmdir**.

Example

To create a directory several levels down from the current directory when the intermediate directories do not exist, use the **-p** option and type the relative pathname of the new directory. For example, suppose that the current directory, called **properties**, has no subdirectories. To create a directory called **georgia**, whose parent directory, called **south**, is a subdirectory of **us**, which is in turn a subdirectory of **properties**, you would type

```
% mkdir -p us/south/georgia
```

Now **mkdir** will create all three directories — **us**, **south**, and **georgia** — properly descending from the current directory.

The more Command

The **more** command displays files one screenful at a time, pausing after each screenful until you press RETURN or one of the **more** internal commands. This command was developed for Berkeley UNIX and may not be available on all System V UNIX systems. If it is not available on your system, use **pg** instead.

Syntax

more [*-options*] [*-n*] [+*linenumber*] [+*/pattern*] *file* . . .

Options

-c	Causes **more** to draw each screen starting at the top instead of scrolling. This way you can start reading a screen before it has completely printed
-d	Causes **more** to prompt with the message "Hit space to continue, 'q' to quit." after each screenful
-r	Causes carriage returns to be printed as ^M (CTRL-M).
-s	Compresses multiple blank lines in the input to just one blank line in the output. When viewing files with many blank lines, such as **nroff** output, this option maximizes the actual text displayed on the screen
+*linenumber*	Starts at *linenumber*
+*/pattern*	Starts two lines before the first occurrence of *pattern*

Notes

■ When **more** pauses after each screenful, you can use one of the **more** commands to do other things besides advancing one screen. These commands are discussed in Chapter 5, "UNIX Command-Line Fundamentals." You can also get a list of these commands by typing **h** or **?** when **more** pauses.

The mv Command

The **mv** command moves and renames files and directories.

Syntax

mv [**-f**] *file1 file2*
mv [**-f**] *directory1 directory2*
mv [**-f**] *file . . . directory*

Arguments

If the arguments consist of two file names, **mv** gives *file1* the new name *file2*. If the first argument is a file name and the second is the name of a directory, the *file* is moved into the *directory*. If both arguments are directory names, two actions are possible. On all systems, if the second name is not the name of a directory already existing, *directory1* is given the new name *directory2*. On some systems, if the *directory2* is an existing directory, **mv** will actually move *directory1* into *directory2*.

Notes

■ If the second file name argument is the name of an existing file, **mv** will replace it with *file1*, and *file2* will be lost. Thus, you should use caution when renaming files and directories.

■ See Chapter 4, "Files and Directories," for more on **mv**.

The newgrp Command

The **newgrp** command temporarily changes your group membership, giving you access to all the files and directories accessible to members of the new group. To be able to change your group identity, your user name must be in the **/etc/group** file.

Syntax

newgrp [*group*]

Giving a *group* as an argument to **newgrp** changes your group identity to that group. Without an argument, **newgrp** reverts your group identity to your normal group (the group specified in the **/etc/passwd** file).

The news Command

The **news** command displays system news items.

Syntax

news [**-ans**] [*items*]

Without arguments, **news** displays the contents of all files in the directory **/usr/news** that were modified more recently than the file **.news_time** in your home directory. Then the **.news_time** file modification time is changed. The result is that you only see files that you have not seen before. The most recently modified file is displayed first.

Arguments

If you specify the names of any items as arguments, only those items are displayed. You can first use the **news-n** command to see the names of the items and then select only certain items to read.

Options

-a	Causes all files in the **/usr/news** directory to be displayed, regardless of when they were modified
-n	Causes **news** to print only the names of the current files, not their contents
-s	Causes **news** to report the number of current items. Does not print the names or contents of the current items, and does not change the modification time of your **.news_time** file

The nice Command

The **nice** command executes commands with a different scheduling priority level than usual. Ordinary users can only use **nice** to lower the priority of a command. The superuser can also raise a command's priority.

Syntax

nice [*-increment*] *command line*

The *command line* is the command line whose priority you want to change. Any shell command line can serve as an argument to the **nice** command.

Options

By default, each process running on a UNIX system is assigned a priority value of 20. With no options, the **nice** command decreases the priority of a process by a value of 10. (A higher number means a lower priority.) You can use the *-increment* option to decrease the priority of your process by a different value, ranging from 1 to 19. See the "Examples" section.

Notes

■ The C shell has its own built-in **nice** command, which behaves differently from the UNIX standard **nice** command. In the C shell, use a plus (+) instead of a minus (-) to decrease the priority of a process.

■ See also the **ps** command.

Examples

The following example shows how you would lower the priority of the process associated with an **nroff** command line by the default value of 10:

```
% nice nroff -mm death > taxes
```

To give the process associated with an **nroff** command line the lowest possible priority, you would decrease its priority by a value of 19, as follows:

```
% nice -19 nroff -mm love > marriage
```

The nohup Command

The **nohup** command makes a command keep running after you log out. If you are using the Bourne shell, all processes you have initiated will normally be killed when you log out. The C shell has a built-in **nohup** command so commands will automatically keep running if you are using the C shell.

Syntax

nohup *command line*

Any shell command line can be an argument to the **nohup** command.

Notes

■ The **nohup** command will only be useful for commands you run in the background. If the command is running in the foreground, you will have to wait for it to finish executing before you can log out.

■ If you do not redirect to a file the output of a command used with **nohup**, the standard output *and* standard error, if any, will be sent to a file called **nohup.out** in the current directory.

Example

To keep an **nroff** command running in the background after you log out, use **nohup** in the following command line. Since the output is not directed to a file, it would be directed to the file **nohup.out** in the directory you were in when you gave the command.

```
$ nohup nroff net.assets &
```

The nroff Command

The **nroff** formats text for printing on a line printer or letter quality printer. See Chapter 7, "Text Formatting with nroff and troff," for a thorough discussion of **nroff**.

Syntax

nroff [-*macros*] [**-o***pages*] [**-T***type*] [*file. . .*]

Options

-*macros*	Specifies the macro package you want to use in formatting the file
-o*pages*	Causes **nroff** to output only the *pages* you specify. Pages may be listed separated by commas (for example, 1,2,3), or a range of pages may be separated by a hyphen (for example, 1-10)
-T*type*	Specifies the type of terminal on which the output is to be printed. For example, to format a file for a printer, you would use the *type* 1p

The paste Command

The **paste** command merges lines of files. Each file is treated as a column or series of columns, and the columns are concatenated horizontally. This is done by replacing the newline character at the end of the first line in the first file with a tab and then appending the first line in the second file, and so on. This command is useful for preparing tables.

Syntax

paste [**-s**] [**-d***separators*] *file1 file.* . .

Options

-d*separators*	Without this option, columns in the output of **paste** are separated by tabs. The **-d** option lets you designate a separator or separators to be used instead of tabs.
	The separators can be any single character or a list of characters. If you give a list of separators, the list need be only as long as the number of separators required in a single line (see example)
-s	This option converts a file in columnar format into a row. That is, it replaces the newline characters within a given file with tabs (or a character designated with the **-d** option) so that the items are listed across rather than down the page

Notes

■ The **paste** utility does not work on files that are not in columnar format.

■ If you redirect the output of **paste** to a file, you can use it to create tables.

Examples

The following example shows how you would paste together two files, one containing a one-column list of countries and the other a one-column list of cities. Since the output is not redirected to a file, it appears on the standard output.

```
% paste countries cities
U.S.A.  London
Japan   Beijing
Mexico  Minsk
England Tokyo
China   Vancouver
Canada  Tiller
```

The next example shows how you would paste together the same files using # as a separator:

```
% paste -d# countries cities
U.S.A.#London
Japan#Beijing
Mexico#Minsk
England#Tokyo
China#Vancouver
Canada#Tiller
```

The following example shows how you would paste three files — **countries**, **cities**, and **units**. Following the **-d** option is a list of field separators. The field separator **1** will separate the first two fields and the field separator **2** will separate the second and third fields.

```
% paste -d12 countries cities units
U.S.A.1London2Rupee
Japan1Beijing2Yen
Mexico1Minsk2Drachma
England1Tokyo2Dollar
China1Vancouver2Pound
Canada1Tiller2Ruble
```

This example shows what would happen if you pasted the files **countries** and **cities** with the **-s** option. Notice that the countries and cities are now in rows instead of columns.

```
% paste -s countries cities
U.S.A.  Japan   Mexico  England China   Canada
London  Beijing Minsk   Tokyo   Vancouver       Tiller
```

The pg Command

The **pg** command displays files for reading one screenful at a time. Each screenful is followed by a prompt at which you can press RETURN to see the next screenful. You can also use one of the **pg** internal commands, which allow you to view different parts of the file, search for patterns, or modify the viewing environment.

Syntax

pg [-*number*] [-**p** *string*] [-**cefn**] [+*linenumber*] [+*/pattern*] *file* . . .

If you don't specify a file, the standard input is assumed. If you specify more than one file, the files are displayed in the order in which they are typed and the name of each file is displayed before that file is displayed.

Options

-*number*	The *number* specifies the size of the window. By default, the window is the size of the screen minus one line. If you specify a number that is less than the default, less than one screenful is displayed at a time
-**p** *string*	Specifies a *string* to be used as a prompt instead of the default prompt, : (colon)
-**c**	Clears the screen before each screen instead of scrolling. This way you can read each line as it prints.
-**e**	Causes **pg** not to pause at the end of a file
-**f**	Keeps **pg** from splitting long lines in the output. Without this option, **pg** splits lines longer than the screen, but nonprinting escape characters may split some lines that actually would fit on the screen

-n	Ordinarily, you must press RETURN after typing any of the **pg** internal commands. This option causes commands to be executed as soon as they are typed
+*linenumber*	Starts displaying the file at *linenumber*
+*/pattern*	Starts displaying the file at the first occurrence of *pattern*

pg Internal Commands

You can use the **pg** internal commands to skip to a new screen or line number, search for a pattern in the file being displayed, or skip to the next file. For example, you can use the **q** command to quit **pg**. To see a list of these commands, type **h** (for help) and press RETURN at the **:** prompt.

Notes

■ See also Chapter 5, "UNIX Command-Line Fundamentals," for more on **pg**.

■ See also **more**.

The pr Command

The **pr** command paginates files. By default, a file is split into pages, each headed by the page number, date, time, and name of the file. Lines are not wrapped or filled, so **pg** cannot be used as a text formatter.

Syntax

pr [*options*] [*file* . . .]

Options

+n	Begins printing with page n instead of page 1
-n	Produces output with n columns. With the - option, as with other options that produce columnar output, lines that are too long to fit in a column are truncated. Thus, these options are not good for text files unless the lines of text are quite short. If you use this option, the **-e** and **-i** options are assumed as well
-a	Prints multiple-column output with lines ordered across the page instead of down a column. That is, input lines are placed in columns across the page until column n is reached, and the next input line is placed in the first column on the next line of output
-m	Merges and prints all input files side by side, one file per column. The number of columns is determined by the number of files given as arguments
-d	Double spaces the output
-ecn	Replaces input tabs with the specified character. The character can be a number n, in which case tabs will be expanded to $n+1$, $2n+1$, $3n+1$, and so on. If n is omitted or is 0, tabs are set to every eighth position. The character can also be a nonnumerical character c, in which case the character c is replaced with a tab in the output. If c is omitted, the tab character is assumed. If both a number n and a character c are specified, the character c is replaced with tabs that are n characters long. Note that the nonnumerical character c must precede the number n
-ncn	Numbers the output lines, allowing for n digits. If no n is specified, allows for five digits. The line number is separated from the text by the nonnumeric character c. If no c is specified, a tab character is the separator
-wn	Sets the line length to n characters. This does not change the length of input lines, but it does change the length of output lines. Useful when you are printing in multiple columns
-on	Offsets, or indents, each line by n characters

-l*n*	Sets the page length to *n* lines. By default, page length is set to 66 lines
-h *name*	Uses *name* instead of the file name as the header printed on each page. If *name* includes any spaces, it must be enclosed in quotes
-p	Pauses after each page if the output is directed to a terminal. The bell will ring and **pr** will wait for you to press RETURN

Examples

The following example shows how you would paginate a file called **report** with numbered lines, allowing for three digits. The numbers will be separated from the text by a hyphen.

```
% pr -n-3 report
```

The next example shows how you would print the file with three-column output.

```
% pr -3 report
```

The ps Command

The **ps** command reports process status. See Chapter 12, "The UNIX Multiuser Environment," for more information about **ps**.

Syntax

ps [*options*]

Options

-e	Displays information about all processes on the system
-d	Displays information about all processes except process group leaders
-a	Prints information about all processes except process group leaders and those not associated with a terminal
-f	Prints a full listing of processes. Ordinarily only a short list of information is displayed. With the **-f** option, however, **ps** attempts to determine the command name and arguments that initiated each process
-l	Prints a long listing, which includes status, priority, location, and memory usage for each process
-t*tlist*	Lists only those processes associated with terminals in *tlist*. The *tlist* can be either a list of terminals separated by commas or a list enclosed in double quotes and separated by commas and/or spaces
-u*ulist*	Lists only those processes initiated by users whose user names appear in *ulist*. The *ulist* follows the same format as the *tlist*. In the listing, the user's numerical ID is printed instead of the user name. If you use the **-f** option with the **-u** option, the user name will be displayed

Display Columns

Each column in a **ps** listing has an abbreviated heading. These abbreviations are listed in order next, where the information displayed in the various columns in a **ps** listing is also explained. The letter in parentheses after the abbreviation indicates what type of listing includes that column: (f) indicates columns displayed only with a full listing, (l) indicates columns displayed only with a long listing, and no letter indicates columns displayed with all listings.

F (l)	This column displays octal numbers representing flags associated with each process. The octal number is the sum of the numbers for all of

	the associated flags. The numbers for the flags are
	01 In core
	02 System process
	04 Locked in core
	10 Being swapped
	20 Being traced by another process
S (l)	This column shows the state of the process. The possible states and the codes that represent them are
	O Nonexistent
	S Sleeping
	R Running
	I Intermediate
	Z Terminated
	T Stopped
	B Waiting
UID (f,l)	The user ID number of the process owner, or, with the **-f** option, the user name up to seven characters
PID	The process identification number. Use this number when you want to kill a particular process
PPID (f,l)	The process ID of the parent process
C (f,l)	The processor utilization for scheduling
STIME (f)	The starting time of the process
PRI (l)	The priority of the process (the higher the number, the lower the priority)
NI	The nice value of the process
ADDR1,ADDR2 (l)	The memory addresses of the process, or the disk address
SZ	The size in blocks of the image of the process in the core
WCHAN (1)	If a process is sleeping or waiting for another event, that event is displayed in this column
TTY	The terminal from which the process was initiated
TIME	The cumulative processing time for the process

CMD   The name of the command (and arguments) associated with the process

Notes

■ The options discussed here do not necessarily behave the same way on Berkeley UNIX systems.

■ See also **kill** and **nice**.

The pwd Command

The **pwd** command prints the full pathname of the working, or current, directory.

Syntax

pwd

Notes

■ See Chapter 4, "Files and Directories," for more on **pwd**.

■ See also **cd**.

The rm Command

The **rm** command removes files or directories.

Syntax

rm [**-fir**] *file* . . .
rm **-r** *directory* . . .

Options

-f   With this option, **rm** does not ask for confirmation when you attempt to remove a file on which you do not have write permission. Instead, it simply removes the file

-i   Causes **rm** to ask for confirmation before removing a file

-r   Recursively removes all files and subdirectories from a directory, finally removing the directory. Be very careful when using this option

Notes

■ It is safer to use **rmdir** to remove a directory than to use **rm -r**, since **rmdir** refuses to remove a directory if it is not empty. You should use **rm -r** only if you are absolutely sure that you want to remove the contents of a given directory.

■ See Chapter 4, "Files and Directories," for more about **rm**.

The rmdir Command

The **rmdir** command removes directories.

Syntax

rmdir [**-ps**] *directory* . . .

Options

-p   Enables you to remove directories and their parent directories
        that become empty when the subdirectories are removed

-s   Suppresses the error message normally printed when you use
        -p

Notes

■ You cannot use **rmdir** to remove a directory that is not empty. To
remove a directory containing any files or subdirectories, you must use
rm -r.

■ See Chapter 4, "Files and Directories," for more on **rmdir**.

The sed Command

The **sed** command edits files noninteractively. See Chapter 5, "UNIX
Command-Line Fundamentals," for more on **sed**.

Syntax

sed [**-n**] [**-f** *scriptfile*] [*file* . . .]
sed [**-n**] [**-e** *editing command*] [*file* . . .]

Options

-e *editing command*   Causes **sed** to use the *editing command* following
                           the option. This option may be used more than
                           once on a command line, each with its own
                           following command

-f *scriptfile*	Causes **sed** to use the editing commands found in the file *scriptfile*
-n	Suppresses the output of **sed**. This allows you to print only certain lines of the file

sed Editing Commands

Editing commands used on the command line with the **-e** option, or in a *scriptfile* with the **-f** option have the format

[*address*[,*address*]] *instruction*

Addresses are either line numbers or regular expressions enclosed in slashes (*/expression/*). You may precede a **sed** instruction by one address to edit one line, by two addresses to edit all lines between and including the two addressed lines, or by no address to edit all lines in the input.

As **sed** examines each input line, that line is copied to a *pattern space*. Any changes to be made to the line are made here, and the line is then copied to the standard output. Some of the **sed** instructions copy lines to or from a *hold space,* where lines are stored for later retrieval.

sed Instructions

a	
text	Appends *text* to the addressed line. All lines of *text* except the last must be followed by ****. You can only use one address with this command
c	
text	Changes addressed lines to *text*
d	Deletes the addressed lines
D	Deletes from the address to the first newline character
g	Replaces the addressed lines with the contents of the hold space
G	Appends the contents of the hold space to the last addressed line

h	Replaces the contents of the hold space with the addressed line. You can only use one address with this command. If you give more than one address, only the line addressed by the last address is put in the hold space
H	Appends the addressed lines to the hold space. You may append more than one line
i *text*	Inserts *text* before the addressed line. You can only use one address with this command
l	Prints the addressed lines with nonprinting characters printed as two-digit ASCII codes with long lines wrapped
n	Copies the addressed line to the standard output and goes to the next line of input. You can use this command to make changes to the lines *after* lines matching a certain pattern, even if you don't know the contents of the next lines. For example, by enclosing the **n** and **d** commands in braces, you could delete all lines following lines containing a particular word (see "Examples")
N	Copies the addressed line to the standard output and appends the next line of input with an embedded newline character. Any commands enclosed in braces with the **N** command will affect both the addressed line and the next line
p	Prints the addressed lines on the standard output. This is useful when you use the **-n** command-line option, which normally suppresses the output of **sed**. Using this command with the **-n** option causes only selected lines to be printed as output
P	Prints from the beginning of the addressed line to the first newline character
q	Quits **sed** without starting a new cycle. That is, the rest of the file is ignored. This is useful if you want to edit only part of a file

r *file* Reads in *file* below the addressed line. You can only use one address with this command

s/*oldpattern***/***newpattern***/***flags*

Substitutes *newpattern* for *oldpattern* on the addressed lines, where *oldpattern* is any regular expression and *newpattern* is the replacement pattern. The possible *flags* are

n Substitutes only for the *n*th occurrence of *oldpattern* on a line, where *n* is any number from 1 to 512

g Substitutes for every occurrence of *oldpattern* on the addressed lines. By default, only the first occurrence of *oldpattern* on a line is replaced

p Prints every addressed line on which a substitution is made

w *file* Writes every addressed line on which a substitution is made to *file*

w *file* Writes the addressed lines to *file*

x Replaces the addressed lines with the contents of the hold space, and puts the addressed lines in the hold space

!*instruction* Applies the *instruction* only to lines not selected by the addresses

= Places the current line number on the standard output as a line

{ Used to begin a group of commands to be executed on the same selected lines. Each command within the group should be on a separate line, and a } on its own line should end the grouping

Notes

■ To save the output of **sed**, you must either pipe it to another command or redirect it to a file.

■ Since the **sed** utility is a very complex program, you should read the section on **sed** in Chapter 5, "UNIX Command-Line Fundamentals."

You should also practice with some simple files and simple commands.

Examples

The following examples show **sed** editing commands only, not entire command lines. You can either type these editing commands on the command line with the **-e** option or enter them in a script file for use with the **-f** option. See Chapter 5, "UNIX Command-Line Fundamentals," for examples that use entire command lines.

The following editing commands would delete each line that followed a line containing the pattern **.PP** (an **nroff** macro). Remember, the **.** must be preceded by a backslash since it is a magic character in regular expressions. The address finds lines that contain this pattern. Then **sed** goes to the next line of input and deletes that line. These two commands are enclosed in braces. Notice that when you enclose commands in braces the second brace must be on a new line.

```
/.PP/ {
n
d
}
```

The following commands switch the positions of lines in the input. The address first finds a line that begins with the pattern **Begin Listing.** Then **sed** stores that line in the hold space (with the **h** command) and deletes the line from the output (with the **d** command). The next address then selects the next input linethat begins with the pattern **Listing #**, and **sed** appends to this line (with the **G** command) the contents of the hold space, which will be the previously selected line. Then the next cycle will begin. As a result, in every place where a line beginning with **Begin Listing** once preceded a line that began with **Listing #**, the two lines will be switched.

```
/^Begin Listing/ {h
d
}
/^Listing #/ G
```

The sh Command

The **sh** command invokes the Bourne shell command interpreter. For more details, see Chapter 9, "The Bourne Shell."

Syntax

sh

The shl Command

The **shl** command manages shell layers, which are multiple shells being run simultaneously from a single terminal. You control which layer you interact with at any given time by using **shl** internal commands.

Syntax

shl

shl Internal Commands

You can use the following **shl** internal commands to create new shell layers, switch between layers, and more. You type these commands at the **shl** prompt. To return to the **shl** prompt from one of the layers, you can use the **stty** character **swtch**, which is CTRL-Z if not set to another character.

create [*name*]	Creates a new shell layer called *name*. If you give no *name*, the layer is numbered (1, 2, and so on). You can later refer to the layer by this name or number. After you create a layer, you will see the prompt for that layer, which **shl** sets to the name of the layer
block *name* . . .	Blocks the output from each layer indicated by *name*
delete *name* . . .	Deletes each layer indicated by *name*
help	Prints a list of the **shl** commands
layers [**-l**] [*name*]	Displays information about each layer indicated by *name*. The **-l** option displays a listing like that displayed by **ps**
resume [*name* . . .]	Makes the layer indicated by *name* the current layer. If you don't specify a name, resumes the last current layer
toggle	Resumes the layer that was current before the last current layer
unblock	Reverses the effects of a **block** command for the layer indicated by *name*
quit	Exits **shl**. Sends the **SIGHUP** signal to each layer
name	Makes the layer indicated by *name* the current layer

Notes

■ In order for the **shl** layers to work on a system, the kernel must be specially configured. If your system is not configured for **shl** layers, you will not be able to use this command.

The sleep Command

The **sleep** command suspends execution of a process for a specified interval.

Syntax

sleep *number*

The **sleep** command causes processing to be suspended for *number* seconds before the next command is executed.

Notes

■ The **sleep** command is often inserted in a shell script to leave some time between the execution of two commands. You can also place it in a **while** loop to execute a command at regular intervals. See Chapter 9, "The Bourne Shell," and Chapter 10, "The C Shell," for more on shell scripts and looping commands.

■ If the number of seconds you specify is longer than 65,536, *number* will automatically be set to a shorter time.

Examples

The following sequence of commands might appear in a shell script. The first command echoes "You have no mail." The second command suspends processing for five seconds to give the user a chance to read the message, and the third command clears the screen.

```
echo "You have no mail."
sleep 5
clear
```

The following **while** loop uses **sleep** to execute the **date** command at five-minute intervals:

```
while (1)
date
sleep 300
end
```

The sort Command

The **sort** command sorts files according to the ASCII collating sequence and merges files. All files specified on the command line are sorted together and placed on the standard output. See Chapter 5, "UNIX Command-Line Fundamentals," for more on the **sort** command.

Syntax

sort [*options*] [+*pos1*] [-*pos2*] [*file* . . .]

Options

-b	Causes **sort** to ignore leading whitespace characters. Without this option, whitespace characters are considered to be part of the field they precede, and the field is sorted accordingly
-c	Checks whether a file is already sorted. If it is, **sort** simply returns a prompt; if it is not, **sort** prints a message showing the location of the first out-of-order line
-d	Causes **sort** to use dictionary ordering, in which all nonalphanumeric characters (punctuation and CTRL characters) are ignored
-f	Folds lowercase into uppercase letters. That is, each lowercase letter is ordered immediately after the corresponding uppercase letter, rather than all lowercase letters coming after all uppercase letters
-i	Ignores nonprinting characters in a nonnumeric sort
-m	Only merges files, which are assumed to be already sorted
-M	Sorts a field by month. The first three nonwhitespace characters in the field are considered as uppercase letters and compared in the order JAN < FEB < MAR . . . < DEC

-n   Causes **sort** to use the arithmetic values of digits, mi-
                 nuses, and decimal points for sorting instead of the
                 ASCII collating sequence

-ofilename   Specifies an output file to be used instead of the stan-
                 dard output. The output file can be the same as one of
                 the input files. You can achieve the same result by
                 redirecting the output to a file with the redirection
                 symbol >

-r   Sorts lines in reverse order

-tx   Sets the field delimiter to the character x. Ordinarily, a
                 field is delimited by whitespace characters or the begin-
                 nings or ends of lines. If you set the delimiter to a char-
                 acter x, every occurrence of x is significant, so that the
                 sequence xx is treated as an empty field

-u   Prints only one of each set of lines with identical sort
                 fields. If you specify no sort fields with the +pos1 and
                 -pos2 options, whole lines are compared. This ensures
                 that the output will contain no duplicate lines

-zrecsz   Determines the longest allowable line length when
                 merging files. Otherwise, **sort** will use a default size,
                 and will terminate abnormally if any lines in the files to
                 be merged are longer than this default. Use this option
                 only in conjunction with the **-c** or **-m** option

+pos1   Specifies the position on a line where the sort is to be-
                 gin. The position (pos1) can specify both a field and a
                 character within that field (see "Fields")

-pos2   Specifies the position on a line where the sort is to end.
                 The position (pos2) can specify both a field and a char-
                 acter within that field (see "Fields")

Fields

A *line field* is a sequence of characters bounded by spaces or the beginning or end of a line, or by a special character that you designate as the
field delimiter (see the *-tx* option in the previous section). A *sort field* may
include all or part of a line field. Sort fields, specified with the +pos1 and
-pos2 options explained in the previous section, are of the form f.c, where

f is the number of a line field, and the optional *c*, separated from *f* by a period, is a character position within the field. For example, you would specify a sort field that started on the third character of the second line field as

2.3

If no *c* is specified, *f* is interpreted as the first character of that field.

Notes

■ See Chapter 5, "UNIX Command-Line Fundamentals," for more on **sort**.

The spell Command

The **spell** command finds spelling errors in a file or the standard input. All words in the input are compared with a list of words in the system dictionary and in any other files you want included. The output is an alphabetized list of all words that cannot be found in the dictionary files or derived from one of the words in these files.

Syntax

spell [*options*] [+*local-file*] [*file* . . .]

Arguments

Ordinarily, all words not found in the system dictionary are printed as output. You can supplement this dictionary with words of your choice stored in a file in one of your own directories. The file must contain a sorted list of words, one word per line. To remove any words in this list from the output of **spell**, use the +*local-file* argument, where *local-file* is the file containing the list. If that file is not in the current directory, you must specify its pathname.

If you specify more than one *file* as an argument to **spell**, only one list of misspelled words will be generated for all of the files.

Options

-b	Causes **spell** to accept British spellings
-v	Causes **spell** to print all words that are not literally in the dictionary. If a word can be derived from a word in the dictionary, a possible derivation of each word is also printed
-x	Causes **spell** to print every possible stem for each word, following an equal sign (=)

Notes

■ Don't use the **spell** utility as a substitute for proofreading. Although it will probably find all misspelled words, it cannot tell if you used the wrong word. For example, it will not tell you if you have written "two" where you should have written "too."

■ Some UNIX systems have their own interactive spelling checkers. These are generally more useful than **spell**, which does not show you where the misspelled words are in a file or change them for you. Ask your system administrator if there is such a program on your system.

■ The options for Berkeley UNIX systems vary substantially from the System V options.

■ Some systems have a command related to **spell** that is called **look**. The **look** command enables you to look up words that you are not sure how to spell. To look up a word, type

look *string*

where *string* is all or the first segment of a word. Then **look** will report all words it finds that begin with the sequence you have typed. For example, if you weren't sure how to spell the word "argument," you could type the following command, which would display the list shown:

```
% look argu
argue
argument
argumentation
Argus
```

Examples

The following example shows how you would run **spell** without any options on a file. A sample output follows the command line.

```
% spell outline
POLS
Mazone
McGillivray
finanse
mannagement
tge
```

The following example shows how you would make **spell** include a file in the current directory called **sp.dict** to remove the words in that file from the output. Suppose that you include the words "POLS" and "Mazone" in **sp.dict**, the output would now be as follows:

```
% spell +sp.dict outline
McGillivray
finanse
mannagement
tge
```

The split Command

The **split** command splits a file into pieces of equal length.

Syntax

split [*-n*] [*file* [*name*]]

Arguments

Unless you specify a number of lines (see "Options"), a file that you specify (or the standard input if you specify no file) is split into as many 1000-line sections as necessary. If you specify a name on the command line, the pieces of the original file will be placed in files named *name***aa**, *name***ab**, and so on, up to *name***zz**. By default, *name* is **x**.

Option

-*n*   Splits files into pieces *n* lines in length instead of the default 1000

Examples

The following example shows how you would split a file called **m.list** into pieces 100 lines long. Since no name is specified, the resulting files will be named **xaa**, **xab**, and so on.

```
% split -100 m.list
```

The following example shows how you split the file **m.list** into pieces 500 lines long. In this example, the name **l.chunk** is specified after the file name, so the resulting files will be named **l.chunkaa, l.chunkab,** and so on. Note that you can specify only one file name as an argument to **split,** so any other argument is automatically interpreted as a name prefix for the resulting files.

```
% split -500 m.list l.chunk
```

The stty Command

The **stty** command displays and sets terminal parameters. For example, you can use **stty** to change the line-kill and erase keys for your terminal.

Syntax

stty [**-a**] [**-g**] [*parameters*]

Without any arguments, **stty** displays certain parameters (listed under "Parameters") that determine the behavior of the terminal. To set these parameters, you can specify them as command-line arguments.

Options

These options may not be used together, nor may either of them be used in conjunction with any parameters.

-a	Displays all of the parameter settings
-g	Displays the parameter settings in a compact format that can be used as input to another **stty** command

Parameters

Some parameters take numerical values, some take character values, and others are binary. The parameters here are grouped by function.

Special Keys   The parameters in this section determine which keys serve the erase, line-kill, and interrupt keys, as well as other special keys. These keys take character values. To indicate a control character (for example, CTRL-C or CTRL-D), you would precede a letter with a caret (^) and enclose both in single quotes. For example, to indicate CTRL-C, you would use

`'^c'`

One parameter that does not fit into any of the following categories is **sane**. This parameter sets all the other parameters to reasonable values in the event that your terminal's settings are scrambled. You should try the command **stty sane** if you are ever faced with a frozen or odd-looking terminal.

erase *x*	Sets the erase key to *x*, where *x* is a regular or control character of your choice. The two most commonly used erase keys are CTRL-H and **#**, either of which may be the default on your system
kill *x*	Sets the line-kill key to *x*, where *x* is a regular or control character of your choice
ek	Sets the erase and line-kill characters to the default for your system
intr *x*	Sets the interrupt key to *x*, where *x* is a regular or control character of your choice
eof *x*	Sets the end-of-file character to *x*, where *x* is a regular or control character of your choice. The end-of-file character is the character that you use to signal the end of input to commands like **cat** and also to log out. CTRL-D is usually the default end-of-file character

Interpretation of Characters

[-]nl	When **nl** is set, only the newline character is accepted as a line terminator. When **-nl** is set, the system accepts a RETURN as a line terminator and gives as output a RE-TURN followed by a linefeed as output in place of a new-line character
[-]echo	Echoes characters to the screen as they are typed. If your terminal is in half duplex mode, and each charac-ter you type is echoed to the screen twice, you should set **-echo**
[-]echoe	Echoes the erase character as a space. That is, the char-acter you erase is replaced by a blank space, so that the erased character actually disappears from the screen. If **-echoe** is set, erased characters will remain on the screen but will be ignored by the shell
[-]echok	Echoes a newline character after the line-kill character. If **-echok** is set, the cursor remains on the same line when you press the line-kill key
[-]lcase	Translates all uppercase letters into the corresponding lowercase letters on input, and vice versa on output, as is necessary for uppercase-only terminals
[-]tabs	Transmits each tab character received to an actual tab character. When **-tabs** is set, tabs are translated into the appropriate number of spaces

Job Control Parameters The following two parameters are used by the **shl** shell layer manager. See **shl** for more information.

swtch *x*	Sets *x* as the character you use to switch from a layer back to the shell layer manager
[-]loblk	Blocks the output from the layer you set this parameter in when any other layer is the current layer. When **loblk** is set, output from this layer will be suspended until you make the layer current again. Setting **loblk** is the equivalent of giving the **block** command within **shl**. When you set **-loblk** within a layer, the system will send output from that layer to the terminal whether the layer is current or not

Data Transmission Parameters

[-]parenb   Enables parity generation and detection. If **-parenb** is set, the system neither uses nor expects a parity bit when communicating with the terminal

[-]parodd   Sets odd parity. Setting **-parodd** sets even parity

[-]raw   Causes the system to interpret data from the terminal in its raw form. That is, the erase, line-kill, interrupt, and eof characters do not have special meaning. By default **-raw** is set

[-]cstopb   Uses 2 stop bits per character. If **-cstopb** is set, uses 1 stop bit per character

Data Line Parameters

[-]hupcl   Sends a HANGUP signal to all processes upon logout

0   Hangs up phone line immediately

50 75 110 134 150   Sets terminal baud rate to the number you
200 300 600 1200   select
1800 2400 4800
9600 19200

Transmission Delay Parameters   The parameters in this section determine the transmission delays following various special characters. For each of these parameters, a final 0 indicates no transmission delay. All other numbers indicate transmission delays of increasing length.

cr0 cr1 cr2   Sets a delay following a RETURN

nl0 nl1   Sets a delay following a newline character

tab0 tab1   Sets a delay following a tab

ff0 ff1   Sets a delay following a form feed (for line printers)

bs0 bs1   Sets a delay following a BACKSPACE

vt0 vt1   Sets a delay following a vertical tab

Examples

The following example shows a sample output of **stty** with the **-a** option:

```
% stty -a
speed 9600 baud; line = 0; intr = ^C; quit = ^; erase = ^H;
kill = ^U; eof = ^D; eol = ^\; swtch = ^\
-parenb -parodd cs8 -cstopb hupcl cread -clocal -loblk
-ctsflow -rtsflow -ignbrk brkint ignpar -parmrk -inpck
-istrip -inlcr -igncr icrnl -iuclc ixon ixany -ixoff
isig icanon -xcase echo echoe echok -echonl -noflsh
opost -olcuc onlcr -ocrnl -onocr -onlret -ofill -ofdel
cr0 nl0 tab3 bs0 vt0 ff0
```

The following example shows how you would assign the character CTRL-C
to the interrupt key:

```
% stty intr '^c'
```

The next example shows how you would reset all the parameter values
if your terminal settings were scrambled:

```
% stty sane
```

This example shows how you would turn off the echo of characters to
your terminal screen:

```
% stty -echo
```

The su Command

The **su** command temporarily switches your effective user ID to that of
another user and executes a new shell. To be able to switch user iden-
tities, you must either know that user's password or be the superuser.

Syntax

su [-] [*user* [*arg* . . .]]

Arguments

With no arguments, **su** changes your effective user ID to that of the superuser. You must know the **root** password to do this. If you specify a user, **su** will change your effective ID to that user's ID. You may follow the user name with one of the following two *args:*

-c *"commands"*	Causes the shell invoked by **su** to execute the commands enclosed in quotes following the **-c** and then exit immediately. This is useful if you just want to execute a few commands with the permissions of another user
-r	Invokes a restricted shell for the user

Additionally, if the user's login shell is the Bourne shell, you can specify a **-** as the first argument to the **su** command and the shell that is invoked will behave as if you had originally logged in as that user. That is, you will be placed in that user's home directory, and that user's **.profile** file will be executed.

Examples

To switch to the user ID of a user called **ramsay**, you would type

```
% su ramsay
```

You would then be prompted for the password for that account. If you typed it correctly, a new shell with a new prompt would be invoked.

To switch to the user ID of **ramsay** and have the new shell execute the **.profile** file in the home directory of **ramsay**, you would type

```
% su - ramsay
```

Remember that this will only work if **ramsay**'s login shell is the Bourne shell.

To switch temporarily to the user ID of **root**, then kill process number 5277, and, finally, exit, you would type

```
% su root -c "kill 5277"
```

The tail Command

The **tail** command takes a file or the standard input and gives the last part as output.

Syntax

tail [+ or *-number*[**lbc**]] [**-f**] [*file* . . .]

Options

±*number*   By default, **tail** prints the last ten lines of the input as output. You can change this by specifying the distance from the beginning or end of the file at which **tail** is to start. A number following a **+** indicates the distance from the beginning of the file, while a number following a **-** indicates the distance from the end of the file. You can specify this distance in lines, blocks, or characters, with the letter l (lines), **b** (blocks), or **c** (characters) appended to the number. You must type these letters immediately following the number on the command line, with no intervening spaces or hyphens

-f   If the input to **tail** is a file and not the standard input, this option causes **tail** to loop endlessly, pausing for one second and then displaying any new lines at the end of the file. This is useful for monitoring the progress of a file created by another command. For example, if the output of **nroff** or **find** is directed to a file, that file will grow as the process executes. To stop the loop, you must press the interrupt key

Notes

■ See Chapter 5, "UNIX Command-Line Fundamentals," for more on **tail**.

■ If you use **tail** to view a very long segment of a file (longer than the number of lines on the screen), the text will scroll off the screen quickly, just as with **cat**. To prevent this, you can pipe the output of **tail** to **pg** or **more**.

Examples

The following example shows how you would view the file **stats** starting at line 575:

```
% tail +5751 stats
```

The next example shows how you would view the last 25 lines of the file **stats** in an endless loop:

```
% tail -25 -f stats
```

The tar Command

The **tar** command saves and restores files to and from archive media, usually storage devices such as floppy disks or magnetic tapes. You can also use **tar** to copy files to other files. This command is usually used to make backups of files or file systems.

Syntax

tar *key*[*options*] [*files*]

Arguments

The key argument determines what action **tar** will take. It may consist of one of the function letters explained next and one or more options that modify the function.

The *files* are any files (or directories) that you want to save or retrieve to or from the archive. If you specify no files, all the files in the current directory (or in the archive) are stored or retrieved. A directory name refers recursively to all files and subdirectories in that directory.

Function Letters

r   Appends the named *files* to an existing archive. Any ex-
             isting files in the archive are left intact. This option will
             not work with most tape drives

x   Extracts the files from the archive. If you do not specify
             any files, the entire contents of the directory are ex-
             tracted. If you name a directory, it is recursively ex-
             tracted. The owner, modification, and permissions of
             the files are preserved if possible

t   Prints the names of the specified files each time they
             occur in the archive and extracts these files. If you do
             not specify any files, the entire contents of the archive
             are listed and extracted

u   Adds any specified files to the archive only if they are
             not already there or if they are more recently modified
             than those in the archive

c   Creates a new archive and writes the named files to it,
             destroying any existing files in the archive

Function Modifiers   You may append any of these letters to the function letters described in the previous section. Although the function

modifiers are optional, they are not preceded by a hyphen as are most options.

number	Selects the tape or disk drive with the number you select. If you do not select a number, the default drive is used
v	Causes **tar** to display the name of each of the files it reads or writes. If used with the function **t**, causes additional information about each file to be displayed
w	Displays the action (reading or writing) to be performed on each file and waits for you to confirm before proceeding
f *argument*	Causes **tar** to read from or write to the next device or file you name as the next argument instead of the default device, which is usually a tape or disk drive. If you type a - instead of a device or file name, **tar** reads from or writes to the standard input instead of a device or file
l	Causes **tar** to display a message if it cannot resolve all the links to a file it is reading. Without this option, no error messages are displayed
m	Causes **tar** to set the modification time of files to the time of extraction from the archive rather than preserving their original modification times
k *number*	Specifies the size of the archive as *number* kilobytes. The minimum allowable number is 250. If you do not specify a number, the size specified in the **/etc/default/archive** file is used
e	Prevents files from being split across backup volumes (tapes or floppy disks). If a file will not fit on the remaining space in the present volume, **tar** prompts you for a new volume before proceeding. This option will only work if you also specify the **k** option.

Notes

■ If you write a file with its short name, its full pathname will not be preserved when you write it to an archive. When you read that file back from the archive, it will appear in the current directory (the directory you are in when you give the command). If you specify a file's relative pathname, (for example, **debts/big/personal**), the file will have that pathname relative to the current directory.

Examples

The following example shows how you would append all the files and directories (recursively) to the archive on the default disk drive. Since the **v** option is given after the function letter **r**, the names of all the copied files are given as output.

```
% tar rv
accounts
accounts/anderson.pp
accounts/engwall.doll
accounts.list
accounts/martino.sct
accounts/velasquez.ss
accounts/wall.coffee
accounts/webst.royjel
man.styles
plethora
search
sed.acc
```

The next example shows how you would extract files from an archive on drive 3. The **w** option following the function letter **x** allows you to select only certain files by confirming them and not confirming the others.

```
% tar x3w
```


The tee Command

The **tee** command pipes the standard input to both the standard output and any files you specify. The **tee** utility is usually used as part of a pipeline (see the following "Examples" section). If not used in a pipeline, **tee** behaves like **cat**, taking lines of input and giving them as output.

Syntax

tee [**-iau**] *file* . . .

Options

-a	Causes the output to be appended to the named files instead of overwriting the existing contents
-i	Causes the interrupt signal to be ignored
-u	Causes the output to be unbuffered

Examples

The following example shows a possible use of **tee** in a pipeline. The output from **nroff** is piped to **tee**, and the output of **tee** is piped to **lp**, which sends the formatted version of the file to the default printer. A copy of the formatted file is also saved in the file **report.n**.

```
% nroff report | tee report.n | lp
```

If you pipe the standard output of **tee** to another command, the standard output cannot also go to the terminal screen. You can, however, send the output to the screen as well if you specify the device file associated with your terminal as the output file, as in the following example, where the terminal device name is **/dev/ttyi1c**:

```
% cat list* | sort | tee /dev/ttyi1c | pr
```

The test Command

The **test** command evaluates expressions, returning a zero exit status if the expression is true and a nonzero exit status if the expression is false. The **test** command is built into the Bourne shell on System V UNIX systems. See Chapter 9, "The Bourne Shell," for more on **test**.

Syntax

test *expression*
[*expression*]

The time Command

The **time** command times a command. The command you specify is executed, and then four pieces of information are reported: the time elapsed during execution of the command, the time the command spent in the system, the actual processing time spent on the command, and the percentage of system resources used for the command.

Syntax

time *command*

The touch Command

The **touch** command updates a file's access and modification times.

Syntax

touch [**-amc**] [*time*] *files*

Without any options, **touch** modifies both the access time and the modification time of the named files.

Arguments

You specify the time in the format *mmddhhmm[yy]*, where the first *mm* is the number of the month (01-12), *dd* is the day of the month (01-31), *hh* is the hour (00-23), the second *mm* is the minute (00-59), and the optional *yy* is the last two digits of the year. If you do not specify a time, the current time is used as the modification and/or access time.

The files are any files whose modification and/or access times you wish to update.

Options

-a	Updates only the access time, leaving the modification time unchanged
-m	Updates only the modification time, leaving the access time unchanged
-c	Ordinarily, **touch** will create any of the named files that do not exist, setting their creation time to the current time. The **-c** option prevents this

Examples

To set only the modification time of a file called **forms** to the current time, you would type

```
% touch -m forms
```

To set both the modification time and the access time of a file called **forms** to 3:15 P.M., November 28, 1990, you would type

```
% touch 11281515 forms
```

The tty Command

The **tty** command prints the pathname of your terminal's device file.

Syntax

tty [-s]

Option

-s   Causes **tty** not to print any output. However, the command still returns an exit code

Notes

■ If the standard input is not a terminal, **tty** prints the message "not a terminal."

Examples

The following example shows the **tty** command without the **-s** option:

```
% tty
/dev/ttyi1c
```

The umask Command

The **umask** command sets the file-creation mode mask. This mask determines the original permissions for all files and directories that you create.

Syntax

umask [*number*]

The **mask** number is a three-digit octal number, the first digit indicating the permissions of the owner, the second indicating the permissions of the owner's group, and the third indicating the permissions of other users. These numbers are like the numbers used in absolute mode with the **chmod** command. The difference is that the **mask** number specifies permissions *not* to be granted. That is, each digit is subtracted from the total possible 7 and the remaining number indicates the permissions the files are to have. For example, with the **chmod** command, you would use the number 777 to indicate all permissions for all users, but with **umask** 777 would mean no permissions for any users.

Notes

■ The **umask** command is usually a line in the **.login** or **.profile** file so that it will be executed every time you log in.

■ See also **chmod**.

Examples

Setting the file-creation mask to 177 will remove only execute permission (1) for you and all permissions (4 for read, 2 for write, and 1 for execute) for other users. The only permissions set for files that you create will be read and write permission for you. To set the file-creation mask this way, you would use the command:

```
% umask 177
```

Remember that this command is more often used in the **.login** or **.profile** file than on the command line.

To set the file-creation mask so that you will have read and write permission on all files, and all other users will have read permission, you would use the command:

```
% umask 133
```

The uniq Command

The **uniq** command prints one occurrence of each line that occurs in the input, even if the input contains duplicate lines. However, the duplicate lines in the input must be adjacent to be counted as duplicate.

Syntax

uniq [**-udc**] [*-fnum*] [*+cnum*] [*input-file* [*output-file*]]

Arguments

If you specify an *fnum* following a **-**, **uniq** will ignore the first *fnum* fields in each input line, where a field is a sequence of nonwhitespace characters bounded by whitespace characters. If you specify a *cnum* following a **+**, **uniq** will ignore the first *cnum* characters. If you specify both an *fnum* and a *cnum*, **uniq** will ignore the first *fnum* fields and the first *cnum* characters after that. These two arguments can be useful if, for example, each line in the input is numbered, but the text after the numbers may be the same. You could have **uniq** ignore the field(s) that contained the line numbers and still find duplicate lines.

The **uniq** utility is unique in that you can specify both its input and output as arguments on the command line. If you specify one file name, that file is taken as the input, and the output is sent to the standard output, which may be redirected to a file or piped to another command. If you specify two file names, the first is taken as the input and the second as the output. You may also pipe the output from another command to **uniq**, but in this case you must send the output of **uniq** to the standard output as well (see the following "Examples" section).

Options

-c	Causes **uniq** to precede each line of the output with the number of times that that line occurred in the input
-d	Causes **uniq** to display one occurrence of only those lines that are repeated in the input
-u	Displays only those lines that are *not* duplicated in the input. Remember that if duplicate lines are not adjacent, they are counted as unique

Notes

■ Since you can only compare adjacent lines of input, you should first use **sort** on the input if you really want to find only unique lines. This will ensure that all duplicate lines are adjacent. However, this may not be practical if the input is a text file.

Examples

In the following three examples, the **uniq** command will take as input the file **logdates,** which is shown here:

```
% cat logdates
martino    Jan 01
martino    Jan 01
kraz       Jan 02
anderson   Jan 10
anderson   Jan 10
kraz       Feb 01
kraz       Feb 01
martino    Feb 05
kraz       Feb 06
anderson   Feb 06
```

The following example shows the output that **uniq** (with no options) gives when it takes the file **logdates** as input:

```
% uniq logdates
martino    Jan 01
kraz       Jan 02
anderson   Jan 10
kraz       Feb 01
martino    Feb 05
kraz       Feb 06
anderson   Feb 06
```

The next example shows the output of **uniq** with the **-d** option. Only those lines in **logdates** that are duplicated are printed as output.

```
% uniq -d logdates
martino    Jan 01
anderson   Jan 10
kraz       Feb 01
```

The following command shows how you would make **uniq** ignore the first two fields of each line in the input file **logdates**—that is, the user name and the abbreviated month name. Thus **uniq** will compare only the date portion of these lines.

```
% uniq -2 logdates
martino    Jan 01
kraz       Jan 02
```

```
anderson  Jan 10
kraz      Feb 01
martino   Feb 05
kraz      Feb 06
```

This example shows how you would pipe the output of **sort** to **uniq**. Since the input to **uniq** is not specified as a file on the command line, the output cannot be either. To save the output to a file, you would have to use the redirection symbol >.

```
% sort printers | uniq > new.printers
```

The vi Command

The **vi** command invokes the visual text editor, **vi**, which is discussed in detail in Chapter 6.

Syntax

vi [-*options*] [*file*]

Options

+*linenumber*	Starts **vi** at *linenumber*
+/*pattern*	Starts **vi** at the first occurrence of *pattern*
-w*n*	Sets the default window size to *n* lines
-R	Sets a read-only option so the file can be viewed but not edited
-L	Lists all files saved during an editor or system crash
-r	Recovers the buffer copy of the file after an editor or system failure.

The w Command

The **w** command displays information about all users currently on the system. See Chapter 12, "The UNIX Multiuser Environment," for more on **w**.

Syntax

w [*options*] [*users*]

Arguments

Without any arguments or options, **w** prints a heading that contains information about the system and then some information about each of the users currently logged in on the system. If you specify one or more users, only information about those users will be displayed (if the users are currently logged in).

Options

-h	Suppresses the heading and title lines and displays only information about the current users
-q	Causes **w** to display information in a quick format. That is, for every user **w** displays only their login name, their current terminal, the number of minutes they have been idle, and the name of the process that they are currently running
-t	Prints only the heading line

The wc Command

The **wc** command counts the number of lines, words, and characters in a file or the standard input.

Syntax

wc [**-lwc**] [*file* . . .]

Without any options, **wc** prints three columns of output. The first column shows the number of lines, the second shows the number of words, and the third shows the number of characters. If the input is a file or a group of files, an additional fourth column shows the name of each file. When the input is more than one file, **wc** displays an individual count for each file and a total count for all the files.

Options

-l	Displays only the number of lines in the input
-w	Displays only the number of words in the input
-c	Displays only the number of characters in the input

Examples

The following example shows the output of **wc** with no options. The input file, **willis**, has 170 lines, 825 words, and 4949 characters.

```
% wc willis
    170    825   4949 willis
```

The following example shows the output of **wc** when its input is a group of files—in this case all the files in the current directory beginning with "w."

```
% wc w*
    838   3345  19576 wanda
    427   2032  12104 webster
   1358   6014  36173 wharton
    690   3109  18488 willis
    922   4542  28203 wilson
```

```
 572   2610  15726 wylder
4807  21652 130270 total
```

The next example shows how you would use **wc** to count the number of files in the current directory. The output of **ls** is piped to **wc**. Since the output of **ls** contains only one file name per line, only the number of lines is important and you can use the -l option.

```
% ls | wc -l
```

The who Command

The **who** command lists the users currently logged on to the system.

Syntax

who [*options*]
who am i

Arguments

With no arguments, **who** prints the name of each user currently logged in, the device name of the terminal that the user is using, and the time the user logged in. With the arguments **am i**, **who** prints this information only for you.

Options

-b	Displays the time the system was last booted
-H	Causes **who** to print a header before the ordinary output

-l	Lists all data lines that are waiting for someone to log in. You could use this option to find out which terminals on your system are free
-q	Displays only the number of users currently logged in
-t	Displays the time the system clock was last reset
-u	Causes **who** to display some additional information about each user currently logged in. In addition to the name, terminal, and login time of each user, the **-u** option displays the process ID number of the user's login shell and the time the user has been idle. If you use this option with the **-H** option, a header will show which column corresponds to each of these things.
-T	This is the same as the **-u** option except that an additional column displays the state of the terminal. A **+** in this column indicates that the terminal is writable, while a **-** indicates that it is not writable (except by the superuser)

Notes

■ See Chapter 3, "Getting Started," and Chapter 12, "The UNIX Multi-user Environment," for more on the **who** command.

The write Command

The **write** command writes to another user's terminal. For you to be able to write to another user, that user's terminal must be writable. The **write** command is also discussed in Chapter 12, "The UNIX Multiuser Environment."

Syntax

write *name* [*tty*]

Arguments

The name is the login name of the user you want to write to. If that user is logged in at more than one terminal, you will have to specify a tty to write to.

Notes

■ See also **mesg**.

■ Users often establish a routine to let each other know that they have finished writing. For example, you could use a slash when you had finished typing your message, and the other user would then know to respond.

Trademarks

ACCELL®	Unify Corporation
Hewlett-Packard®	Hewlett-Packard Company
IBM® PC®	International Business Machines Corporation
Informix®	Relational Database Systems, Inc.
INGRES™	Relational Technology, Inc.
Intel®	Intel Corporation
Lotus® 1-2-3®	Lotus Development Corporation
Macintosh®	Apple Computer, Inc.
Microsoft® Word	Microsoft Corporation
MS-DOS®	Microsoft Corporation
Multiplan®	Microsoft Corporation
NFS™	Sun Microsystems, Inc.
ORACLE®	Oracle Corporation
PDP®	Digital Equipment Corporation
SCO™ Lyrix®	The Santa Cruz Operation, Inc.
SCO™ Multiview™	The Santa Cruz Operation, Inc.
SCO™ Office Portfolio™	The Santa Cruz Operation, Inc.
SCO™ Professional®	The Santa Cruz Operation, Inc.
SCO™ UNIX®	The Santa Cruz Operation, Inc.
SCO™ VP/ix™	The Santa Cruz Operation, Inc.
Toshiba®	Toshiba America, Inc.
UNIX®	AT&T
VAX®	Digital Equipment Corporation
VP/ix™	Interactive Systems Corporation
WordPerfect®	WordPerfect Corporation
XENIX®	Microsoft Corporation

Index

The manuscript for this book was prepared and submitted to Osborne/McGraw-Hill in electronic form. The acquisitions editor for this project was Elizabeth Fisher, the technical reviewer was Ross Oliver, and the project editor was Dusty Bernard. Text design by Stefany Otis, Lynda Higham, and Roger Dunshee, using Baskerville for text body and Swiss for display. Cover art by Bay Graphics Design, Inc. Color separation and cover supplier, Phoenix Color Corporation. Screens produced with InSet, from InSet Systems, Inc. Book printed and bound by R.R. Donnelley & Sons Company, Crawfordsville, Indiana.